FROM NATIONAL LIBERATION TO DEMOCRATIC RENAISSANCE IN SOUTHERN AFRICA

Edited by
Cheryl Hendricks
& Lwazi Lushaba

COUNCIL FOR THE DEVELOPMENT OF
SOCIAL SCIENCE RESEARCH IN AFRICA

© Council for the Development of Social Science Research in Africa, 2005
Avenue Cheikh Anta Diop Angle Canal IV, BP 3304 Dakar, 18524, Senegal
Web site: www.codesria.org
All rights reserved

ISBN: 2-86978-162-8   ISBN-13: 978-2-86978-162-7

Typeset by Daouda Thiam

Cover designed by Ibrahima Fofana

Printed by Lightning Source

Distributed in Africa by CODESRIA

Distributed elsewhere by
African Books Collective, Oxford, UK
Web site: www.africanbookscollective.com

The Council for the Development of Social Science Research in Africa (CODESRIA) is an independent organisation whose principal objectives are facilitating research, promoting research-based publishing and creating multiple forums geared towards the exchange of views and information among African researchers. It challenges the fragmentation of research through the creation of thematic research networks that cut across linguistic and regional boundaries.

CODESRIA would like to express its gratitude to African Governments, the Swedish Development Co-operation Agency (SIDA/SAREC), the International Development Research Centre (IDRC), OXFAM GB/I, the MacArthur Foundation, the Carnegie Corporation, the Norwegian Ministry of Foreign Affairs, the Danish Agency for International Development (DANIDA), the French Ministry of Cooperation, the Ford Foundation, the United Nations Development Programme (UNDP), the Rockefeller Foundation, the Prince Claus Fund and the Government of Senegal for support of its research, publication and training activities.

Contents

Contributors v

Preface vii

Introduction: Southern Africa – Continuities and Disjunctures in the Discourse and Practices
Cheryl Hendricks and Lwazi Lushaba 1

Chapter 1
Swaziland and South Africa Since 1994: Reflections on Aspects of Post-Liberation Swazi Historiography
Balem Nyeko 23

Chapter 2
Problems and Prospects of Democratic Renewal in Southern Africa: A Study of Statecraft and Democratisation in South Africa, 1994-2003
Adekunle Amuwo 38

Chapter 3
Legacies and Meanings of the United Democratic Front (UDF) Period for Contemporary South Africa
Raymond Suttner 59

Chapter 4
The 1987 Zimbabwe National Unity Accord and its Aftermath: A Case of Peace without Reconciliation?
Terence M. Mashingaidze 82

Chapter 5
Race and Democracy in South Africa
Cheryl Hendricks..93

Chapter 6
From Apartheid Social Stratification to Democratic Social Divisions: Examining the Contradictory Notions of Social Transformation between Indian and Black South Africans
Lwazi Siyabonga Lushaba..111

Chapter 7
Negotiating Nationalism: Women's Narratives of Forced Displacement
Ingrid Palmary...140

Chapter 8
Wilgespruit Fellowship Centre: Part of Our Struggle for Freedom
Monique Vanek..152

Chapter 9
Curfew and the 'Man in the Middle' in Zimbabwe's War of Liberation with Special Reference to the Eastern Areas of Zimbabwe, 1977-1980
Munyaradzi Mushonga...171

Chapter 10
'Your Obedient Servant or Your Friend': Forms of Address in Letters Among British Administrators and Batswana Chiefs
Mompoloki Bagwasi...191

Contributors

Adekunle Amuwo is currently the Executive Secretary, African Association of Political Science (AAPS) based in Pretoria, South Africa. He holds a BSc and an MSc from the University of Ibadan, Nigeria and a PhD. from the University of Bordeaux, France in Comparative Public Policy & Governance, Civil-Military Relations/Francophone Africa. He is a Senior Lecturer in the Department of Political Science, University of Ibadan.

Cheryl Hendricks is currently the Head of the Southern Africa Human Security Program at the Institute for Security Studies. She was previously a Political Analyst at the Institute for Justice and Reconciliation and the Academic Manager at the Centre for Conflict Resolution in Cape Town. Prior to this she spent years as a lecturer in the Political Studies Department, University of the Western Cape. She has been an active participant in the established regional and continental research institutions. Hendricks has written extensively on issues of race and identity in South Africa.

Balem Nyeko is an Associate Professor of History at the University of Swaziland, Southern Africa, having previously taught at the National University of Lesotho, the University of Zambia, and Makerere University in Uganda.

Raymond Suttner is a former political prisoner. He has published extensively and especially on questions of South African resistance and democratisation, most recently editing the autobiography of Ray Alexander Simons, *All my life and All my Strength* (STE Publishers, 2004). Currently he is attached to the College of Humanities at the University of South Africa in Pretoria.

Terence M. Mashingaidze is a Zimbabwean historian. He was educated at the University of Zimbabwe from where he obtained a BA general in history and economic history, a BA in history, and an MA in African history. He has taught at the University of Zimbabwe and is currently teaching in the Department of History and Development Studies at the Midlands State

University where he is also the Head of Department. His research and teaching interests include gender and development, youth and governance, Zimbabwean history, governance and African electoral issues.

Lwazi Lushaba is currently completing his doctoral degree at the University of Ibadan, Nigeria. Between 2001 and 2003 he worked as a Programme Assistant at a Ford funded Programme on Ethnic and Federal Studies, housed in the Department of Political Science. He has been a recipient of several awards and fellowships including Ford Foundation Young African Scholar Award, Social Science Research Council (New York) Youth in a Global Age Fellowship and National Research Foundation, (Pretoria) Scholarship for Doctoral Study Abroad. His research interests range from youth politics, political economy of the South African transition to identity and citizenship politics in transitional societies.

Ingrid Palmary is a former Researcher in the City Safety Project at the Centre for the Study of Violence and Reconciliation.

Monique Vanek is the business content editor for the *Citizen*, at Moneyweb, South Africa, and a producer for several radio programmes. She completed her MA at the University of Witwatersrand, South Africa. She has written several articles for the *Citizen*.

Munyaradzi Mushonga holds an MA in History and lectures in the History Department of the University of Zimbabwe. His areas of expertise and research interests are historiography (Western and non-Western) and African History with special emphasis on race, class and ethnicity, gender and sexuality, identity and nationalism. He has done consultancy work in education, gender, human rights and democracy.

Mompoloki Bagwasi is currently a lecturer in the English Department at the University of Botswana. Her area of specialization is language and linguistics. She did her masters at the University of Leeds (UK) in 1992 and doctorate studies at Indiana University (USA) in 2002. Though a languages major, she is currently involved in the kind of language research that attempts to link language to history, politics, sociology and economics.

Preface

The Council for the Development of Social Science Research in Africa (CODESRIA) celebrated its 30th anniversary in 2003. Established in 1973, through the collective will of African social science researchers, the Council was created to be a forum through which scholars could transcend barriers to knowledge production and, in doing so, play a critical role in the democratic development of the continent.

As part of the series of events marking the anniversary, five sub-regional conferences were organised in Central, East, North, Southern and West Africa. These sub-regional conferences were followed by a grand finale held at the Council's headquarters in Dakar, Senegal, in December 2003. The papers in this volume were first presented at the Southern Africa sub-regional conference which convened in Gaborone, Botswana, on 18 and 19 October 2003, under the theme of 'Southern Africa: From National Liberation to Democratic Renaissance'.

Southern Africa, as a region, has known some of the most interesting political developments in the history of Africa. In the period prior to the onset of formal colonial domination, the area was host to major projects of state formation, dissolution and recomposition which were characterised by interesting and well-documented experiments in statecraft. Home to some of the most prolonged and vicious forms of settler colonial rule, the sub-region was also the site for the most systematic, institutionalised system of racism, racial domination, and racially-based exclusion known in recent human history. Partly on account of the racial structuring of opportunities integral to the establishment and consolidation of colonial domination, the sub-region witnessed an intense intra-regional flow of labour to the key mining and agro-business centres mainly located in South Africa. The demographic outcomes associated with widespread labour migration and the racially-based systems of labour control established in the colonial mines and plantations had consequences not only for the organisation of state power and rural society but also for that of the family and citizenship. They also established the foundations for the pattern of urbanisation that developed—and the violence associated with it.

Given the violent history of the establishment of colonial rule and white racial domination in the sub-region, it is not surprising that Southern Africa was also one of the earliest sites of resistance to foreign and minority rule in Africa. The African National Congress (ANC) has the distinction of being the oldest liberation political party in Africa; once adopted, its Freedom Charter fed into the pan-African quest for the liberation of the continent from colonial oppression. The example of the ANC and its Freedom Charter was to inspire virtually all other key nationalist politicians of the sub-region in their campaign for national liberation. Several of these countries, such as Zambia, Botswana, and Malawi, were able to achieve independence earlier than others. For most, however, the struggle for liberation became a long-drawn-out and increasingly violent affair which the East-West Cold War did a great deal to complicate in the light of the strategic geo-political advantages and mineral resources which the sub-region enjoys. Not surprisingly, armed struggle became an important and almost ubiquitous instrument in the quest for the termination of settler colonialism and institutionalised racism. It was to play a major role in delivering liberation first to the former Portuguese colonies of Angola and Mozambique and then to Zimbabwe and Namibia, and, finally, to South Africa, with the inauguration of Nelson Mandela in 1994 as the first president to be elected by South Africans of all races and the first person from among the black majority to rule the country.

The achievement of national liberation and installation of majority rule in Southern Africa was always considered as an important project of the pan-African movement within the continent and in the Diaspora. Not only were the key leaders of the sub-region active participants in the pan-African meetings convened to discuss the future of the continent and the black race from 1945 onwards; the first set of African countries to attain their independence and all the others that subsequently joined them were to offer solidarity and material support to the Southern Africa liberation project. Indeed, the mandate of the Organization of African Unity, at its foundation, consisted in promoting continental unity and liberation. For the latter purpose, the OAU set up a Liberation Committee which was a key player in the struggle for independence and majority rule in Southern Africa. Following the end of apartheid in South Africa and the installation of a black majority government, Southern Africa has been pre-occupied with efforts at democratisation, regional co-operation and integration, and continental renaissance. The processes of democratisation, regionalism and renaissance point to a determination to create more open, inclusive and fair societies built on representative governance, the inventive energies of the peoples and a shared pan-African community. But it is a project confronted by a host of historical and contemporary difficulties. These states, and South Africa, in particular, must somehow manage the complex equation of race, rights and justice; address the vexed issue of post-liberation xenophobia; reverse the persistent, ever-deepening problems of social exclusion; tackle unresolved problems of historical dispossession and present-day challenges of representation; and come to grips with the structure of labour migration in the sub-region and the unidirectional conquest of new economic terrains in the sub-region by South African capital.

Taken collectively, the chapters in this volume constitute critical reflections on the Southern African component of the pan-African ideal through the entry points offered by the sub-region's struggle for national liberation and the ongoing quest for a democratic renaissance which includes a greater investment of efforts in regional co-operation and integration. The book should thus be seen as part of an ongoing effort by scholars in the region to re-visit the theories, historiographies and experiences of national liberation; and the various ideological currents and contestations which underpinned the struggle for liberation in the period before and after the publication of the Freedom Charter, including the Black Consciousness Movement. Today much research is being devoted to the key actors and factors in the Southern African liberation project; the labour processes that defined the colonial labour economy and the political policies and responses which they elicited; the dynamics of post-liberation statecraft, including the pursuit of truth and reconciliation, affirmative action, black economic empowerment, and various policies of social inclusion; the negotiation of post-liberation identity and citizenship; the place of land in the political economy of national liberation; the rise of post-liberation xenophobic tendencies, the forces and factors that account for them; the problems and prospects of democratic renewal in Southern Africa, including the change and renewal in Southern African civil society; post-liberation economics and economic policy-making as read from the point of view of a national liberation project; the search for regional co-operation and integration; the quest for an African renaissance project and its connections to the pan-African ideal; Southern Africa and the NEPAD initiative; Africa in the foreign policies of the countries of Southern Africa; and Southern Africa's Diaspora linkages. CODESRIA hopes that this collection of essays is able to enrich policy, scholarship and understanding of Southern Africans and their pan-African aspirations.

Introduction

Southern Africa: Continuities and Disjunctures in the Discourse and Practices[1]

Cheryl Hendricks and Lwazi Lushaba

In 2003 the Council for the Development of Social Science Research in Africa (CODESRIA) celebrated its 30th anniversary with a series of sub-regional conferences that fed into a continent-wide meeting in Dakar in December. This volume contains revised versions of papers initially presented at the Southern Africa sub-regional conference held in Botswana in October 2003. The theme of the conference, 'Southern Africa: From National Liberation to Democratic Renaissance' attested to the current preoccupation of African intellectuals and political leaders with defining new goals and strategies for a positive African trajectory. The emergent vision in Africa is one of development that focuses on human security, in which poverty alleviation and democratic participation are key pillars. The conference was an occasion for critical reflection on how the colonial and postcolonial experiences of the sub-region define the challenges and opportunities for the realisation of this vision.

The production of knowledge on Southern Africa has been rich and diverse, its contours reflecting the changing dynamics of the region and theoretical developments from within and without the continent. The primary post-colonial concerns of intellectual writing on Africa were, and remain, dominated by the quest for liberation and the development of stable, just national orders. The evolution of perspectives which sought to address these issues, and critiques thereof, have been extensively dealt with in the literature (see Rothchild and Chazan 1988; Apter and Rosberg 1994; Himmelstrand, Kinyanjui and Mburugu 1994; Osaghae 1994; Sandbrook 2000; Berman, Eyoh and Kymlicka 2004; and numerous others). Here we merely flag the pre-occupations, debates and contestations that evolved in the attempt to understand the nature of post-colonial African states and chart a development path. We then briefly explore its play in the Southern African context.

From the 1950s to the 1970s scholarship on Africa focused on analysing the birth of nationalist thought, the rise of African nationalist movements, the processes of decolonisation and the formation of nation-states. Nationalism, therefore, constituted the primary focus of intellectuals and was constituted as the driving force for political renewal on the continent. Political theorists, in particular, sought to provide recipes which would enable these states both to cohere as viable political communities and to embark on the journey of development. This scholarship was generally optimistic about the potential of African societies to restructure themselves in the dominant image of developed western nation-states. The nationalist historiography of this period tended to conflate political protest with nationalism and/or largely romanticised the form and content of African liberation struggles (Young 1994; Ranger 2004). There was a distinct interplay between intellectuals and activists (the two often inseparable) during this period which shaped the content of African nationalism (self-determination, self-representation, unity and development) and posited the guardians of the ideology and practice, predominantly African elites, as those best able to fulfil those objectives for post-colonial states (see Young 1994).

Modernisation theory was the dominant development paradigm of this era. It focused on the institutions, practices and policies required to move from one system of governance, 'the traditional', to another, 'the modern,' and maintain stability whilst doing so (Apter and Rosberg 1994). The newly formed African governments were to play a central role in effecting this progress. This paradigm resonated with African elites who wanted both to consolidate and legitimate their rule: rule based on their being the bearers and harbingers of progress. They interpreted development as industrialisation and nation-state building. Central to their discourse and practice of nation-building was the need to suppress sub-national identities and create primary allegiance to a national identity.

By the 1970s the fissures in this nationalist vision were evident. Authoritarian rule, corruption, politicised ethnicities and a general malaise of development became the dominant features of many African countries. Scholars, predominantly of African descent, in the light of a perception of a 'betrayal of independence', began to question the representations of nationalist struggles, the content of nationalism and the perceived wisdom of the path of development outlined by modernisation theory.

This revisionist approach, popularised by scholars such as Walter Rodney, Immanuel Wallerstein, and Samir Amin, became known as Radical Political

Economy (RPE). Their intellectual gaze turned to a re-examination of the colonial period, and the formation of a world economy, to make sense of the lack of development that had transpired. RPE theorists argued that Africa's woes stemmed from the way in which it was incorporated into the world economy, as a dependent formation webbed in a set of unequal exchange relations. Contrary to imperial historians, they argued that the colonialists deliberately underdeveloped African societies. These theorists also concentrated on the processes of class formation and/or fragmentation in the colonial and post-colonial contexts. The inheritors of the post-colonial state (the nationalist elite) were revealed as a 'compradorian bourgeoisie'/'under-developed middle-class' cum parochial nationalists unable and/or unwilling to develop these societies. This portrayal led to a rethinking of the relevance of this class in the decolonisation process and a concomitant emphasis on peasant and worker struggles to break the pattern of neo-colonial rule and embark on alternative development paths. The RPE theorists therefore offered a materialist interpretation of the post-colonial state, pointing to the systemic structural impediments inhibiting transformation, and to class conflict as the motor of change. They remained optimistic about the potential for breaking the cycle of dependency and creating the modern nation-states envisaged at independence.

Radical Political Economy was an important theoretical contribution to the debates on the development of African states. However, it suffered from some of the same ills that plagued modernisation theory, namely, creating a false dichotomy between the modern and traditional, and the centrality of the role of the state in the development process. Eyoh points out that these theorists were unable 'to advance a more subtle and credible analysis of the manner in which the mixing of traditional and modern economic, cultural and institutional relations underscored the complexity of power relations in post-colonial society...' (1998a: 116). The theory was therefore too reductionist, ignoring the impact of other salient social divisions, such as gender, ethnicity and religion, on the processes of state formation and development.

By the mid 1980s, African societies were described as being in 'crisis' and a distinct Afro-pessimism was discernible in the literature. Both capitalist and socialist states (in all their African variants) suffered the same fate of economic decline and political illegitimacy. Statist models of development appeared to have been exhausted with few results yielded. At the same time, the world witnessed the collapse of communism, disillusionment with nationalism and the rise of neo-liberalism. The new discourse on development began to concentrate on free markets and democracy. African countries, heavily indebted to the World Bank and International Monetary Fund (IMF), were forced to embark on this new development path via the imposition of Structural

Adjustment Programmes (SAPs). African scholars had long argued that democratic reform was needed and they were in broad agreement that the state was a central component of the crisis, but they differed on the frameworks for democracy and development. Many disputed the reduction of democracy to multi-partyism and the feasibility of simultaneously embarking on political and economic reform (Mkandawire 1999; Nzongola-Ntalaja 1997; Olukoshi 1998). SAPs were critiqued for their effects on the poor (erosion of social-welfare policies) and their inherent liberalisation thrust was thought to exacerbate the African 'crisis'. A number of important African scholars thus sought to elaborate more substantive, just and sustainable transformation agendas.

There was a new burgeoning multidisciplinary literature on the role of women in development, identity politics, the role of civil society, the rise of new social movements, and so forth. In the 1990s post-colonial and post-modernist perspectives entered the discourse. They re-directed our conceptual lenses and epistemologies to give voice to those previously marginalised, to deconstruct totalising narratives, interrogate representations, and to discern the manifestations and reproduction of power relations in varied spaces. The 'Janus face' of nationalism was highlighted and a new discourse on diversity/multi-culturalism gained currency.

Democratic renewal is now foremost on the African agenda. African governments, through the formation of the African Union (AU) and the New Economic Partnership for African Development (NEPAD) framework, currently claim to seek to finally deliver the 'fruits of independence'. Scholars, such as Nabudere (2002) and Wanyeki (2002), have already pointed out the limitations of these institutions and development frameworks, but their inauguration has increased the optimism and engagement of African scholars, which is in and of itself a positive development.

Southern African discourses

The trajectory of Southern African scholarship is shaped by, and shapes, the debates outlined above. The decolonisation process for many of the states in Southern Africa occurred when the RPE paradigm was at its peak. This influenced the interpretation of decolonisation, and, indeed, the mode of achieving independence and development. Many scholars working within this tradition were also closely aligned to the liberation movements and guilty of the same form of romanticisation of the liberation struggles. They focused predominantly on the racialised accumulation of power and wealth and/or class formation and often presented the violent overthrow of the colonial state and the creation of an equitable/classless society as the desired method for, and form of, liberation. Their analyses also accorded with the aspirations of the nationalist elite for state-driven modernist projects of nation-building and development.

The race-class debate that emerged in South Africa in the 1970s provides an example of the types of arguments advanced by RPE theorists in the region. Liberal historiography had portrayed race-relations in South Africa as anachronistic and irrational and contended that economic development was key to the transformation of these relations. A 'revisionist school' influenced by the work of E.P. Thompson, Walter Rodney, Giovanni Arrighi, Eric Hobsbawn, Eugene Genovese and others challenged this narrative (see Cobley 2001 for an overview). Martin Legassick, Shula Marks, Stanley Trapido, Harold Wolpe, Colin Bundy and John Saul were key protagonists of the sub-regional school, illustrating the functionality of apartheid for the development of capitalism. In short, their argument was that institutionalised racism developed to ensure a cheap labour system and, therefore, capitalism itself would have to be overthrown in order to transcend racism. For Saul and Gelb, writing in the 1980s, the time for revolution was imminent as an 'organic crisis' existed: both capitalism and apartheid were in crisis. These 'revisionists' were thus primarily seeking to expose the material basis of Southern African societies.

In the latter part of the 1980s, this materialist historiography was critiqued as 'top-down', deterministic and reductionist. The focus of RPE, in vogue continentally, was on the state, class formation and class conflict, to the exclusion of other social categories. In Mafeje's critique, for example, the point was advanced that there was a need to 'filter the Marxist vocabulary through local history' (cited in Ranger, 1988: 480). A more general critique was on the lack of agency afforded to Africans and a need to focus on the many intra-African struggles that had taken place, or were taking place (Lushaba's chapter elaborates on this aspect).

The rapid decline into civil war of those countries that embarked on a socialist path of development, and the general lack of development of countries in Africa that pursued state-led development, challenged the hegemony of this body of knowledge. By the mid 1980s the scholarly field had opened to produce a knowledge base that was more methodologically, conceptually and epistemologically varied. The lives of ordinary people became worthy of scholarly attention, women were made visible, sub-national organisations, identities and struggles were provided textual space, and the modes of operating and agendas of African nationalist movements, and those turned ruling party, were increasingly interrogated. Africans were accorded with agency in the making of their lived experiences and the construction of their identities, and the complexity of the relations that were revealed rendered the oppressor/oppressed binaries or victim tropes inaccurate and limiting. A plethora of analyses emerged, with differing foci of time and space, teasing out the interconnections between race, gender, nationalism and ethnicity. This currently remains the dominant form of theorisation.

The implementation of SAPs across the region, which coincided with the movement for democratic reform, beginning with the rise of the Movement for Democratic Change in Zambia and including the formation of a post-apartheid democratic state in South Africa, produced a concentration of development studies literature on democratic renewal. Here, too, scholars challenge the viability of SAPs, extensively critique the now hegemonic neo-liberal approach to development and contest the form and content of the democratic processes underway (see Solway 1995; Matlosa 1998; Nkiwane 1998; Bond 2000; Buthelezi 2000; Habib and Padayachee 2000; Marais 2001; Alexander 2002; Mhone 2003 and opinion pieces in the *Southern Africa Political and Economic Monthly*).

Scholarship in Southern Africa, therefore, remains committed to finding new approaches to understanding the past and to showing how the past impacts on the choice of goals and strategies for alternative development trajectories. The scholarship in the region has matured and is now able to advance more subtle and complex analyses of social, political, economic and power relations, both past and present, and their linkages. The ten chapters in this book are broadly concerned with aspects of the development of the sub-region's political economy, and, in particular, the ways in which colonial legacies and the nature of the liberation movement imprint on post-liberation patterns of change and the continued challenges confronting the sub-region.

The authors are representative of both mature and emerging scholars, predominantly from within the sub-region. Drawing on new discourses and theoretical innovations, they address, from different theoretical perspectives, issues of identity, citizenship, reconciliation, gender, post-liberation state building, democratisation and the politics of knowledge production. While collectively paying homage to the contributions by past regional scholarship, the chapters are oriented by the need to advance critical knowledge of socio-political, economic and cultural conditions that define the struggle for a more positive developmental path in the current African conjuncture. In other words, the authors consider it imperative to rethink old ideas and theories in the light of today's vocabularies and realities. Before providing a broad overview of the arguments in the chapters and how they link with broader debates, it is important to indicate the ways in which Southern Africa coheres as more than a mere geographic unit.

Deconstructing Southern Africa

Southern Africa has a shared colonial history which accounts for the similarities in socio-economic and political structures, and simultaneously differentiates the region from other African sub-regions. In a classic study of the colonial shaped political economy of the continent, Samir Amin (1972) designated the sub-region as part of a macro-region called 'Africa of the labour reserves': a region marked by the intertwined processes of white settler colonialism, proletarianisation, dispossession and subjugation. This shared history shaped the nature of the resistance by the colonised and the challenges for state-reconstruction. These challenges include land alienation, racialised distribution of resources, politicised ethnicities, reconciliation, migrant labour (which has increased the HIV/AIDS pandemic in the region), and centralised state structures (informed by the organisation of power in the liberation movements).

Despite these similarities, it is misleading to treat the sub-region as a homogeneous entity; the variations between its constituent states are as great as the ties that bind them. Southern African states experienced different degrees of white settlement that would later define the fault lines within countries such as South Africa, Namibia and Zimbabwe. There were different methods of achieving national liberation: for example, Angola and Mozambique were liberated through the pressures of the barrel of the gun, Botswana, Lesotho and Swaziland were granted independence without much struggle, and Zimbabwe and South Africa became majority-ruled states via negotiated settlements. In the immediate post-colonial phase Mozambique and Angola, whose liberation movements had embraced Marxist-Leninism, became socialist states, Tanzania and Zambia adopted what they called African Socialism, whilst Malawi, Botswana and Lesotho espoused capitalism even though they lacked an industrial base. Zimbabwe and South Africa, relatively industrialised countries, had to contend with the processes of reconciliation and reconstruct racially inclusive states. There are also marked differences in the levels of socio-economic and political development which continue to inform both intra-state and inter-state relations in the region. For example, Swaziland remains under the tutelage of a monarchy and multi-partyism in Zimbabwe is stifled, leading to civil unrest in these countries. South Africa's Gross Domestic Product (GDP) and infrastructure make it the dominant economic player in the region, but it is also the country with the largest socio-economic inequities. We will more closely examine the characteristics and challenges for the construction of post-colonial societies, of the sub-region's defining feature – white settler colonialism.

White settler colonialism

White settler colonialism is characterised by the permanent settlement of a large number of colonialists and their appropriation of space, power and wealth. Angola, Mozambique, Namibia, South Africa and Zimbabwe were subjected to this form of colonialism. The institutionalisation of a system geared to the protection and reproduction of white settler interests remains a matter of concern for the latter three countries.

For the present purpose we focus on four of the features of settler colonialism in Southern Africa: the co-existence of the colonisers and the colonised within the same geographical space over an extended period of time; the violence inherent in this form of colonialism; the racialisation of inequality; and the construction of identities in the furtherance of this colonial project. We briefly flag what these mean and the challenges they present for post-liberation development.

Mamdani's 1996 study, *Citizen and Subject*, concluded that indirect rule was the generic form of rule for all colonies in Africa. That being said, however, white settler colonialism was distinct in that the visible presence of the colonialist, the racialised class formation and the racialisation of space made the colonial encounter directly oppressive. Blacks were herded into virtual dormitories (rural reserves with little potential for capital accumulation and/or where excess labour was contained or urban townships) – with the train line often symbolising the border between spaces of privilege and spaces of deprivation. Moreover, white settlement meant that, post-liberation, there would be no 'Great Trek back to a Motherland'. The re-ordering of the societies therefore had to take cognisance of a continued presence of whites and their control over the 'commanding heights of the economy'. Not surprisingly, non-racialism and reconciliation became the platform and process for the construction of more inclusive post-liberation nations in the sub-region. However, these post-colonial societies are confronted with the problematic of practising non-racialism in profoundly race-based societies and the limitations of reconciliation when structural cleavages, coinciding with race, continue to exist.

White settler colonialism was a violent form of rule. Physical violence was the means through which land was seized and it structured the form of resistance to dispossession: all of this is inscribed in 'colonial wars', to use the shorthand. Settler colonialism could only be maintained by the sort of structural violence which permeates everyday life and governs the interaction between coloniser and colonised, and psychological violence which strips people of dignity and respect and renders them inherently inferior. Violence then also became the means through which the oppressed, excluded from their societies, and unable to effect change through peaceful avenues, fought for self-rule and an equitable distribution of resources: hence the resort to armed struggle in Angola, Mozambique, South Africa, Namibia and Zimbabwe. Violence has thus become normalised ('a culture of violence') patterning itself in the ordering of the post-colonial societies and the methods through which differences are resolved.

The consequences of the armed struggle include centralised, commandist, loyalist, non-transparent organisational cultures which continue to resonate in the post-colonial states where organisations which gained control of the state continue to function more as liberation movements than political parties (see Suttner and Amuwo's chapters for an elaboration on these aspects). Secondly, the cache of arms from this period has fuelled the high levels of crime in the region and, in the case of Mozambique and Angola, development has been retarded in rural areas littered with mines. Thirdly, there is the phenomenon of war veterans, many with expectations of the state which remain unfulfilled. Fourthly, more positively, the role played by women within the armed struggles and the broader liberation movement, has, to some extent, enabled women to assert their rights in the restructuring of their societies. Though gender discrimination still persists, Southern Africa now has the largest percentage of women's representation in government in Africa.

The racialisation of inequality that was a hallmark of white settler colonialism constitutes *the* source of continued tensions within 'post-white settler societies' (to employ the terminology of Mandaza 1987). The economies were premised on a racial division of labour where whites owned the industrial and commercial agricultural means of production, whilst blacks filled the ranks of the unskilled labour category. In the case of South Africa, large-scale agriculture, mining, and, later, industrialisation, required cheap black labour to be supplied by a migrant labour system. This system involved all the countries in the region, creating a 'skewed, integrated regional economy' (Marais 1998:11). It explains the high rate of urbanisation and proletarianisation in Southern Africa. The migrant labour system is also a major factor in the spread of HIV/AIDS in the region.

Land alienation, political exclusion and racial domination were the pillars of the National Question. The liberation struggles in Southern Africa were not merely about deracialisation, they were centrally concerned with getting back the land. A direct link was made between black poverty and the lack of access to fertile tracts of land, in other words, unequal land ownership. Negotiated settlements in Zimbabwe, Namibia and South Africa, occurring as they did when the neo-liberal paradigm was becoming influential, left the National Question unresolved. Although these settlements created the conditions for the deracialisation of the political environment they left largely to the vagaries of the market and land (and broader economic) reform.

Only limited remedial measures were put in place to bring about transformation. The principle of the 'willing buyer, willing seller' conditioned the pace and scale of land reform, and land ownership in Zimbabwe, Namibia and South Africa remained largely in white hands, although the new black bourgeoisie also acquired some access to this land. Sam Moyo (2003) has argued that throughout Southern Africa land alienation and control over land constitutes a threat to the security of the region. He has also broadened his argument to include the black elite and foreign investors making other countries in the region vulnerable to the same threats of instability. This threat became a reality in Zimbabwe in 2000, when 'war veterans' began to seize land by violent means. The formation of the Landless People's Movement in South Africa indicates the urgency for land reform if the country does not want to walk the same road as Zimbabwe.

Ten years after South Africa's transformation, racialised inequality persists despite the nationalists' strategy of creating a black bourgeoisie through access to state power, policies of affirmative action and black economic empowerment. Blacks remain largely trapped in apartheid's ghettos and urban shanty towns, populating the unskilled, unemployed and underemployed economic sectors. Moreover, the level and scale of inequality is increasing as democratisation proceeds (see Amuwo's chapter). The vexing challenge here is to transform the national economy to serve the interests of a majority black citizenry under conditions of continued domination by a powerful white bourgeoisie and in a global environment that allows little deviation from neo-liberal policies and principles. Other countries in the region have been constrained by SAPs for much longer than South Africa and have also registered increased levels of deprivation among the poor, even though their GDP appears to indicate economic growth.

Our last focus is on the construction of identities under white settler colonialism and the challenges this presents for post-colonial states in the region. Much has been written on the role played by colonialists in the construction of ethnic identities in Africa (see Vail 1989; Mamdani 1996; Ranger 1983; Berman 1998; Hendricks 2001 and 2004; and Lushaba in this volume). Of particular importance has been the politicisation of identities through the dual processes of hardening the boundaries of previously more fluid cultural identities (through legal codification, for example) and making identity the basis upon which access to resources is determined. Mamdani (2003) has elaborated upon the 'technology of colonial rule', noting that the census divided the populations into races (non-natives) and tribes (natives/ indigenes), the former governed by civil law and the latter by customary law which reinforced cultural difference. Ekeh (1975) made a similar argument, elaborating the notion of 'two publics,' the civic and the primordial, constructed to safeguard colonial interests in the continued subjugation of the population under colonial rule. The strategy of compartmentalisation contained the idea that 'races were meant to have a common future; different ethnicities were not' (Mamdani 2003: 455). The consolidation of communities into a plethora of ethnic minorities, according to colonial logic, would disrupt the easy emergence of a national consciousness and the quest for self-determination.

The construction of identities in Southern Africa, though hardly unique, took this logic to extremes. In South Africa, for example, the Apartheid State, through to its policy of separate development, sought to turn ethnic groups into nations, each with their own homeland. The South African state also sought to differentiate those of 'mixed descent' from both African and white identities and invest this differentiation with a materiality that would reinforce this identification (see Hendricks 2000, 2001, 2004). This resonates in other white settler societies (see Mandaza 1997), the larger point being that, though these identities predate colonial or apartheid rule, much of their contemporary character and social and political significance developed under colonial rule.

This fragmentation of these societies impacted on the quest for unity during the struggles for liberation and in the immediate post-independence phase, as well as the often-noted problematic of the post-colonial African state where the 'unity project took on the form of a unitary project' (Olukoshi and Laakso 1996:13). Fragmentation in the liberation struggles in Angola, Mozambique and Zimbabwe had ethnic dimensions and catapulted these societies into civil wars after independence (see Mashingaidze's chapter which highlights the case of Zimbabwe). A repeat performance was feared in South Africa where the Inkatha Freedom Party (IFP), a predominantly Zulu-based party, threatened secession after clashes between it and the African National Congress (ANC) supporters had already left thousands dead in Kwa-Zulu Natal. However, aware of the failure of the nation-building strategy encapsulated by Samora Machel's oft-cited statement, 'For the nation to live, the tribe must die', South Africa and Namibia adopted multi-culturalism and/ or civic nationalism as the basis for constituting new political communities. The phrase, 'rainbow nation' was coined to signify the 'unity in diversity' approach that sets these countries apart from other states in the region, indeed, on the continent.

It is, however, through ideological struggles within South Africa, particularly struggles about the basis for citizenship, rather than through intra-African ethnic tensions, that a vision of a multi-cultural non-racial nation-state was constructed. Simply put, the question to be resolved was who is a citizen or what are the lines for inclusion and exclusion? Mamdani has captured this problematic under his oft-cited question 'when does the settler become a native?' For the ANC, this question had been resolved in 1955 at the historic Kliptown conference which produced the Freedom Charter. This charter, though not uncontested, noted that 'the land belonged to all those who lived in it'. In the 1980s, the United Democratic Front (UDF) popularised the principle of non-racialism. Non-racialism's discourse is primarily about rights, asserting that an 'individuals citizenship, legal rights, economic entitlement and life chances should not be decided on the basis of "racial ascriptions" (Marks 1994: 2). These ideas diluted the categorisations of 'indigene' and 'settler' in the South African context and made possible a negotiated settlement in which all could see themselves as an integral part of a post-apartheid state.

Breaking out of the worldview of the settler and the native (which Mamdani, 2003, deemed necessary to solve the problematic) has not, as the social history of the sub-region demonstrates, completely abated the problem of racism. The limitations of liberal democracy, now dominant in the sub-region, as the measure of political accommodation and social integration in 'post-white settler colonies', has already been analysed (see Hendricks's chapter). Liberal democracy's celebration of a narrow form of political equality conceals and further perpetuates white dominance and privilege. Protest against this state of affairs inadvertently turns into a race question, hence the continued salience of race in the region. The features of the sub-region highlighted above constitute the spectrum of issues within the scope of contemporary analysis of Southern African politics and history. In various ways the ten chapters outlined below tease out, and read anew, the problematic of these features for development in the region.

Situating the chapters

Broad themes that emerge in the chapters of this volume are: the production of knowledge on Africa; alternative sites of struggle for national liberation; democratisation\democratic renewal; and post-liberation identity politics and social transformation. Read together, the chapters make a modest contribution towards filling the gaps in Southern African scholarship and identifying alternative approaches to democratic renewal.

The production of knowledge on Africa

Post-colonial studies has revealed a close relationship between the writing of history and broader societal power relations. In other words, historical narratives are often embedded within existent power relations and are reflective of the values of the dominant socio-political forces. For example, colonial/imperial history was concerned to rationalise and legitimate colonialism through a discourse that pitted the 'civilised' against the 'savage': a discourse that constructed the colonised as an inferior 'other'. There have been numerous works exploring and/or analysing these constructions (see, for example, Said 1978; Mudimbe 1988, 1994; Pieterse 1992). During the decolonisation process, we saw a corresponding shift in African history to the retrieval and celebration of Africa's pre-colonial glories and civilisations. A nationalist history developed, capturing the rise of nationalism and the moments of liberation. These histories often amounted to uncritical celebrations of both Africa's past and the gallant struggles for independence by African nationalist movements.

Within these historical narratives, other equally important dynamics of struggle were glossed over: for example, the divisions within the liberation movements, different forms of struggle, and race, class, ethnic and gender cleavages among the dominated. As earlier alluded to, the post-nationalist historiography of the 1980s began to tease out these complexities. This disrupted the static binary categories of coloniser/colonised, tradition/modernity, white/black, producing new narratives in which Africans of all genders were provided with agency, the fluidity of relations was revealed, and the internal cleavages and contradictions within homogenised categories brought to the fore. Some of the chapters in this volume continue this exercise.

In chapter 1, Nyeko provides an overview of the historiography of Swaziland and contests the positioning of the country vis-a-vis the liberation struggle in Southern Africa as a 'willing bedfellow of apartheid South Africa' (pg 25). Pointing to the emergence of a new social history, he notes that there is a need to make a distinction between the policies and actions of the Swazi government and those of the ordinary citizens: a 'bottom-up history' reveals very different forms of Swaziland's interaction with, and contribution to, the national liberation struggles in the region. Through an analysis of the topics of post-graduate students and historians at the University of Swaziland, Nyeko highlights the concerns now dominating historical investigation in the country, such as, gender and society, race relations, labour relations, and HIV/AIDS. This research places Swaziland within the context of larger continental processes and scholarship shifting from the earlier emphasis on Swaziland exceptionality. However, this scholarship still has a glaring gap with regard to the democratisation process (or lack of it).

Mushonge's chapter points to the need for a broader analysis of the history of armed struggle that not only focuses on the main protagonists but shows how non-combatants\unarmed civilians were drawn into the struggle as willing or unwilling participants. In the logic of the armed struggle the highest price that could be paid for liberation was death on the battle fields. Nationalist historiography tended to concentrate on the deaths and sacrifices that were directly related to the armed struggle. Mushonga's chapter takes us to the other, uncelebrated sacrifices that were made. He considers how curfew laws, imposed by the white Rhodesian regime during Zimbabwe's liberation war, led to the death of many peasants and placed them between a rock and a hard-place. The exigencies of the war meant that they were forced to be on the wrong side, either by the liberation/guerrilla fighters or by the state security forces. This chapter provides a situational analysis of the liberation struggle through the lens of the experiences of the peasants caught between the demands of the liberation movement and those of the state. It is a refreshing reminder that things were never simply black and white and that ordinary people had to negotiate their lives in the context of these complexities.

Alternative sites of struggle for national liberation

Nationalist history tended to concentrate on the strategies and tactics of the liberation movements and how they responded to the manoeuvrings of the settler colonial regimes. It ignored the contributions and sacrifices made by ordinary civilians and any other forms of challenging the colonialists or the apartheid government. The chapters by Bagwasi and Vanek address this issue.

Bagwasi employs a textual analysis to show how language is used as an instrument/site of struggle and/or as a register of power relations. For a long time research on language focused on the imposition of foreign languages on the peoples of the continent. This chapter draws our attention to language as an inter-subjective space within which a contest between the colonisers and the colonised is played out. Bagwasi analyses the salutations, beginnings and endings of letters exchanged between British administrators and chiefs in Botswana. Through this process she is able to show how British administrators invest themselves with superiority that is reflected in the ways in which they address letters to chiefs, and the resistance by chiefs to their perceived place in the hierarchised colonial society. This preliminary investigation indicates the need for further exploration of different forms of resistance, as well as the need for a closer look at the role of language in power struggles, and for greater complexity in our analyses of the relationships between chiefs and administrators.

Vanek, in a case study of the Wilgespruit Fellowship Centre (WFC), looks at the internal and external difficulties faced by a predominantly white liberal faith-based organisation in its quest to counter apartheid ideology and practice in South Africa. She focuses the reader's attention on the way white liberals dealt with the challenge of racial segregation. The chapter, by elaborating on attempts by the state to close the WFC, once again shows the white supremacist obsession with racial degeneracy. The centre was constructed as a 'den of iniquity'. It was the possibility of interracial sex, always constituted in racist discourse as capable of destroying the fabric of white society (Dubow 1995), that caused the greatest concern for the authorities.

Vanek lists a number of influential Black Consciousness Movement people whose politicisation began through an encounter with the teachings of the WFC. She argues that the WFC's emphasis on 'self-definition' shaped their ideological stance. This analysis is at variance with the portrayal of a decisive break, through the emergence of Black Consciousness, in the development of liberation thought in South Africa and instead indicates a logical progression. However, Vanek's analysis can only be understood in the context of an elaborate discussion of the differences between a race-relations paradigm and a non-racial or anti-racist paradigm.

Democratisation/democratic renewal

Since the late 1980s, the continent has been engulfed in struggles for democratic renewal. This has generated an abundance of scholarly debate on the appropriate form of democratisation and the conditions for its consolidation. Eyoh (1998b) divided African scholarship on the topic into three categories 'universalist', 'popular democratic' and 'nativist'. The 'universalists' dominated the debate at first, emphasising universal procedures for democratic rule, with multi-partyism as the most important component. The 'popular democratic' theorists questioned the conflation of democracy with multi-partyism and argued that too much emphasis was placed on democratic procedures with a subsequent neglect of substantive issues of socio-economic rights. 'Nativists', according to Eyoh, also questioned the reductionist view of democracy and highlighted the need for African societies to build on democratic values that are culturally germane. It is noteworthy that despite their differences, all three groups of scholars accept democracy as the best form of governance. However, the neo-liberalism that has gone in tandem with political democracy has been widely rejected. There is a plethora of literature on structural adjustment in relation to democratisation that stresses the impoverishment of the poor and the deepening of class cleavages. The linkage of economic liberalisation to political liberalisation is seen as undermining the latter, giving rise to what Mkandawire referred to as 'choice-less democracies' (1999).

South Africa's democratisation process has been subject to a similar trajectory and concomitant analytical debate. The left argues that the self-imposed, neo-liberal informed macroeconomic policy, Growth, Employment and Redistribution (GEAR) has compromised the democratic transition. This policy has meant a shift in the emphasis on redistribution to, and development of, the poor that guided the aims of the liberation movement. Instead, it facilitates the emergence of a new black middle class which is increasingly beginning to resemble Fanon's depiction of the post-colonial nationalist bourgeoisie.

Amuwo (chapter 2) and Suttner (chapter 3) probe the nature of politics in post-apartheid South Africa, inquiring into the meaning and content of democracy in the country and the reasons why it assumes its particular form. Amuwo argues that while there is 'formal democracy (in terms of institutions and procedures of a neo-electoral democracy), substantive democracy partly explicated in terms of "redistribution of power – the degree to which citizens can participate in the decisions which affect their lives" [citing Luckham 2003] remains largely a shrinking province' (page 39). He further argues 'that the problem of a de facto one-party state seems to loom large on the horizon' (page 40). Amuwo's arguments can be situated within the 'popular democratic' school of thought on democratisation as outlined above. His concern is to show how the neo-liberal democratic paradigm results in the institutionalisation of an elite-driven formal democracy, what he calls the 'political science of democracy', to the detriment of the more urgent and empowering 'political economy of democratisation'. Against the expectations of independence raised by the long and excruciating fight against apartheid, the chapter points to the ANC's capitulation to domestic and international capital and the consequent alienation and impoverishment of the masses and political demobilisation of civil society. Amuwo sees continuities in autocratic decision-making in the national liberation and post-liberation phases. While he applauds South Africa's progress at the super-structural level he warns against the danger of autocracy and the backlash that may result if substantive issues are not addressed.

Suttner's chapter closely examines a period in the South African struggle when the United Democratic Front (UDF) was dominant. His intention is to uncover the meanings and practices of democracy during this period, contrast these with current conceptualisations and modes of enactment, and identify the lessons of the UDF period. In so doing, he offers a nuanced and introspective interpretation of the liberation struggle and the factors that have shaped the current state of democratic practice in South Africa. Suttner contends that during the UDF period, democratic accountability and popular power informed democratic practice. The concept of 'prefigurative democracy' is employed to depict an understanding of democracy, operative during the UDF's heyday when people 'understood that their daily practices were part of the process of building the 'new South Africa' (page 63). His overview is not a romanticisation of the period for he is well aware that along with this conceptualisation came forms of abuse and an intolerance of diversity. His analysis provides agency to the populace who, he contends, played a substantial part in determining the ways in which extra-parliamentary governance unfolded. His explanation of the demobilisation of society differs in emphasis from Amuwo's. Instead of focusing on the ANC's predilection for authoritarianism, he concentrates on the UDF's self-conceptualisation –

as 'curtain raisers' – providing the 'opportunity structure' for the 'real liberation movement' (who by the very nature of their modus operandi were less inclined to tolerate dissent from below) to assume power. The shape of South African democracy today can largely be attributed period. In this chapter we see the complexity of the process of arriving at the current conjuncture in South Africa: the process cannot be reduced to either the machinations of globalisation, capitalism and/or neo-liberalism. Suttner also alludes to the necessity for taking identity seriously and argues that its corresponding organisational forms, even if race-based, should not necessarily be taken as racist or reactionary. It is to the issue of identity politics and social transformation that the discussion turns in Mashingaidze, Hendricks, Lushaba and Palmary.

Post-liberation identity politics and social transformation

Earlier we noted that settler colonialism, as a form of rule, was sustained in the sub-region through the twin processes of divide and rule (separate development) and violent repression. Consequently, its dismantling also took a violent form. These societies therefore faced the task of post-conflict reconstruction or rebuilding: fashioning a social and political system where former enemies, in this case, the colonisers and the colonised, can co-exist harmoniously in a 'politics of accommodation'. In these societies a transitional notion of justice emerged in which the emphasis is on revealing and forgiving, in an attempt to heal the nation's psychological wounds and move on with the task of nation-building. The ultimate goal, therefore, is to foster unity and a sense of belonging among the different sections of the population.

In his critique of the 1987 Zimbabwean National Unity Accord, Mashingaidze addresses the issue of transitional justice in Zimbabwe, arguing that its failure was mainly because, in both spirit and content, it remained elitist, and, therefore, bereft of integrative elements. According to him, 'the Unity Accord had a poor post-conflict peace-building framework that encompassed the aspirations and demands of the grassroots' (page 88). The consequences for the post-conflict era are that war memories continue to inform and shape political opinion and choices in those regions that were devastated when the state's forces quelled the 'rebellion'. Against this background, he concludes that the failure of the Accord to close the fissures caused by the Matabeleland conflagration is a 'case of peace without reconciliation' (page 82). This chapter is, therefore, concerned with the role of memory, an area of study that is increasingly yielding important insights into how our understanding of the past impacts on the present. Richard Werbner notes that there is a 'post-colonial memory crisis' and contends, in relation to Zimbabwe, that 'In many places, people bring powerful, sometimes intimately painful traces of the colonial as well as the postcolonial past to bear on their present politics' (1998: 1-2). Mashingaidze's chapter puts forward a similar argument to explain the discord that currently disrupts the easy constitution of a democratic order in this country.

A closely related question focuses on social transformation in post-settler colonies where differential racialisation imbued identities with a materiality that made them inter-subjective spaces within which privilege and deprivation were lived and experienced, thereby reinforcing the boundaries of those identities. Through the policy of differential racialisation and a host of other laws, settler colonialism created first- and second-class citizens. Post-liberation societies are confronted by the challenge of fashioning a social transformation agenda to break down the artificial barriers to social mobility that coincide with social and group identity boundaries, if they are to escape group-based agitations against marginalisation and domination. That group-based discrimination is antithetical to sustainable democratic governance is axiomatic. However, liberal democracy, widely embraced by almost all countries in the region, has proved its weakness in the face of such group-based discrimination.

The contribution by Hendricks deals with an analysis of the compatibility between liberal democracy and group-based deprivation\marginalisation. In her analysis of the interplay between race/racism and liberal democracy in the South African context, she brings to our attention liberal democracy's ability to legitimise and reproduce unequal social relations. In her view, it does this through its limited focus on political equality, thereby neglecting the structural foundations of socio-economic inequality. Liberal democracy, premised as it is on the individual, thus requires domestication in racialised societies, that is, group-based corrective measures must be brought to bear. Implied in Amuwo's chapter is a similar form of democracy that recognises unequal group relations.

In virtually all settler colonies, being white meant being privileged while being non-white meant inescapable poverty and marginality. The conspicuous gap between the living conditions and opportunities of the two social strata has been captured in neo-marxist studies of white settler colonies in the region. However, this kind of analysis has the unintended consequence of glossing over the protean nature of social relations entailed in settler colonial social structuration. Contrary to what the Marxist class analysis suggests, the social transformation challenge in post-white settler colonies involves far more than the equalisation of opportunities between whites and blacks. Lushaba's intervention problematises further this already complex imperative for democratising social relations by pointing to the unequal social relations within subjugated groups. Drawing on both Marx and Weber, he locates the construction of an Indian identity in the apartheid government's structuration of the society and shows how the differential allocation of resources to Africans and Indians in Durban leads to tensions between the two dominated communities. His conclusion, supported by evidence from South Africa, that mere legislation is not enough to transform the identities and interaction of their bearers in the post-apartheid state, can be generalised to other settler colonies.

Scholars like McClintock (1995) have analysed the exclusionary, racialised and gendered nature of nationalism, drawing on Anderson's (1983) concept of 'imagined communities' that posits the nation as constructed through discourses of nationalism, as well as post-modernist and post-colonial interventions which deconstruct identity representation and the power relations they conceal, Palmary's chapter contributes to this scholarship by analysing the identity narratives of women refugees in South Africa. She considers 'how women make sense of the events leading up to their forced displacement to South Africa within the context of South African and their own nationalist rhetoric' (page 140). Using the private/public dichotomy, expounded upon at length by various feminist theorists, she notes how women remain stereotyped within the private domain within these nationalist discourses, and how refugee women often subvert their own political agency by presenting themselves as politically inactive and disengaged. Noteworthy here is that this is done as a conscious strategy for survival. Palmary's chapter eloquently explores the debates that have transpired around nationalism and begins to shift our scholarly gaze to the new theoretical interventions on transnationalism.

In conclusion, despite the overall unity of the subcontinent, the chapters reveal temporal and spatial variations in the actual processes of colonial and post-colonial development. Radical Political Economy provided a powerful analytical framework to comprehend the overall contours of Southern African development, but, as subsequent literature and these chapters demonstrate, it was too blunt an instrument to do justice to the subtleties and complexities of actual experiences. The chapters point to the contradictions and alternative paths taken in the movement toward democracy. Moreover, they question the very nature of democratisation and turn our attention to the continuing need to problematise and interrogate this fundamental goal and process. We hope that this volume succeeds in opening up and/or extending debates on issues that have long pre-occupied the sub-region and that it contributes to the realisation of new visions and practices in the continent as a whole.

Note
1. The authors would like to thank Dickson Eyoh and Jacky Solway for comments on an earlier draft.

References

Alexander, N., 2002, *An Ordinary Country: Issues in the Transition from Apartheid to Democracy in South Africa*, Pietermaritzburg: University of Natal Press.

Amin, S., 1972, 'Underdevelopment and Dependence in Black Africa: Origins and Contemporary Forms,' *Journal of Modern African Studies*, Vol. 10/4.

Anderson, B., 1983, *Imagined Communities: Reflections on the Origin and Spread of Nationalism*, London: NLB.

Apter, D. and Rosberg, C., 1994, 'Changing African Perspectives', in Apter and Rosberg (eds) *Political Development and the New Realism in Sub-Saharan Africa*, Charlottesville and London: University of Virginia.

Berman, B., 1998, 'Ethnicity, Patronage and the African State: The Politics of Uncivil Nationalism,' *African Affairs*, Vol. 97.

Berman, B., Eyoh, D. and W. Kymlicka eds., 2004, *Ethnicity and Democracy in Africa*, Oxford: James Currey.

Bond, P., 2000, *Elite Transition*, London: Pluto Press.

Buthelezi, S., 2000, 'Globalisation and the Process of Democratisation in Southern Africa' in, D.W. Nabudere (ed.) *Globalisation and the Post-Colonial African State*, Harare: AAPS Books.

Cobley, A., 2001, 'Does Social History have a Future? The Ending of Apartheid and Recent Trends in South African History', *Journal of Southern African Studies*, Vol. 27/3.

Dubow, S., 1995, *Scientific Racism in Modern South Africa*, Cambridge: Cambridge University Press.

Ekeh, P., 1975, 'Colonialism and the Two Publics in Africa: A Theoretical Statement', *Comparative Studies in Society and History*, Vol. 17/1.

Eyoh, D., 1998a, 'Representations of Power in African Nationalist Discourse' in *Research in African Literatures*, Summer, Vol. 29/2.

Eyoh, D., 1998b, 'African Perspectives on Democracy and the Dilemmas of Post-colonial Intellectuals, *Africa Today*, Vol. 3/4.

Habib, A. and Padayachee, V., 2000, 'Economic Policy and Power Relations in South Africa's Transition to Democracy, *World Development*, Vol. 28/2.

Hendricks, C., 2000, '"We knew our Place": A Study of the Constructions of Coloured Identity in South Africa', PhD. Thesis, University of South Carolina.

Hendricks, C., 2001, '"Ominous Liaisons": Tracing the Interface Between Race and Sex at the Cape', in Z. Erasmus (ed.) *Coloured by History, Shaped By Place*, Cape Town: Kwela Books.

Hendricks, C., 2004, 'The Burdens of the Past and the Challenges of the Present: Coloured Identity and the Rainbow Nation,' in B. Berman, D. Eyoh, and W. Kymlicka (eds) *Ethnicity and Democracy in Africa*, Oxford: James Currey.

Himmelstrand, U., Kinyanjui, K. and E. Mburugu, eds., 1994, *African Perspectives on Development: Controversies, Dilemmas and Openings*, Nairobi: East African Educational Publishers.

Mamdani, M., 1996, *Citizen and Subject: Contemporary Africa and the Legacy of Late Colonialism*, Princeton, NJ.: Princeton University Press.

Mamdani, M., 2003, 'Race and Ethnicity,' in Paul Tiyambe Zeleza and Dickson Eyoh (eds) *Encyclopedia of Twentieth-Century African History*, London: Routledge.

Mandaza, I., 1987, 'Introduction: The Political Economy of Transition', and 'The State and Politics in the Post-White Settler Colonial Situation', in Ibbo Mandaza, (ed.) *Zimbabwe: The Political Economy of Transition 1980-1986*, Zimbabwe: CODESRIA.

Mandaza, I., 1997, *Race, Colour and Class in Southern Africa*, Harare: Sapes Books.

Marais, H., 1998, *South Africa Limits to Change: The Political Economy of Transition*, London: Zed Books.

Marks, S., 1994, 'The Tradition of Non-Racism in South Africa', paper presented at the History Workshop 'Democracy: Popular Precedents, Practices, Culture,' University of Witwatersrand, 13-15 July.

Matlosa, K., 1998, 'Democracy and Conflict in Post-Apartheid Southern Africa: Dilemmas of Social Change in Small States', *International Affairs*, Vol. 74/2.

McClintock, A., 1997, 'No Longer in Future Heaven: Gender, Race and Nationalism' in A. McClintock, A. Mufti, and E. Shohat (eds) *Dangerous Liaisons: Gender, National and Postcolonial Perspectives*, Minneapolis and London: University of Minnesota Press.

Mkandawire, T., 1999, 'Crisis Management and the Making of Choiceless Democracies', in R. Joseph (ed.) *State, Conflict and Democracy in Africa*, Boulder: Lynne Rienner.

Mhone, G., 2003, 'Democratisation, Economic Liberalisation and the Quest for Sustainable Development in South Africa', in G. Mhone and O. Edigheji (eds) *Governance in the New South Africa: The Challenges of Globalisation*, Cape Town: University of Cape Town Press.

Moyo, S., 2003, 'Land Reform in Zimbabwe', *New Agenda* issue 9.

Moyo, S., 2003, 'The Land Questions in Africa: Research, Perspective and Questions', paper presented at the CODESRIA Conference in Gaborone, Botswana, 18-19 October.

Mudimbe, V.Y., 1988, *The Invention of Africa: Gnosis, Philosophy and the Order of Knowledge*, Bloomington and Indianapolis: Indiana University Press.

Mudimbe, V.Y., 1994, *The Idea of Africa*, Bloomington and Indianapolis: Indiana University Press.

Nabudere, D. W., 2002, 'Nepad: Its Historical Background and Its Prospects', at www.worldsummit2002.org/texts/DaniWNabudere.pdf

Nkiwane, T., 1998, 'Opposition Politics in Zimbabwe: The Struggle within the Struggle' in A. Olukoshi (ed.) *The Politics of Opposition in Contemporary Africa*, Uppsala Nordiska Afrikainstitutet.

Nzongola-Ntalaja, G., 1997, 'The State and Democracy in Africa' in G. Nzongola-Ntalaja and Margaret Lee (eds) *The State and Democracy in Africa*, Harare: AAPS Books.

Pieterse, J.N., 1992, *White on Black: Images of Africa and Blacks in Western Popular Culture*, New Haven and London: Yale University Press.

Olukoshi, A. and Laakso, B., eds., 1996, *Challenges to the Nation-State in Africa*, Uppsala: Nordiska Afrika Institutet.

Olukoshi, A., 1998, 'Economic Crisis, Multipartyism, and Opposition Politics in Contemporary Africa' in A. Olukoshi (ed.) *The Politics of Opposition in Contemporary Africa*, Uppsala: Nordiska Afrikainstitutet.

Osaghae, E., 1994, 'Ethnicity in Africa or African Ethnicity: The Search for a Contextual Understanding', in U. Himmelstrand et al. (eds) *African Perspectives on Development: Controversies, Dilemmas and Openings*, Nairobi: E.A.E.P.

Ranger, T., 1983, 'The Invention of Tradition in Colonial Africa' in Eric Hobsbawm and Terence Ranger (eds) *The Invention of Tradition*, Cambridge: Cambridge University Press.

Ranger, T., 1988, 'Review Article: Africa Looks at Southern Africa: A Review of Journals', *Journal of Southern African Studies* Vol. 14/3.

Ranger, T., 2004, 'Nationalist Historiography, Patriotic History and the History of the Nation: the Struggle over the Past in Zimbabwe', *Journal of Southern African Studies*, Vol. 30/2.

Rothchild, D. and Chazan, N., eds., 1998, *The Precarious Balance: State and Society in Africa*, Boulder: Westview.

Said, E., 1978, *Orientalism*, London: Routledge and Kegan Paul.

Sandbrook, R., 2000, *Closing the Circle: Democratization and Development in Africa*, London and New York: Zed Books.

Saul, J. and Gelb, S., 1986, *The Crisis in South Africa*, London Zed Books.

Solway, J., 1995, 'Political Participation, Ethnicity and Multiparty Democracy in Botswana' in Dan O'Mear (ed.) *The Politics of Change in Southern Africa*, Montreal: Canadian Research Consortium on Southern Africa.

Vail, L., ed., 1989, *The Creation of Tribalism in Southern Africa*, Berkeley: University of California Press.

Wanyeki, L.M., 2002, 'A Gender Critique of Nepad', paper presented at the Women in Law and Development in Africa (WILDAF) panel during the 46th session of the UN Commission on the Status of Women, 4-15, March, New York, at www.sarpn.org.za/nepad/march2002/women/index.php

Werbner, R., 1998, 'Beyond Oblivion: Confronting Memory Crisis', in Richard Werbner (ed.) *Memory and the Postcolony: African Anthropology and the Critique of Power*, London and New York: Zed Books.

Young, C., 1994, 'Evolving Modes of Consciousness and Ideology: Nationalism and Ethnicity', in David E. Apter, and Carl G. Rosberg (eds) *Political Development and the New Realism in Sub-Saharan Africa*, Charlottesville and London: University Press of Virginia.

1

Swaziland and South Africa Since 1994: Reflections on Aspects of Post-Liberation Swazi Historiography

Balam Nyeko

Introduction: African historiographies

This consideration of the post-1994 historiography of Swaziland seeks to do two things: to provide a general survey of the historical work done since 1994, and to highlight some of the scholarly efforts that have attempted to project Swaziland's position *vis-a-vis* the liberation struggle in Southern Africa. The chapter assumes the status of a kind of interim reportage. An essential first step is to take stock of what has been done and what is currently available. Subsequent research will involve a more intense analysis of the contents of the work, with a view to assessing the extent to which it all contributes to a set of new directions in the scholarly discussion of Swazi history since 1994.

The production of historical knowledge about Swaziland was closely patterned on the way in which Southern African and African historiographies in general evolved. Given the geo-political and historical position of the country, this is scarcely surprising. These historiographies began with the imperialist/colonial school that saw publications written by the colonial administrators within the colonies. Their concern was to provide a basic description of what they called the natives' social and political way of life as well as their economic organisation. Closely following this and intimately allied with it was the school of historians that concentrated on the 'invaders' and their imperial activities. They often sought to justify the colonial state's position through their study of the various administrative policies applied in the colonies. These included programmes such as 'Direct' and 'Indirect Rule', 'Assimilation', 'Native Administration', and so forth. Their history of the

Africans was largely intended to assist the colonial state entrench its rule. As a reaction to this approach, the Nationalist/Africanist school emerged in the late 1950s and early 1960s, as the anti-colonial political campaign gained momentum in nearly all African colonies, to challenge alien control and the colonial presence as a whole. This was the kind of history that sought to place the African at the centre-stage, to trace the origins and development of nationalism in particular African countries, and to focus on the task of recovering the 'African initiative'. Later on, this school was severely criticised by scholars who could be described as representing the post-Nationalist historiography of the 1980s. They pointed out what they perceived as an undue pre-occupation with nationalism even where there were still no 'nation-states'. Among its limitations was the stark reality that, attractive as it was at the time, it could not explain the poverty and instability that confronted Africans everywhere during the post-independence years. Such revisionist scholars were sometimes referred to as the post-colonial pessimists because of their disillusionment with the 'emptiness' of the political independence already acquired by African states at this stage. They suggested a different kind of historiography that would trace and depict the social and economic transformation of Africa more satisfactorily.[1] They generally preferred to frame their questions within a different set of theoretical perspectives. For Slater, post-nationalist historiography is 'that historiography which sought to move beyond the bourgeois limitations of the Africanist historiography of the 1960s, and towards the production of a form of historical knowledge whose objective [was] to understand and present ... Africa's history from the standpoint of the workers and peasants, the oppressed classes of Africa...' (Slater 1986:250). If the early African historical scholarship was mainly concerned to 'demonstrate that African history existed' and was doable, and if the nationalist writers were pre-occupied with producing 'corrective history', certainly by the early 1980s African history had 'come of age'.[2]

South Africa and the BOLESWA countries

Relations between the modern republic of South Africa and its smaller neighbours of Botswana, Lesotho and Swaziland, have attracted serious academic as well as journalistic discussion for almost as long as the enclave countries have existed as separate entities. From the period of the *Mfecane* social upheavals of the early nineteenth century, when the evolution of the modern Nguni and Sotho states began, till contemporary times, the question of their very survival as independent sovereignties has been a major concern for all three. That they have been and are for all practical purposes socially and economically an integral part of their larger and more powerful neighbour goes without saying. That their history was for a long time—and continues to be—treated as a part of the history of South Africa by some scholars is also self-evident.[3]

One of the aspects of South Africa's relations with the enclave states during the 1970s and 1980s that interested many scholars was the question of their role in the anti-apartheid struggle. In the eyes of several observers, these countries had the opportunity of playing the part of a Trojan horse for the liberation movements. Indeed, both Botswana and Lesotho were used as hideouts and/or the first stopping points for liberation fighters fleeing from or infiltrating into South Africa. As is well documented, this often led to retaliatory and punitive responses towards these countries by the South African apartheid regime with very costly consequences for them. Any effort at taking a census of 'apartheid deaths', as some of the ongoing discussion amongst historians of Southern Africa is currently seeking, will have to take into account such casualties inside the affected countries.[4] The general consensus seems to be that, apart from the obvious examples of the more 'traditional' front-line states of the late 1970s and early 1980s, such as Zambia, Zimbabwe, Mozambique or Tanzania, both Lesotho and Botswana played a positive role in all this.

Swaziland, on the other hand, by and large enjoyed a far less flattering image and came under severe criticism from various writers for its alleged indifference and even opposition to the liberation movements operating from inside it. One scholar even went as far as suggesting that in its dealings with the Republic, it was 'a willing bedfellow of apartheid South Africa' in contrast to the position of the other two enclave states of Botswana and Lesotho, which had found themselves reluctantly obliged to co-operate with the enemy (Daniel 1984). Indeed, Swaziland has often been accused of having been overtly hostile to the African National Congress (ANC) and other Southern African liberation movements prior to 1994. The animosity appears to have reached its apex in the so-called four-year *Liqoqo* (inner council of Swazi expert advisers) period following the death of King Sobhuza II in 1982, when the government was under the effective control of this group (Shongwe 1995; Africa Report 1984; Simelane 1999). During this period, by all accounts, the factional in-fighting within the ruling circle saw a group of ruthless Swazi senior politicians not only assume dictatorial powers, but literally declare the ANC unwelcome in the country.[5] These evidently sour relations to which critics such as Daniel drew attention were, however, largely a reflection of the Swazi state's hostility to the organization rather than that of the ordinary Swazi. Available evidence shows that many ANC activists were able to undergo educational and other social training programmes, to work in paid employment in both government and private institutions, and even undertake clandestine political projects within Swaziland in the 1970s and 1980s.[6] A related and important aspect of the relations between the liberation movements and Swaziland was the real possibility that some government officers may have acted without official sanction. Rather, some evidence is now emerging that suggests they may have been acting independently by taking the liberty to harass the ANC men and women living in Swaziland at that point.[7] It was during the same time that the abortive Ingwavuma/Kangwane land deal, made public barely two months before Sobhuza's death, seemed to assume a considerable degree of urgency (Griffitties and Funell 1983).

This chapter does not seek to endorse or promote the official position of Swaziland or any of the 'front-line' states in the region. After all, it would be easy enough for nearly all of them to claim, at the political level at any rate, that they *all* contributed to the struggle to a lesser or greater degree.[8] Rather, we wish to examine critically the claim that Swaziland consistently maintained warm relations with apartheid South Africa and was conversely always less than welcoming to the liberation movements. In doing so, the discussion will briefly revisit the question first posed by Bischoff in the mid-1980s. His argument was that Swaziland's policy towards South Africa had been 'non-conflictual and accommodationist' largely as a consequence of sheer necessity. Not only had the Swazi monarchy historically played a key role in the 'national liberation' (that is, the struggle for the Swaziland's own independence) during the 1960s, but Swaziland had gone ahead and adopted a strategy of accommodating foreign capital in the post-independence years and accepted a policy of multi-racialism (Henri-Bischoff 1988, 1986). The intimate relationship between the Swazi ruling group and South Africa, the dominant power in the region, was seen as an insurance for the survival of the Swazi state in the face of the impending radical change in the region. This, in Bischoff's view, made the country different. It can be argued further that this was one explanation of why Swaziland appeared to have taken a somewhat low-key posture on the liberation issue. The question becomes even more significant in view of the long acknowledged fact that at the beginning of the twentieth century Swazi rulers were intimately involved in the launching of the original South African Native National Congress (SANNC). Queen Regent Gwamile Labotsibeni provided financial support to the party's newspaper and her son, Prince Malunge, who was an important political actor in the Swazi ruling circle, attended the early meetings of the ANC. Scholars from the region have continued to be mostly silent on this question and related themes since 1994. Has there been a recognition that Swaziland is indeed a component part of a wider world, and that it should see itself as part of this rather than an isolated country insisting on being different? What are the principal attributes of recent historical studies from Swaziland itself? To what extent have they been shaped by the changing regional relations since 1994?

Pre-1994 analyses of Swaziland's relations with South Africa

As already pointed out, the historiography of Swaziland's relations with South Africa can be traced to the turn of the nineteenth century when, at the end of the negotiations following the Anglo-Boer War of 1899–1902, the Union of South Africa was created. Then, as Hyam and other writers wrote some time ago, the possibility of the eventual incorporation of Swaziland and the other two High Commission territories of Basutoland and the Bechuanaland Protectorate was left open. The question continued to hang over the little states throughout the twentieth century and was a major consideration in determining their political attitude towards South Africa (Hyam 1972). In the discussion of both Lesotho and Swaziland's resistance to South Africa's ambitions to take them over, for instance, several scholars pointed out that the opposition to incorporation in both countries was based upon the African people's fear of South Africa's racial policies. Moreover, Britain, the colonial power in question, was highly critical of the South African authorities' overall outlook towards its African population (Nyeko 1979-81; Mekenye 1996). In recent times, therefore, more attention has been given to the need for a greater appreciation of the African resistance within these territories to South Africa's intentions. Although the decision to retain the status of the former High Commission territories was one that was clearly made in Whitehall rather than Maseru, Mbabane or Gaborone, the attitude of the colonised people contributed significantly to the conclusion made by the British authorities on the question.

If South Africa failed to absorb the neighbouring states politically throughout the twentieth century, the position was quite the opposite in terms of her economic relations with them. Here the available evidence confirms what is generally well known: that through a variety of processes, the economies of these countries were integrated into that of South Africa over the years. The coverage of this theme has been quite extensive in the historiography of the region and continues to grow. The emergence of a dominance-dependence relationship looms large in studies of the modern history of the individual countries as well as in their collective experience. As the political scientist Joshua Mugyenyi (1990) showed, this affected the small countries' foreign policies. Contributing to the discussion of the question why Swaziland seemed to pursue a different kind of policy than the other two states, he identified four factors that shaped the country's attitude to South Africa. These included the role of international capital (which was largely South African), South Africa's own policy of destabilising its neighbours, the white settler interests within Swaziland, and the Swazi ruling group's interests. This particular line of argument was in keeping with the position articulated by Henri-Bischoff (1988). Other related issues that indicate a greater level of economic integration and received scholarly attention include the question of land and the struggle for it, the development of migrant labour and its impact on the ordinary citizens of these countries, the rise of settler economic power, mining, agriculture, capital penetration, worker consciousness, etc.[9]

Swazi historical studies since the 1990s: Contributions from the University of Swaziland (UNISWA)

In a recent review of the Canadian scholar, Gillis's, study of the political history of Swaziland, Jonathan Crush has lamented the author's failure to recognize the new historiography of Swaziland that has emerged in the period c.1971–2001. Gillis is faulted for persisting with the royalty-centred approach previously criticised by other scholars. Rather than produce a history covering the majority of the population, he provided, instead, a 'narrative [that] describes the actions of the great, not the lowly. Swazi kings and queen-regents, colonial governors and officials, and white settlers feature prominently in the narrative'(Crush 2001).[10] Crush goes on to classify the existing historical work on Swaziland as falling under the categories of 'colonial and imperial history', the 'African nationalist' school, and those who are concerned with the 'social and economic' transformation of the country. Whether the more recent work emanating from the University of Swaziland can be fitted into any or all of these categories would seem immaterial. The overall picture, however, is that it has taken due cognisance of Swaziland's historical and contemporary interaction with the rest of society. A brief survey should highlight some of the features of these writings.

If many of the previous efforts at studying Swazi history and culture had been hampered by an undue concentration on the 'Swazi way', a tendency to see it as different and isolated, and a marked reluctance to perceive the country as a part of the wider world, certainly the Department of History at the University of Swaziland has steered its work in a totally distinctive direction over the last decade or so. The overall picture shows a clear move away from a concern with the rulers and pays less attention to political history.

From the early 1990s, undergraduate students undertook staff-supervised research projects that increasingly showed awareness of Swaziland's social and economic ties not only with South(ern) Africa, but also with the rest of the world. Thus, students were encouraged to examine the growth and impact of certain industries such as cotton production, sugar cultivation with special reference to how it has affected Swaziland's economy since independence in 1968, and the maize industry.[11] Other themes that have been covered include the role of co-operatives in the marketing of agricultural produce, and farmers' use of them as a mechanism for developing the rural areas of the country, as well as the introduction of bodies such as the National Agricultural Marketing Board (NAMBOARD) by the government. Worker consciousness and labour issues have also been of central interest in a number of works by the students. Throughout this latter category of research projects, there seems to be an emphasis on the way in which the Swazi ordinary citizen, for a long time marginalised in previous studies, has now been placed at the centre-stage.

Similarly, the researchers show an awareness that the common Swazi always found themselves in a disadvantaged relationship with their employers or competitors in almost any commercial economic activity they undertook, whether jointly or separately. Thus, Mangaliso Nkambule, in his examination of the initiative taken by the Swazi monarchy to help indigenous entrepreneurs, especially commercial transport operators, pointed out, for example, that as far back as 1947, Sobhuza II had founded the organisation known as the 'Swazi Commercial *Amadoda*' following his 'realization that the Swazis were being ignored in commerce by the white settlers ...' (Nkambule 1992). Swazi business men and women set up small shops and groceries in the rural areas of the country. Yet, it soon became clear that laudable as the organization's intentions had been, it was seriously handicapped by internal wranglings, indiscipline, and corruption. Thus, it achieved only limited success and was, by and large a failure. Much of the argument in this work and the others in the same category was couched or formulated in largely nationalistic terms. The general tone is one in which the explanation of historical themes places blame on some extraneous factors—usually the colonial system or its legacy—as being responsible for Swaziland's woes. Then, again, the unit of study, in a number of cases, was frequently a tiny locality in a corner of the country. However, while the focus of these studies seemed understandably local, they all showed awareness of the comparative work from other parts of Africa. For example, the projects undertaken by Manyatsi and Dladla respectively illustrate the point that an understanding of the way in which Swaziland's co-operatives functioned could be enhanced by an appreciation of similar studies carried out in similarly European-dominated areas such as Kenya.

So while the topics themselves may appear narrowly focused or somewhat parochial, there is a distinct recognition that Swazi history has long moved away from being presented as just the exploits of the ruling group and the story of their confrontations with the Boers, British or other African peoples.

It is particularly striking that even the projects that addressed specifically *political* themes were themselves not restricted to the older type of court history but rather dealt with questions that concerned the wider society.[12]

The undergraduate students' research projects appear to have been suspended by the University authorities around the mid-1990s.[13] Consequently, there is a break in the record from 1995 until 2002 when the Department of History resumed its offering of the course. It attracted as many as twenty-six students and the range of the subjects of study once again illustrated the continued preference for social and economic history over the purely political issues. The emphasis seems to have been on what might be described as 'applied history,' seeking to illustrate the relevance of the topics chosen to contemporary society. Many of the studies covered the last two or three decades of the twenty-first century and some carried their discussion up to 2002. Thus, the contribution of the trade unions to Swaziland's recent history, the impact of HIV-AIDS on society, gender relationships, women's changing attitudes to various mechanisms of social control over them in modern Swaziland, the role of Non-Governmental Organizations, (NGOs), the effects of the mass media control regulations, and the impact of co-operation between Swaziland and international organizations such as the European Union on the country's development programmes, the plight of elderly people in Swaziland today, and the significance of national heritage and tourism—all appealed to students who opted for this course during the 2002/2003 academic year.[14] This partiality for the more recent themes of Swazi history as a subject of historical investigation seemed to continue during the 2003/2004 academic year, as the students opted for the course.

The mid-1990s also saw the department embark on a two-part MA degree programme even though it temporarily shelved the BA projects. The main interests of the research portion of the post-graduate course, however, remained largely similar to those pursued in the undergraduate one. During the first year of the degree programme, the students attended taught classes on such optional areas as 'Gender and Society in Africa,' 'Comparative Peasantry,' and 'Comparative Slavery in the World'. They also took the compulsory 'Themes in the History of Swaziland' and 'Historiography of Southern Africa'. They spent the next year researching a topic of their choice dealing with some aspects of Swazi history. While numbers have been small due to obvious financial constraints, the completed dissertations have demonstrated, once again, the shifts in the historiography of Swaziland since the 1980s. Thus, although certain old themes such as the history of missionary endeavours in the country may appear to have been over-studied in the past, they have certainly been worth re-visiting. By focusing on the life histories of some educated women, it is possible to show how the mission-provided training they received, for example, helped change their status and image in Swazi society. One striking feature of a recently completed work under this programme concentrated specifically on the way in which women were affected by the activities of such missionary institutions (Ndwandwe 2000). Yet another MA student, Nhlanhla Dlamini, examined the nature of race relations at a particular mine complex in Swaziland during the colonial period, considering specifically relations between Europeans and Africans at the country's Havelock Asbestos Mine between 1939 and 1964. The author believed that the relevance of his study lay not only in the fact that the mine was a major employer of both European and African workers, but that race relations also occupied an important place in the historiography of Swaziland's economic development. (Dlamini's 2001) work has helped underline the point that, as was the case during the colonial period, race relations are likely to influence the overall attitude of the Swazis and Swaziland towards South Africa even in the post-1994 years. His continuing work on this theme will surely explore this argument further and advance our knowledge on the subject.[15]

If these works focus on social history and steer clear of any discussion of political issues, our third example of the kind of MA study done at UNISWA in the post-1994 period in fact returned to political history. Thus, in seeking to make 'a contribution to Swaziland's post-colonial history', Caanan Simelane initially traces the political developments in the country from the 1960s before turning to the post-independence period. He concentrates on the period from the 1973 repeal of the Independence Constitution onwards. He argues that the country-wide strikes and work stoppages that characterised the period was a manifestation of the 'people's frustration with the late King Sobhuza II's move to reverse [the] democratic process in the country'. Referring to the growing pressure for democratisation in the 1990s, Simelane concludes that the 'popular democratic opposition [had] failed to win majority support' principally because the Swazi leadership had successfully appeased the rural majority and even the traditionalists within the country's urban areas at the expense of those who were demanding multi-party democracy.[16]

Apart from making their obvious contribution through the supervision of both undergraduate and postgraduate work by students, members of the Department of History have, of course, conducted their own individual research that has often found its way into publications. Their particular interests have, not unexpectedly, been closely linked with those of their own students. Thus, agriculture, labour, social history, HIV-AIDS, and other related topics have provided the subject matter for staff research. While BAB Sikhondze has continued to write on the subject of rural change and trade in colonial Swaziland during the last several years, Ackson Kanduza has turned his attention to HIV-AIDS as well as to the role of intellectuals in Swaziland's politics before independence (Sikhondze 2003; Kanduza 2003a, 2003b). The most recent and possibly the best example of these efforts is Hamilton Sipho Simelane's 2003 study of economic relations in Swaziland during the colonial period. It is an illustration of how far the historiography of Swaziland has gone since the adoption by its students of the 'social transformation' and 'political economy' approach that Crush refers to (Crush 2001). Here we see a sustained effort to present the interests of the common Swazi man as distinct from those of the 'traditional leadership'. Simelane points out that he is concerned with 'moments of change [as they] affected the majority of the Swazi people' (Simelane 2003:6). The work starts off with a review of the various theories that different scholars have used in explaining the effects of colonialism on the subject peoples. He identifies two of these in particular— modernisation theory and dependency theory, preferring the latter over the former in his discussion of the economic change that took place in Swaziland during the period 1940–1960. He then proceeds to trace that change through the period after World War II by considering specific British policies on land, agriculture, mining and capital penetration and its attendant consequences for labour and labour relations. Throughout his book, Simelane is evidently mindful of the fact that Swaziland has not been immune to extraneous influences, but he insists that his work is an example of how the country's political economy deserves to be studied in its own right.[17] This is quite a persuasive argument in support of our position that the book has made a most significant addition to Swazi historiography.

Conclusion

This chapter started by re-visiting the efforts of earlier scholars of Swaziland's recent history in which they had offered explanations for the country's different attitude towards South Africa in comparison with the outlook of the other countries in the Southern African region. It pointed out that while at the state level Swaziland may have appeared hostile to the liberation movements in the region in general and the ANC in particular, this was not necessarily the case with the bulk of the Swazi population. There seems to be growing evidence to support the view that the country was probably just as sympathetic to the liberation struggle as the other nations in the region.

The chapter next considered the state of play in the study of history with particular attention to Swaziland-South Africa relations in the post-apartheid period. This survey has concentrated on what work has been done on the history of Swaziland since the 1990s with special reference to studies produced locally. This particular choice of emphasis was not intended to minimise the importance of research done on the country by scholars based elsewhere. In fact, the contribution of such authors has been quite substantial, as can be attested by the work of Bonner, Booth, Crush, and others. It can be argued that they are probably not encumbered by the disadvantage of too narrow a perspective that can so easily affect local scholarship. Yet it is true, at the same time, that not much is known outside of Swaziland of what has been and is being done here. The main avenue for the publication of academic articles, for example, is the *Uniswa Research Journal*, but it does not circulate beyond the University itself. This chapter has attempted to provide a window through which to view this work.

Several glaring gaps remain to be filled. The History Department's efforts have scarcely touched, for example, the political concerns of the region over the question of democratisation in Swaziland since 1994. On the political front, scholars and other commentators still remain unconvinced that the 'Swazi way'—which includes the use of a no-party system of elections, for example—is the best way forward for the country.[18] The trade unions have brought immense pressure to bear on Swaziland to introduce political change. While a start has been made to study their recent history, more detailed research needs to be done.[19] However, by demonstrating that the various social and economic themes the students and staff have investigated since the 1990s transcend national boundaries throughout the region and Africa as a whole, they have shown that Swaziland is no longer the insulated society that earlier studies seemed to suggest it was by laying undue emphasis on the uniqueness of the 'Swazi way'.

Endnotes

1. This short outline of what is commonly known about the 'history of African history' hardly does justice to the complex and much more detailed work of the numerous writers on the subject in the last several decades. See, among others, Denoon and Kuper (1970) and Ranger (1971). On African historiographies generally: Neale (1985); Jewsiewicki and Newbury (1986); Temu and Swai (1981); Vansina (1994).
2. By 1965, as Ranger (1968). noted, 'there was no longer any need to proclaim the possibility of African history'. Ten years later, the authors of a University-level text entitled *African History* and targeted mainly at American students, could state that African history had 'come of age' and that their own volume was itself an indication of this 'maturity' of their discipline. See P. Curtin *et al*, (1978: v).
3. For instance, major works on Swaziland and Lesotho went by titles that suggested this. Examples: Kuper, *The Swazi: A South African Kingdom*, New York: Holt, 1963; and E.A. Eldredge, *A South African Kingdom: The Pursuit of Security in Nineteenth*

Century Lesotho, Cambridge: CUP, 1993. For pertinent comments on the latter, see M. Thabane, review of Eldredge's book, in which he criticises her for describing Lesotho as 'a South African kingdom', *South African Historical Journal*, Vol. 42, 2000.
4. See the (September 2003) discussion of this thread on the H-Net lists on 'African History and Culture' and 'South African History', H-Africa and H-South Africa, respectively.
5. There is a brief but succinct account of this factional in-fighting in Davies, O'meara and Dlamini, *The Kingdom of Swaziland: A Profile*, London: Zed Books, (1985).
6. In mid-2004 both *The Times of Swaziland* and *The Swazi Observer*, the country's two English language daily newspapers, reported on the so-called cleaning ceremonies involving ANC cadres who remembered their struggle while in Swaziland in this period. This was in commemoration of the support that the ANC had received from the Swazi populace during this period. See various issues of both papers from 20 – 25 June 2004.
7. Private conversation with some Swazi academic colleagues at the University of Swaziland, Kwaluseni, who would prefer to remain anonymous, 28 June 2004.
8. During a visit to Swaziland in April 2002, former Namibian Prime Minister, Hage Geingob, praised the country for supporting SWAPO during the liberation struggle, noting that 'some SWAPO freedom fighters made secret visits' to Swaziland. Such assistance extended to diplomatic support at international forums such as the UN.
9. The myriad studies covering these themes—too numerous to be listed here—clearly indicate the extent to which Swaziland, like Lesotho, has become an economic appendage to South Africa over the years.
10. For comparison, see P. E. Lovejoy, 'The Ibadan School and Its Critics', referring to E. A. Ayandele's discomfort, expressed as long ago as 1969, with a 'history focusing on the cream of society rather than the people', in Jewsiewicki and D. Newbury (1986: 2000).
11. Some of the BA research essays include: Muze (1992); Mabuza (1995); and Dlamini, (1994). Co-operatives and their role in post-colonial Swaziland were studied by Dladla (1993), Manyatsi (1992) and (1994).
12. For example, the Shongwe project already mentioned above focused on the post-Sobhuza II political struggle and its wider ramifications, while both T. L. Matsebula's 'The history of the Matsebula clan' and N. Dlamini's 'The Ndwandwe in the history of the Swazi nation' placed far less emphasis on the centrality of the Dlamini clan than the older Swazi historiography spearheaded by H. Kuper had done in previous years.
13. Interview with A. M. Kanduza, Kwaluseni, Swaziland, 26 Sept 2003.
14. For example: J. V. Mayisela, 'A history of the Swaziland Federation of Trade Unions (SFTU) focusing on its formation, objectives, membership, status, disputes with government, achievements and constraints'; S. Mamba, 'The Swaziland – European Union partnership: relations and impact on trade, agriculture and rural development, 1980–2000', Makhosazana Gamedze, 'Journalism versus traditional culture, 1990– 2000'; H. N. Dlamini, 'Socio-economic problems faced by the elderly people in Swaziland, 1990–2002'; G. Dlamini, 'National heritage and tourism in Swaziland'.

15. N. Dlamini is currently (2004) working on a PhD (History) degree at the University of Witwatersrand on the legal abolition of racial discrimination in Swaziland after 1945.
16. Simelane, *Political Reforms in Post-colonial Swaziland*, especially Chapter 7. For another recent examination of the question of democracy, see P. Limb, 'Alliance strengthened or diminished? Relationships between labour and African nationalist/liberation movements in Southern Africa', especially the section entitled 'Swaziland: Liberation without Nationalism?'; a paper from the conference on 'The Dynamics of Change in Southern Africa', University of Melbourne, 18-20 May 1992.
17. Although this work signals a major landmark in the production of historical knowledge on Swaziland (and *from* Swaziland), this is not the place to provide a fully-fledged review of the book, which probably belongs elsewhere.
18. Swaziland held its last general election under the traditional *Tinkundla* system in October 2003, which coincided with the CODESRIA Southern African Regional Conference in Gaborone, Botswana. Participants were curious to know to what extent such an election reflected the majority opinion in the country.
19. Apart from Mayisela's BA (History) research essay, Mavela Shongwe completed an MA (History) in 2002 on the role of the trade unions in Swaziland.

References

Anon, 1984, 'The Post-Sobhuza Power Struggle', *Africa Report*, Vol. 29, No. 1.
Crush, J. 2001, 'Review of D. Hugh Gillis, "The Kingdom of Swaziland: Studies in Political History" (Contributions in *Comparative Colonial Studies*, No. 37), Westport, Conn.: Greenwood, 1999', in *The American Historical Review*, Vol. 106, 3.
Curtin, P., Feierman, S., Thompson, L., and Vansina, J., 1978, *African History*, London: Longmans.
Daniel, J., 1984, 'A Comparative Analysis of Lesotho and Swaziland's Relations with South Africa', *South African Review II*, Johannesburg: Ravan Press.
Davies, R. H., O'Meara, D. and Dlamini, S., 1985, *The Kingdom of Swaziland: A Profile*, London: Zed Books.
Denoon, D. and Kuper, A., 1970, 'Nationalist Historians in Search of a Nation: The New Historiography in Dar es Salaam', *African Affairs*, Vol. 69, No. 277.
Dladla, L.S., 1993, 'The Role of CCU (The Central Co-operative Union) in the Marketing of Agricultural items', unpublished B.A. Project, University of Swaziland.
Dlamini, G., 2003, 'National Heritage and Tourism in Swaziland', unpublished, B.A. Project, University of Swaziland.
Dlamini, H.N., 2003, 'Socio-economic Problems Facing the Elderly People in Swaziland, 1990–2002', unpublished B.A. Project, University of Swaziland.
Dlamini, N., 2001, 'Race Relations in Swaziland: The Case of Havelock Asbestos Mine', unpublished M.A. thesis, University of Swaziland.
Dlamini, N.G., 1994, 'The Impact the Sugar Industry Had on the Economy of Swaziland from 1968–1993', unpublished B.A. Project, University of Swaziland.
Dlamini, P.S., 1994, 'The History of the National Agricultural Board (NAMBOARD) and its Impact on Vegetable and Fruit Entrepreneurs in Swaziland', unpublished

B.A. Project, University of Swaziland.
Dupont-Mkhonza, S.T., Vilakati, J. N., Mundia, L.J.S, (eds.), *Democracy, Transformation, Conflict and Public Policy in Swaziland*, Kwaluseni: OSSREA Swaziland Chapter.
Eldredge, E.A., 1993, *A South African Kingdom: The Pursuit of Security in Nineteenth Century Lesotho*, Cambridge: Cambridge University Press.
Gamedze, M., 2003, 'Journalism versus Traditional Culture, 1990–2000', unpublished B.A. Project, University of Swaziland.
Griffiths, I. and Funnell, D.C., 1983, 'The Abortive Swazi Land Deal', *African Affairs*, Vol. 90, No. 482.
Henri-Bishoff, P., 1988, 'Why Swaziland is Different: An Explanation of the Kingdom's Political Position in Southern Africa', *Journal of Modern African Studies*, Vol. 26, No. 3.
Henri-Bishoff, P., 1986, 'Swaziland: A Small State in International Relations', *Afrika Spectrum*, Vol. 21, No. 2.
Hyam, R., 1972, *The Failure of South African Expansion*, London: Macmillan.
Jewsiewicki, B. and Newbury, D., (eds.), 1986, *African Historiographies: What History for which Africa*, Beverly Hills, London, New Delhi: Sage Publications.
Kanduza, A.M., 2003 a, 'Intellectuals in Swazi Politics', in S.T. Dupont-Mkhonza, et al. (eds) *Democracy, Transformation, Conflict and Public Policy in Swaziland*, Kwaluseni: OSSREA Swaziland Chapter.
Kanduza, A.M., 2003 b, 'Tackling HIV/AIDS and Related Stigma in Swaziland Through Education', *EASSRR*, Vol. XIX, No. 2.
Kuper, H., 1963, *The Swazi: A South African Kingdom*, New York: Holt.
Limb, P., 1992, 'Alliance Strengthened or Diminished? Relationships between Labour and African Nationalist/Liberation Movements in Southern Africa', unpublished paper presented at a Conference on The Dynamics of Change in Southern Africa, Melbourne, May.
Mabuza, M.N.N., 1995, 'The Maize Industry in Swaziland', unpublished B.A. Project, University of Swaziland.
Mamba, S., 2003, 'The Swazi-European Union Partnership: Relations and Impact on Trade, Agriculture and Rural Development 1980–2000', unpublished B.A. Project, University of Swaziland.
Manyatsi, G. S., 1992, 'Farmers Co-operative Societies as a Strategy to Develop the Rural Areas in Swaziland, 1964–1979', unpublished B.A. Project, University of Swaziland.
Mayisela, J. V., 2003, 'A History of the Swaziland Federation of Trade Unions (SFTU)', unpublished B.A. Project, University of Swaziland.
Mekenye, R. O., 1996, 'The African Struggle Against South African Periphery Imperialism, 1902–1966: The Case of Lesotho', unpublished PhD. thesis, UCLA.
Mugyenyi, J. B., 1990, 'Swaziland: The Vagaries of Geopolitics, Subordination and Collaboration', in S. H. Arnold, and A. Nitechi (eds) *Culture and Development in Africa*, Trenton and New Jersey: Africa World Press.
Muze, P.M., 1992, 'Socio-economic Impact of Cotton on Cotton Farmers of Kangcamphalala: 1970–1991,' unpublished B.A. Project, University of Swaziland.
Ndwandwe, S.R., 2000, 'Christian Missionary Activity and the Transformation of the Social Status of Swazi Women', unpublished M.A. thesis, University of Swaziland.

Neale, C., 1985, *Writing 'Independent' History: African Historiography, 1960–1980*, Westport, Connecticut: Greenwood Press.

Nkambule, M., 1992, 'The History and Activities of the Swazi Commercial Amadoda', unpublished B.A. Project, University of Swaziland.

Nyeko, B., 1979–81, 'The African Voice in Colonial Swaziland: The Question of Transfer, 1910–1939', *Mohlomi: Journal of Southern African Studies*, III/IV/V.

Ranger, T.O., ed., 1968, *Emerging Themes of African History*, Nairobi: East African Publishing House.

Ranger, T.O., 1971, 'The "New Historiography" in Dar es Salaam: An Answer', *African Affairs*, Vol. 70, No. 280.

Shongwe, K., 1995, 'The Regency of Queen Regent Dzeliwe and Political Machination in Swaziland 1982–1986', unpublished B.A. Project, University of Swaziland.

Sikhondze, B.A.B., 2003, 'The Poverty of Analytical Models in Explaining Rural Economic Stagnation: The Case of Colonial Swaziland', in S.T. Dupont-Mkhonza, et al. (eds) *Democracy, Transformation, Conflict and Public Policy in Swaziland*, Swaziland: OSSREA.

Simelane, C.M., 1999, 'Political Reforms in Post-Colonial Swaziland, 1973–1992', unpublished M.A. thesis, University of Swaziland.

Simelane, H. S., 2003, *Colonialism and Economic Change in Swaziland, 1940–1960*, Swaziland and Uganda: JAN Publishing Centre.

Slater, H., 1986, 'Dar es Salaam and the Post-nationalist Historiography of Africa', in B. Jewsiewicki and D. Newbury (eds) *African Historiographies: What History for Which Africa?* Beverly Hills, London and New Delhi: Sage Publications.

Temu, A. and Swai, B., 1981, *Historians and Africanist History: A Critique*, London: Zed Press.

The Swazi Observer, 20–25 June 2004

The Times of Swaziland, 20–25 June 2004

Vansina, J., 1994, *Living with Africa*, Madison: Wisconsin University Press.

2

Problems and Prospects of Democratic Renewal in Southern Africa: A Study of Statecraft and Democratisation in South Africa, 1994–2003

Adekunle Amuwo

The problematique

There is little doubt that South Africa's post-apartheid democratic governments (Mandela's, 1994–1999, and Mbeki's, 1999 till date) have made important strides in the delivery of much-needed public goods, values and services to hitherto marginalised constituents, races and ethno-nationalities. By so doing, the post-apartheid state has largely legitimised itself in the eyes of the people, millions of whom have only recently started to recover their citizenship (du Toit 1995:406). In a fundamental sense, the South African state has progressively sought to become constitutional and to anchor itself on the rule of law. The state, to all appearances, may be on the road to becoming a civic culture capable of taking on what Alexis de Tocqueville refers to as 'common objects of common desires'. There are, however, important socio-economic lacunae. The democratising South African state is caught between *procedural* or *formal democracy* and *substantive* or *social democracy*. The dialectics and dynamics of the latter are such that whilst some appreciable progress has been recorded in the sphere of the 'political science of democratisation', this has not been matched at the level of what Saul (in Luckham et.al, 2003:43) refers to as the 'political economy of democratisation'. Several factors have been responsible for this trajectory. These include the nature of the apartheid and post-apartheid state, particularly its enduring institutional framework, mores and values; the character of the elite-pacted democratic transition; a macroeconomic orientation anchored more on growth than on equity and the resultant growing army of poor and unemployed/ unemployable underclasses; the preference for political stability to popular participation; a state that appears strong but which lacks autonomy in relation to historic blocs, key ethno-nationalities (like the Xhosa) and powerful groups and individuals (e.g., the Black Empowerment Group). In short, there are structural constraints in the national and international system that limit the reach of the state and the import of citizenship and, in consequence, render the state not strong enough to make unattractive other forms of public/ social allegiance and identity aside of citizenship.

We seek to critically examine the foregoing dynamics of an emergent constitutional democracy as well as the extent to which public policies have, on the one hand, made the state more autonomous, stronger and inclusive and, on the other, exacerbated its negative attributes of non-autonomy, weakness and exclusion. We also evaluate the impact of this policy praxis on the problems and prospects of democratisation. Expressed differently, beyond the artefacts of an admittedly liberal constitution; fairly representative political institutions and structures; multipartyism and gender representation (interesting and useful developments, no doubt), we are concerned to investigate the politics and economics of South Africa's democratisation process since the 1990s.

Cast within an essentially implicit comparative (Southern African) perspective, the major *problematique* is that a growing and worrisome hiatus between the post-apartheid state and key societal/non-state actors, forces and classes seems to be assuming the character of a permanent impediment to democratic consolidation. Thus, whereas there is formal democracy (in terms of institutions and procedures of a neo-electoral democracy), substantive democracy partly explicated in terms of 'the redistribution of power—the degree to which citizens can participate in the decisions which affect their lives' (Luckham et al 2003: 19) remains largely a shrinking province. Moreover, non-state social forces (particularly labour (Congress of South African Trade Unions, COSATU) and the South African Communist Party (SACP) as allies in power) have lost capacity, expertise and political clout to the state as the latter (encapsulated in a hegemonic African National Congress (ANC) government) increasingly incorporates or stifles actual and potential sites of political opposition. This is coupled with an ambivalent process of democratisation that furnishes a social gap between an institutional design of democracy (that has virtually built a politics of inclusion) and a political economy of democratisation that has multiple bridges to cross in delivering substantive democracy to millions of the dispossessed, landless and unemployed youth and adults alike (Pottie and Hassim 2003:89 and Bastian and Luckham 2003:305-6).

We also examine problems and prospects of democratisation not so much from the prism of a formally institutionalised white political opposition as that of black political parties and civil society groups. As in Zimbabwe, Namibia, Mozambique, Angola and Botswana, the problem of a dominant or *de facto* one-party state seems to loom large on the horizon. This danger is aided and abetted by an unstated assumption (or principle) that former guerrilla combatants and exiled anti-apartheid activists have the right to cling to power for life. In the South African typology, the lack of a potent and immediate threat to the hegemony of the ANC—both from within the black and white/Indian/coloured political formations—may portend danger for substantive democracy: the seeming and palpable arrogance of the party and some of its leading lights may lead the government to ignore, if not suppress, subaltern political ideologies and policy concerns. The latter may eventually be constrained to take actions and forms that are inconsistent with democratic values (Griffiths and Katalikawe 2003:116). In the process, substantive democracy may further be imperilled.

Democracy–democratisation nexus

While democracy is nothing but an ambivalent, contradictory and complex entity, its superiority, however putative some of the time, has tended to be emphasised in the literature. Le Vine (1997: 205), taking his cue from Winston Churchill's famous description of democracy as 'the worst possible system of government, with the exception of all the rest', has argued that 'as practised in various parts of the world, including Africa, democracy is undeniably messy, often frustrating and can certainly be inefficient (and) does not guarantee that the host of problems besetting so many countries can be handled effectively'. But he underscores the salience and essence of democracy in several respects. One, government policies that emerge from established democratic processes have a fair chance of succeeding. Two, leaders that emerge from democratic consultations are likely to be able to lead. Three, political and other institutions fostered by democratic constitutions can function as expected. Finally, the point is forcefully made that 'democracy offers the kind of political flexibility that permits the resolution, if not always the solution, of potentially destructive conflicts without irretrievably rending the social fabric'.

Although there is wide latitude to speculate about the capacity and capability of democracy to achieve the foregoing elements, even in the most developed liberal democracies, there is little doubt that there would be both qualitative and quantitative differences between states that regard democracy as a means to an end and those that conceive democracy as an end in itself. In other words, for emergent electoral democracies that seek to use deliberate and deliberative democratisation to gradually reduce a perceived democracy deficit, the road taken would be one that sees democracy as 'an unresolved and contested process', while their counterparts, content with what they already have, would opt for the notion of democracy as 'a fully achieved end state' (Luckham 2003:13). To be sure, democracy deficits are everywhere observable, but they appear to be most irritating and visible when democratic institutions tend to be constantly imperilled by a lack of democratic politics and, worse, by 'the enduring legacies of undemocratic politics' (Luckham 2003:14, 19). The latter would gradually worsen as states take the democracy project seriously by regarding and treating democracy as not just a matter of process and procedure (however correct, corrective and constitutional), but as an exercise in substantive political economy.

The following would constitute the major elements in the nexus. One, democratic politics and institutions; active citizenship and engagement; dense and intense relationships between the state and citizens through the agency of key civil society organisations as well as by the intermediary of processes (high politics of the state and the deep politics of society) that are at once creative and subversive; the politics of social equity, redistributive policies and people-friendly economic growth; prioritisation of popular participation above the maintenance of order; good institutional design; wise leadership, inclusive forms of political and institutional choices; relevant cultural values and a democratic ethos (Bastian and Luckham 2003: 15-18, 21, 40; Swift 2000; Decalo 1992: 35). Procedural democracy is an insufficient condition for the emergence, let alone consolidation, of social democracy. Yet, it remains a necessary condition in so far as 'procedural democracy can...enhance the legitimacy of democratic governments and clear the way for them to advance substantive democracy' (Pottie and Hassim 2003:63). A core element of substantive democracy is the use of organisations and institutions that citizens understand, and with which they are conversant, with a view to routinising the socially relevant values and norms of democracy (Bastian and Luckham 2003:42). In Africa, such organisations would include the 'second public' of village, town and community associations, moral, ethnic, religious and communal bodies which are more inclusive moral communities than the 'first public' of the nation-state. In view of mass poverty, democracy would begin to have social relevance only to the extent that it goes beyond its rendition as 'a system of government in which the authority to exercise power derives from the will of the people' (Bjornland et al 1992:405). Similarly, democratisation has to be not merely a process of institutionalising democracy (however important this may be for emerging electoral democracies), but one of creating new norms of governance, of cultural change and of robustly addressing the critical issue of the unequal distribution of wealth and power in the society (Bastian and Luckham 2003:51, 23).

Standing in an unstable juxtaposition in the foregoing are elements of both the political science and political economy of democratisation. The former is rooted in institutional and structural formalism as well as in elite-driven procedural democracy. It sets much store by a widespread agreement among political elites on institutional rules from which a large majority of supposed citizens are excluded. But, in so far as formal democracy pays little more than a nodding attention to social democracy, it is regarded as only a shade better than an empty shell by the people. Swift (2000) contends that 'modern political science has inherited this distrust of ordinary people and their capacities to participate in their own self-government'. The reason is often not far to seek. Many a mainstream political scientist stresses 'questions of political management and effective elite systems of government. Participation (except passively during elections) is not to be encouraged'. What the latter does—even in developed liberal democracies—is to give a fillip to Schumpeter's copiously conservative argument (Swift 2000) that 'voters must understand that once they have elected an individual, political action is his (sic) business and not theirs. This means that they must refrain from instructing him about what he is to do'. The political economy of democratisation is about the pertinent issues of equity and power struggles. It is also about the reduction in the intensity of the poverty of the mass majority. Similarly, it concerns a dialectical relationship between political and economic power, such that 'the stranglehold of cash has led to the asphyxiation of honest public debate' (Swift 2000). It is about the perennial struggle of subaltern social classes to make the state and the political elite socially responsible and responsive. In the words of Ayogu and Hodge (2002:278), the power component of this process 'implicates governments in Africa and elsewhere to continue to rig markets as part of the repertoire of devices employed to secure political control over their population and retain power. While imposing collective deprivations, governments confer selective benefits to particular groups of the polity'. The expected *riposte* of dominated classes would be to severely contest this seemingly dominant paradigm of political and economic relations in the society with a view to gradually making the state truly democratic, that is to say, a veritable 'mutual protection association where the community protects all its members' (Baker 2000:237).

Within this context, one can appreciate the declaration of Nadia Leila Aissaovi, an Algerian activist to the effect that 'if democracy is the right to speak out and be heard, as a voice and not just a number, then I am a democrat. But if democracy is the freedom to choose between Coca Cola and Pepsi, Levis and Nike, BBC or CNN, McDonald and Pizza Hut, then I ... don't want to be a democrat' (Swift 2000). There is thus an interesting interface here between the political science of democratisation and its political economy, both internationally and internally as far as the African continent is concerned. On the former canvass, the West (principally the US and the corporate world it controls) and the continent have different motives for pursuing a seemingly similar democratisation agenda: the one to maintain formal democracy or political stability; the other—at least for popular forces and their organisations—to facilitate system reforms or social transformation. The two are often mutually exclusive. As Huntington (in Hearn 2000:816) has argued, 'the maintenance of democratic politics and the reconstruction of the social order are fundamentally incompatible'. Similarly, as Hearn (2000:816) has shown, the essence of Western aid to Africa—on occasion, South Africa during the anti-apartheid struggle, pre-1994—was not so much to support democratisation as to penetrate the vibrant and pluralistic civil society in order to ossify its dynamism, block prospects for fundamental or radical changes and limit damage to Western interests. Internally, formal democracy has tended to imperfectly co-exist with poverty, with the latter diminishing the prospects for democracy and, therefore, for citizenship. To be sure, democratic consolidation or social transformation necessarily has to go beyond formal democracy and, to that extent, is a project of the long haul (Amuwo 2003). Yet, a clearly delineated movement towards a post-polyarchy polity should be discernible. Otherwise, social democracy as well as democracy *tout court* would be endangered. 'The inability to substantially ameliorate acute poverty and reduce inequalities', writes Giliomee, 'puts democratic consolidation in serious jeopardy'. He adds that democratic consolidation is a tenuous process in states where 'there is a contradiction between an institutional system based on the political equality of citizens and a society characterised by extreme inequalities or a process of growing social inequality' (Giliomee 1995:101).

In the South African typology—as in much of the continent—the same largely 'captured' civil society organisations are conceptualised as constituting an important locus of critical social action capable of turning the tables against the state. Of primary importance in this respect are those organisations that, to appropriate Tripp (2000:191), 'do not have a stake in the perpetuation of politics as usual and whose very existence is contingent on more thorough going political reform'. What, for long, held out hope for some form of

South African political 'exceptionalism' was that many anti-apartheid activists saw themselves engaged in the fight for both political freedom and increased control over the economy. In other words, whilst popular franchise was a major demand, 'the key liberation movements subscribed to and spread to their poverty-stricken followers an economic, as opposed to a procedural, view of democracy' (Hearn 2000: 818, 827).

The ambivalence, contradiction and complexity of democracy on which we have remarked, come again to bold relief here. Lodge (1997:349) argues that capitalist or post-colonial class solidarities, as well as industrialisation and urbanisation, have engendered a South African civil society that 'is richer, complex and more conducive to liberal democracy than the social cohesion produced by those pre-colonial institutions which continue to shape communal life in rural Botswana and Zimbabwe', Lowe (1999:415), on the other hand, cautions that the South African civil society has been a locus of both democratic and anti-democratic struggles. As Amy and Patterson (1998:439) have demonstrated in their study on rural Senegal, civil society often has constituent parts that do not add up to a coherent and a cohesive whole. Different economic and educational experiences and multiple gender roles and social norms tend, they claim, to slow down communication, participation and the construction of trust networks in civil society. Similarly, deepening poverty worsens material divisions in civil society and drives a wedge between members and leaders alike who have access to the state and those who don't. What this scenario logically suggests is a networking of like-minded democrats and nationalists from both the state and civil society. The one is incomplete without the other.

The dynamics of an emergent liberal democracy

South Africa's hybrid post-apartheid politics has been the product of a myriad of historical, political and cultural influences. On account of procedural continuity, backward legitimacy, controlled transformation, elite-pacted democracy and transition as 'transplacement', the social reach and political import of post-apartheid politics necessarily have to be limited. The latter refers to a process where, as in Poland and Chile, amongst others, both government and opposition have more or less equal strength and learn, *willy-nilly*, the art and science of political compromise since neither of the two can, on its own, determine the future trajectory of the polity (Giliomee 1995:94). To be sure, popular organisations, such as trade unions, took an active part in the transition (Cawthra 2003:32), but that impacted little on the general orientation of the post-transition settlement as an elitist democracy undergirded by the logic of national liberation (Southall 2003:30). Political elites, admittedly multiracial, crafted pacts that helped to minimise feared political violence and to achieve a rather unexpected electoral democracy, but seemingly at some great social costs: amongst others, containment of the radicalising or revolutionary pressures of the mass of the people and the assumption of state power by the black majority (as rightly projected), but one that remains largely divorced from economic power that continues to reside in the hands of the white minority (Southall 2003:18, 47).

The reality, not unexpectedly, has been a mixed grill. On the one hand, there is, by all accounts, a good institutional design of democracy. Anchored on the African National Congress's 'broad, inclusivist nationalism', the latter has sought to reverse apartheid's legacy of exclusion as well as the sophistication of its institutions of control and repression by developing institutions of democracy and inclusion (Cawthra 2003:49; Pottie and Hassim 2003:61). A major institution in this respect is a deliberate robust liberal constitution (considered by many an analyst as the most liberal in our global hamlet, in tandem with a rich Bill of Rights) whose provisions constitute a 'constitutionally-mandated check to concentrated power' (Butler 2003:94). These include real and symbolic concessions to minorities, affirmative actions, respect of basic human rights and political representation (including the right of citizens to participate in local level decision-making affecting their lives) and related constitutional provisions meant to improve the lot of hitherto disadvantaged racial and ethnic communities. South Africans are also protected legally through an array of legal instruments: the Constitutional Court; the Human Rights Commission; Office of the Public Protector; the Gender Equality Commission; the Heath Special Investigation Unit empowered to investigate cases of corruption and to recover lost assets and funds (Lester et.al, 2000:266). Curiously, the latter was disbanded during 2001 notwithstanding its success in either recovering or protecting some US $150 million of assets and money by the end of 1998. Furthermore, the post-apartheid government has put in place what has been regarded as the legislative pillars of a new post-apartheid labour market. These include the Labour Relations Act, the Employment Equity Act and the Basic Conditions of Employment Act (Marais 2001:193).

There is ample evidence to show that, whatever the lacunae otherwise observed, Pretoria has, within a decade, recorded monumental achievements in the areas as varied as rural and urban housing accelerated by a housing subsidy (by 1999 no less than 40 percent of approved subsidies went to women); rural and urban electrification; safe supply of water; more telephone lines; an extensive primary school nutrition programme; and free medical health for pregnant women and children under six years. On the whole, according to a pertinent source, since 1994 on average each day 'another 1300 homes were electrified; another 750 telephones installed and another 1700 people gained access to clean water' (Marais 2001: 190). A major impetus for this 'success story' has been the country's trade union movement that has managed to retain much of its vibrancy notwithstanding its status as a partial state organisation. It has been observed, for instance, that the rate of unionisation South Africa recorded between 1985 and 1995 is one of the highest globally (Good 2002:89).

There are other interesting achievements. Careful attention has been paid by the South African constitution to salient issues such as the democratic control of the security forces, full recognition of presidential authority as well as objective civilian control of military institutions. Silva also claims that although South Africa remains largely defined in ethnic and regional terms, 'much greater national consensus has been achieved about the need to concentrate on the present and the future of the nation' (Silva 2003:103, 118).

The foregoing indices are no mean achievements for a country that was expected to implode under the weight of racial and ethnic hatred a little over a decade ago. In this respect Marais has argued that:

> enormous changes have been wrought since 1994. The progress made at the superstructural level in many respects has been astounding: the constitution, new legislation, new policies and frameworks, overhauled state structures and refurbished state systems, are examples. Hitches and logjams identified inside government are constantly being addressed, with the power concentrated at the apex of the executive apparently intended to facilitate those efforts... social delivery proceeds at a pace and in a manner unprecedented in most South Africans' lives (2001:305).

Yet, the vote for political realism and stability, moderation, pragmatism and compromise which were the buzzwords of the negotiation and immediate post-transition years (and were actually counselled) has virtually become an albatross on the neck of the ANC government. In a fundamental sense, the structural legacy of apartheid haunts the transformation agenda (Butler 2003:94). The ANC itself has, both wittingly and unwittingly, surrendered the relative or embedded autonomy of the South African state to both domestic and international capital. The point to underline is that without social transformation, superstructural changes amount to little. What this suggests is that, to borrow from Cawthra (2003:43), 'it is easier to change policies and structures than values and practices'.

Almost a decade into multi-racial elections, the post-apartheid state has hardly been able to satisfactorily resolve the structural crisis engendered by the apartheid system. For one, the ANC's lofty objective was to use liberation politics and struggle to seize both political and economic power. But, for reasons already alluded to, what it got was a partial transfer of power. This singular phenomenon has been at the source of the dilemma of the former liberation movement. Given its undue emphasis on the state as the citadel of power in society, once it was assimilated into power rather than seizing it and transforming it as it had expected (Marais 2001:2), the ANC lost its major weapon of statecraft and transformation. For another, with a culture of suppression of dissent that it honed during the liberation struggle, the ANC has barely tolerated its alliance partners (COSATU and SACP) and other non-state organisations and actors that militate for a more pro-poor economic and allied policy framework. Whatever the merits otherwise in COSATU and SACP's continued stay in government (more in office than in power), they have allowed the ANC to combine ideological pre-eminence with organisational superiority and, *mutatis mutandis*, to treat its junior partners with scant respect and sometimes with contempt (Marais 2001:73).

While the ANC and its partners sometimes speak the same language of social transformation, the ruling elite pays little more than a nodding attention to it in practice. Good (2002:89, 94) argues that South Africa's predominant ruling elite is weakening the country's democracy to the extent that whereas 'they speak easily of the opportunities supposedly offered but seem dangerously complacent about the inequalities and injustices it entails'. A major reason for this development, for Good, is that the most important hierarchy in the ANC's decision-making structure continues to function, as in the exile days, as 'a secretive, autocratic organisation'. Expressed differently, the ANC, not unlike its counterparts in the Southern African sub-region, has been hard put to shed the toga, logic and orientation of a national liberation movement. Yet, that appears indispensable if the organisation is serious about becoming a key agent in societal transformation and modernisation. Senior officials and cadres of the party alike have to learn to abandon the culture of docile conformity and obeisance to party hierarchy and pressure the party to cultivate a culture of consent and popular legitimacy. Indeed, one reason why COSATU, amongst others, has been reined in is that the trade union organisation itself has been afflicted with the same culture of lack of authentic internal political debate. It has thus been easy for the ANC to stifle leftist critics within its ranks and amongst its alliance partners (Butler 2003:105).

At the core of the massive demobilisation of hitherto vibrant civil society organisations has been the fact that the value of direct and participatory democracy that the United Democratic Front (UDF) and the Mass Democratic Movement (MDM) did much to propagate and diffuse has hardly become routinised in the political system. As Gibson (2001:72) has shown, between the late 1980s and 1994, those values and expressions remained ensconced in celebratory politics. They were not 'translated into a radical rethinking of liberation theory that mapped out paradigms of social and ethical practices for a post-apartheid society'. This ideological and value gap would be exploited by the ANC which captured these narratives and celebrated the idea of people's power 'while remaining the self-appointed future negotiators'.

There is little doubt that the more or less successful demobilisation of popular social forces has aided and abetted the ANC in imposing a politics of compromise in relation to both domestic and international agents of capital and big business. Now, to understand the dominant project in post-apartheid South Africa, it is necessary to look at 'the domestication and assimilation of the key organisations of the socialist left into a neo-corporatist framework dominated by the state and capital' (Marais 2001). The introduction of the neo-liberal/conservative Growth, Employment and Redistribution (GEAR) macroeconomic policy framework (christened 'Greed Entirely Avoids Redistribution' by its critics, Lester et al, 2000:319) in 1996 confirmed the effective marginalisation of the Left in its political romance with the ANC. Increasingly since 1994, as the nexus between the state and capital grows, the authority and influence of ANC's alliance partners has waned even as the influence of its partners in government [Inkatha Freedom Party (IFP) and the New National Party, (NNP)] has become substantial (Marais 2001:271).

A communist would lament that the problem of the allies is that 'ANC policy is still determined by the leadership and few grassroots members can challenge them'. The allies have not been docile or timid altogether, though. At its July 2002 Congress, the SACP agreed that the tripartite alliance should be led by the working class. It also purged itself of the pro-privatisation elements in the leadership. But there has been little beneficial effect of this bold initiative in the politics of the alliance. The ANC has not always had its way in the dynamics of the alliance, either. For instance, during 2002, the party provincial chairs sympathetic to the Left were elected in the North-West, Mpumalanga and the Free State provinces. This was reminiscent, almost in all material particulars, to the Mafikeng conference that was called in response to the unexpected severe critique of GEAR shortly after its release to the public (Lekota, a grassroots politician won the chairmanship election ahead of the late Steve Tshwete, the preferred candidate of the party hierarchy (See Kindra 2002:19). On balance, however, neither COSATU nor SACP nor the voluntary sector has been able 'to impose (its) alternative economic ideas on either the state or domestic and international capital' (Marais 2001:281). Whenever COSATU gets too vocal, the ANC and business resort to blackmail:

they tend to portray the Congress as a special interest group that does no more than protect and enhance its corporate interests and sets little store by the larger interests of the rest of the South African society.

The so-called 'Rainbow Nation' and the promised new dawn for the mass majority have suffered in the process. It would seem that as the process of transformation becomes increasingly state-driven, the country's politics is getting less consensual and more conventional (Johnson 2000:34). This is another way of saying that the negative impact of the gradual disintegration of the critical core of the civil society on statecraft and democratic consolidation can hardly be over-emphasised. The clarion call to transit from resistance to reconstruction, cooperation and transformation has tended to confuse these organisations, particularly in terms of appropriate relations with the state in the new dispensation. The new politics has also had the effect of dulling their radical instincts and sensibilities. Moreover, on account of their histories, it has been difficult to understand the notion of 'critical support' that the ANC government and its supporters demand. By subjugating some of the most critical segments of the civil and political society to the state and its market-friendly policy matrix, with no visible, clear and immediate challenge from other parties, the ANC clearly shows that it has a firm grip of power. But as Cawthra (2003:33) has noted, 'many features of the South African political economy remain much the same'. Invariably, they unwittingly get incorporated into the post-apartheid state. The problem is not so much the incorporation (to the extent that the state and civil society need each other) as that such an intimacy 'carries the risk of a potentially drab relationship that lacks the necessary dynamism of difference and contestation that can give rise to the kinds of innovations and plurality of endeavours a successful popular project requires' (Marais 2001:286).

Social engineering and its limits

To understand the foregoing, one has to come to terms with the ANC's historic capitulation to capital. What happened? Why was it so easy for the ANC, given the immense sacrifice of its many denizens, leaders and organisational chieftains on behalf of popular forces and masses, to succumb to the logic and demands of capital and capitalism? Marais offers an explanation:

> Having neglected the economic realm for decades, the ANC's resistance levels were low, particularly in an era advertised as the 'end of history'. With the organisation's earlier makeshift reference points either crushed or badly dented, its appetite for risk was weak. The low road of accommodation to orthodoxy held great appeal (2001:135).

Marais is also critical. The claim that capitalism is developing a black economic empowerment group is, for him, a weak compensation since this merely enriches the minority black capitalist class, not the general black population. By the same token, it was unacceptable both to the leadership and the ranks and file of the liberation movement that the ANC government could so easily ignore class analysis and the structural realities of the post-apartheid heritage to deal with labour 'as if the process was politically and ideologically neutral and could be appended to a set of strategies and politically palatable social objectives' (Marais 2001:136). There is no doubting the negative impact of global structural constraints and late capitalism on developing and semi-industrialising states, but the decision to vote for capital instead of the people was nothing but premeditated. Nobody entered the economic battlefield blindfolded. What is more, it is a choice that has been regularly and stoutly defended by the ANC, often against the grain of rationality and empirical evidence. By voting with its heart for market economy and with its head for the people, the ANC did some violence to the relative autonomy of the democratic state. However one explicates contemporary globalisation, it does provide some elbow room for manoeuvring and for a more nationalistic and pro-poor economic orientation than the ANC was ready to admit. A semi-industrialised state such as South Africa enjoys enough economic muscle to lessen the somewhat homogenising, hegemonising and integrating logic of globalisation with a view to getting a better deal for its capital and commerce in the international market. The ANC chose to ignore all of this and to opt for the least line of resistance. By so doing, it limits its ability to redistribute opportunity, infrastructural resources and access to productive activity and institutional power in favour of the popular classes (Marais 2001:96). The ANC has, almost *in toto*, bought into the notion that South Africa's democracy was inaugurated in an international ecology that is 'hostile to big government programme and in a global economy that prompts states to remain competitive by reducing expenditures on social welfare programmes and lowering wages' (Evans in Lester et al 2000:321). It was easy for the organisation to do so largely because it entered the pre-1994 CODESA talks and negotiations without a coherent programme committed to dismantling the structural foundations of apartheid.

The GEAR policy, welcomed by both domestic and international capital, became the ANC government's official economic paradigm as from 1996. Its main tenets and elements include export performance, foreign investment, competition and control of wage increases and interest rates, but excluding 'significant state-led redistribution' (Lester et al 2000:320, 322). What effectively comes into bold relief here is that the re-insertion of South Africa into the circuits of the global economy acts as a 'further constraint on the capacity of democratic institutions to alleviate poverty and respond to emergent sources of insecurity and conflict' (Bastian and Luckham 2003:36). Being pro-capital is tantamount to appropriating the paradigm of exclusion and exploitation. Within this framework, there is neither 'a more far-sighted panoramic view of the routes to such states' economic objectives nor, for that matter, an adherence to a basic tenet of true reconciliation, whose logic imposes the striving to ensure that economic benefits 'are distributed as widely as possible' (Dommen 1997:491). And the major contradiction is not so much that of redressing the poverty of the majority as that between capital and labour, of which the latter is a major consequence. It is precisely because of this primary contradiction that the post-apartheid state cannot give wealth and privilege to blacks as the apartheid state did to whites (Judson 2001:67, 69).

Similarly, South Africans are forced to live with economic institutions and financial regimes designed to promote Western interests, not those of their country. Tied to this is the fact that rather than give justice to the country's black majority (as well as other non-black victims of apartheid), the ANC government has been more receptive to white pressures both from within and from outside (Williams 2001:656). On account of this, South Africa's transformation project, 'even with a radical and widely welcomed revision of its political constitution... has been more of a transition to a new social and economic order which is "acceptable" to key metropolitan and local constituencies than a radical break with past socio-economic structures' (Lester et al 2000:320). Lester and his associates add that 'it is those key local and global constituencies which make it so difficult for the new South African state to deploy the universalist notion of "development" in a way which acts against the exclusions and inequities that have been associated with the term' (2000:320).

The dynamics of South Africa's political economy is such that it does some violence to three of the most important ingredients of successful transition that one finds in the contemporary literature on democratisation: the relatively favourable internal political and societal conditions; the internally driven character of the process, and its relatively inclusive and participatory character (Bastian and Luckham 2003:6). While the structural legacies of apartheid are undoubtedly formidable, they are by no means insurmountable. But the politics has to be got right for the proposed economic solution—a supremely political question also—to be correct. From that premise, what remains is for reformers to not derail or backslide. If genuinely democratic leaders are interested in taking pro-poor social decisions and are willing to set much store by public accountability, transparency and responsiveness and by a social explication and interpretation of market injunctions, the goal of democratic renewal would be kept in view. In the case of South Africa, 'when it left apartheid behind, (it) did not leave behind the structures and processes which generate inequality' (Lester et al 2000:322). Rather than confront this structural legacy with the seriousness and single-mindedness that it deserves, the ANC government has, on the contrary, sought relief in a wretched amalgam of a seemingly leftist discourse favourable to the poor and a rightist political and policy praxis beneficial to capital and the corporate world. In other words, whilst the ANC continues to talk 'left', it acts 'right'. In his 1990 address to the US Congress, Mandela was clear:

> the process of reconstruction of South African society will... entail the transformation of its economy. We require an economy that is able to address the needs of the people of our country; that can provide food, houses, social security and everything that makes life joyful rather than a protracted encounter with hopelessness and despair. We must also make the point firmly that the political settlement and democracy itself cannot survive unless the material needs of the people; the bread and butter issue are addressed as part of the process of change as a matter of urgency (cited in Awe 1999:15).

On May Day four years later, he had changed gear: 'In our economic policies... there is no single reference to things like nationalization and this is not accidental. There is not a single slogan that will connect us with any Marxist ideology' (Marais 2001:122).

The politics of democratic consolidation becomes severely flawed in this respect. While there is a perception that the black majority government has done fairly well in meeting some of the basic needs of the historically disadvantaged, the thinking persists that Mandela, for all the goodwill and iconoclasm he enjoyed (and continues to enjoy out of power), is 'widely considered to have failed the test of "delivery"' (Butler 2003:94). The paradoxes and contradictions have virtually become inescapable. South Africans have on their hands a democracy that is simultaneously largely elite-driven, one-party dominant (see below), progressively respectful of the constitution and the rule of law, but, paradoxically, seemingly undergirded by the politics of entitlement. The latter has, for all practical purposes, become a common denominator of former guerrilla fighters in power in the Southern Africa sub-region. Those who, yesterday, gave their prime years in sacrifice to their country and their compatriots deem themselves, today, to be entitled, in perpetuity, to political power and the immense privileges and luxuries that come in its trail. They do not mind becoming sacred cows and virtual untouchables in the process. In the celebrated Tony Yengeni case, with regard to the multi-billion rand arms deal, a corporate analyst was worried, on the occasion of the judiciary's acceptance of a plea bargain for the ANC former Chief Whip at the point that his conviction was virtually secured, that the South African justice system may be a long shot away from being able to deal 'appropriately with well-connected and moneyed criminals'. More specifically, the case was seized upon to remind the hierarchy of the ANC of the essence of the anti-apartheid struggle. The latter was not about replacing white dominance and self-aggrandising greed with demographically representative greed. On the contrary, 'it was about legitimate government, about redistributing the resources of the country more equitably and about respect for the people' (Cf. 'The Fat Cat Mentality' (Editorial) *Mail and Guardian* (Johannesburg), February 21 to 27, 2003, p.24).

To all appearances, a new black elite authoritarianism is developing even as the bastions and ramparts of the old order remain unassailable in certain fundamental ways. According to Good (1997:573), 'the new authoritarianism, built on predominance and power-sharing among the elites, backed by corporate power and the patriotic bourgeoisie has potentially greater permanency than apartheid'. In view of Pretoria's hegemony in the sub-region, it may be that a potent explicatory schema for the inability of South Africa to articulate a foreign policy anchored, *inter alia*, on commitment to human rights, democracy, multipartyism, let alone 'export its democratic governance, its conflict resolution models and its core democratic values' (Cawthra 2003:52-54) is because her own record is nothing but mixed—and this tends to be more supportive of authoritarian tendencies than democratic tenets.

Within this context, one can interrogate the merits and demerits of the ANC's ascendancy and hegemony. There are two emerging schools of thought on this subject. The first sees the hegemony as essentially positive to the extent that the party is perceived as playing a 'hold on' role in the country's democratisation politics. The argument is that the country needs a dominant party in the midst of a fluid multiparty system to help build enduring, legitimate and trusted institutions that, in the long run, will facilitate the construction of a robust democracy (Butler 2003:100). Furthermore, it is argued that beyond providing political stability, the ANC is needed to furnish an 'enabling environment' for the attraction and retention of both domestic and foreign investment. The hope has been expressed that 'an extended period of ANC electoral dominance, over, perhaps, ten or fifteen years, will entrench the legitimacy of democratic institutions' (Butler 2003:100). The hope is perhaps not entirely misplaced. Cawthra (2003:49-50) has contended that the ANC government's achievement in controlling political violence and entrenching democratic processes has resulted in a state system that functions fairly effectively. Elements of a functional state include the following: transformation of the public service; provision of basic services virtually nation-wide; fiscal discipline; effective policy-making; fairly efficiently managed budgets; and deliberate and deliberative measures to make the state more transparent, accountable and responsive. In essence, therefore, the ANC's more than average performance justifies its continued hegemony, even though implementation performance (including some key departments that lack capacity to deliver) remains a sore point. The second school is a little more sceptical and cautious. Its proponents seem wary that an extremely powerful ANC capable of making its many competitors appear politically ordinary portends a grave danger for South Africa's political future—as well as for the entire sub-region, already unsettled by the political *faux pas* of a Mugabe and a Nujoma, amongst others, who seem bent on honouring their countries' constitutions more in the breach than in the observance. The major critique is that 'the ruling party (ANC) is representing itself as the state rather than as a temporary incumbent while other groups are losing the autonomy they require to compete' (Butler 2003:110). Such fears are hardly lessened by the ANC's seeming interest in party (as against state) accountability, as seen, for instance, in the on-going arms deal scandal; the emerging politics, since 2002, of silencing Leftist critics of the ANC and the Mbeki presidency both within and outside the government, and a conscious policy of promoting pro-capitalist groups within the ruling party as well as Mbeki's acolytes (Butler 2003:102, 105). To be sure, the ANC can justify its tight grip on state power on the grounds that the polity requires political cohesion and stability in order to mitigate possible negative fall-outs of a lack of national identity and incipient ethnicity (the 'Xhosa mantra,' for instance) (cf. Austin 2001:501). As Johnson (2000:35) has averred, what South Africa's democratisation agenda calls for is to seek a balance between the temptation to accumulate power ostensibly to better the lot of the poor and the cultivation of a culture of robust democracy that goes beyond electoralism (a defining feature of the sub-region, including Botswana). An important requirement for robust democracy is, in the words of Seepe (2000:29), the creation of 'an environment that encourages a flourishing and flowering of ideas... an environment that promotes robust and vibrant intellectual engagements'.

Conclusion

What the foregoing analysis boils down to is that whatever the ennobling virtues of South Africa's many superstructural achievements, a pro-market macroeconomic orientation that, wittingly and unwittingly, perpetuates inherited structural inequities and inequalities, has prevented the ANC government from undertaking bolder and more innovative systemic reforms. Expressed differently, whilst the political science of democratisation has been important for ordinary South African folk, in view of their long march to freedom, the people's lot is likely to improve further and have a solid foundation if their leaders, spokespersons and carriers of the torch of progress will agitate for the political economy of the same polity. It is this singular phenomenon that has resulted, since 1994, in little economic growth, little redistributive economics and politics, little racial reconciliation and national unity. To the extent that this is so, post-apartheid South Africa has a long road ahead before social democracy could emerge as the only game in town. While for the first time democratisation in the country has translated to the poor having the same formal political power as the rich (Nattrass and Seekings 2001:485), the country remains, *mutatis mutandis*, 'one of the most unequal societies on earth' (Lester et al 2000:230). Similarly, whilst it is true that the ANC government inherited a fairly reasonable macroeconomic system, a fairly redistributive system (that multiple political struggles forced the apartheid government to incrementally arrive at) and a fairly low foreign debt (Lester et al 2000:242), it has hardly been able to build on it. The route to expected massive redistribution having been foreclosed, critical issues such as justice (a major component of social transformation), dignity and autonomy have received little more than a nodding attention (Manzo in Lester et al 2000:230).

In this respect, land reforms and land redistribution would need to be treated with the caution and the urgency they deserve. It is not enough to say, like Lester et al (2000:265) that the land issue is not so important (unlike in, say, Zimbabwe and Namibia) because South Africa's population is largely urbanised. Nor can the country afford to continue to handle the land issue bureaucratically or—which amounts to the same thing—in an extremely slow, painful and tortuous manner. Not only has a mere one percent of land been redistributed by 1999 (as against the 30 percent promised), during the same year only 33 out of 22,500 land claims by people who wanted to reclaim their dispossessed land were settled (Lester et al 2000:265-266). If not sped up, it may snowball into a veritable time bomb ticking away.

As in Brazil, South Africa's transition to social democracy—a social desideratum if the notorious poverty question would have to be progressively (and satisfactorily) addressed and resolved—is being blocked by a combination of powerful vested domestic and international business and capitalist interests; conservative bureaucrats and technocrats (whose incomes are staggering compared to the poverty wage that so ill-befits those lucky enough to find jobs) and elected politicians determined to preserve their control of privilege and patronage (Nattrass and Seekings 2001:494-495).

It is difficult to see how entrenched political, economic and bureaucratic interests and powers can be dislodged without a combination of intellectual work and renewed and reactivated political activism. To begin with, a rethinking is necessary in order to free the democratic and liberating energies of the country's (latent) popular social forces for democratisation. The goal would be to wean democracy from 'self-interested democracy promotion by the West and develop sustainable domestic roots' (Luckham 2003:7). In the words of Swift (2000), 'undemocratic concentration of power will always form and need dissolving. Cliques and cabals will need challenging. Civil service empires will need to be deconstructed'.

Civil society organisations, mass movements, the ANC's tripartite allies and a hopefully reactivated Pan-Africanist Congress (much assailed in recent years by leadership crisis) and similar bodies would need to recover their voice. This would be with a view to pressuring the ANC government to halt those policies 'that keep the economy growing along an inegalitarian path', one that results in 'a large section of the poor being shut out of income-generating activities' (Nattrass and Seekings 2001:495) to embrace growth with equity as well as the 'post-Washington Consensus' which advocates a greater degree of state involvement in a national economy (Lester et al 2000:47).

Furthermore, South Africa would do well with a large number of democrats—from the ranks of current political and other leaders and civil society alike—to move the polity away from the sphere of liberal imperfection (Williams 2003:2) to ensure democratic consolidation and societal transformation. 'Democracy can be installed without democrats, but it cannot be consolidated without them', write Bratton and van de Walle (cited in Haynes 2001: 31). They continue: 'democracy will truly last only when political actors learn to love it. Until elites and citizens alike come to cherish rule by the people and exhibit a willingness to stand up for it, in Africa as elsewhere, there will be no permanent defence against tyranny'. The process of political statecraft and societal transformation would no doubt benefit from sustained cooperation between the tripartite alliance and the opposition parties (Butler 2003:112). While this paradigm may help entrench South Africa's 'highly imperfect democracy', it will do little to bring the mass majority of the poor 'back in'.

As we have tried to show in this essay, the democracy in question has to be that which improves the quality of living of the people. It cannot be one that purely and simply increases the quantum of power, opulence and privileges of the ruling classes and their elastic set of hangers-on—even if it is claimed that this is being done in the name of the 'people'.

References

Amuwo, K., 2003, 'From Transition to Transformation: The State, Social Forces and Democratic Development in South Africa and Nigeria', paper presented during the 19th World Congress of the International Political Science Association (IPSA) conference, 29 June to 4 July, 2003, Durban, South Africa.
Amy, S. and Patterson, 1998, 'A Reappraisal of Democracy in Civil Society: Evidence from rural Senegal', *Journal of Modern African Studies*, Vol. 36, No. 3, September.
Austin, D., 2001, 'Good Governance?', *Round Table*, 361.
Awe, B., 1999, 'Conflict and Divergence: Government and Society in Nigeria', *African Studies Review*, Vol. 42, No. 3, December.
Ayogu, M and Hodge, J., 2002, 'Understanding Telecommunication Sector Reforms in South Africa: A Political Economy Perspective', *Journal of Contemporary African Studies*, Vol. 20, No. 2, July.
Baker, B., 2002, 'When the Bakassi Boys Came: Eastern Nigeria Confronts Vigilantism', *Journal of Contemporary African Studies*, Vol. 20, No. 2, July.
Bastian, S. and Luckham, R., 2003, *Can Democracy Be Designed? The Politics of Institutional Choice in Conflict-Torn Societies*, London and New York: Zed Books.
Bjornlund, E., Bratton, M. and Gibson, C., 1992, 'Observing Multiparty Elections in Africa: Some Lessons from Zambia', *African Affairs*, Vol. 91, No. 364, July.
Boafo-Arthur, K, 1999, 'Ghana: Structural Adjustment, Democratization and the Politics of Continuity', *African Studies Review*, 42, 2, September.
Butler, A., 2003, 'South Africa's Political Futures', *Government and Opposition*, 38, 1, Winter.
Cawthra, G., 2003, 'Security Transformation in Post-Apartheid South Africa', in G. Cawthra and R. Luckham (eds) *Governing Insecurity: Democratic Control of Military and Security Establishment in Transitional Democracies*, London: Zed Books.
Decalo, S., 1992, 'The Process, Prospects and Constraints of Democratisation in Africa', *African Affairs*, 91, 362, January.
Dommen, E., 1997, 'Paradigms of Governance and Exclusion', *Journal of Modern African Studies*, 35, 3, September.
du Toit, P., 1995, *State-Building and Democracy in Southern Africa: Botswana, Zimbabwe and South Africa*, Pretoria: Human Sciences Research Council Publishers.
Gibson, N., 2001, 'Transition from Apartheid', *Journal of Asian and African Studies*, xxxvi, 1.
Giliomee, H., 1995, 'Democratisation in South Africa', *Political Science Quarterly*, 110, 1.
Good, K., 2002, *The Liberal Model and Africa: Elites Against Democracy*, London: Palgrave.
Good, K., 1997, 'Accountable to Themselves: Predominance in Southern Africa', *Journal of Modern African Studies*, 35, 4, December.
Griffiths, A. and Katalikawe, J., 2003, 'The Reformulation of Ugandan Democracy', in S. Bastian and R., Luckham (eds) *Can Democracy be Designed? The Politics of Institutional Choice in Conflict-Torn Societies*, London and New York: Zed Books.
Haynes, J., 2001, *Democracy in the Developing World: Africa, Asia, Latin America and the Middle East*, Cambridge: Polity Press.
Hearn, J., 2000, 'Aiding Democracy? Donors and Civil Society in South Africa', *Third World Quarterly*.

Johnson, K., 2000, 'The Tradeoffs between Distributive Equity and Democratic Process: The Case of Child Welfare Reform in South Africa', *African Studies Review*, 43, 3.

Judson, F., 2001, 'The Dynamics of Transition Governance in South Africa: Voices from Mpumalanga Province', *Africa Today*, 48, 2, Summer.

Kindra, J., 2003, 'South Africa Buys into Zimbabwe Lie', *Mail and Guardian*, 7 to 13 March.

Lester, A., Nel, E., and Binns, T., 2000, *South Africa: Past, Present and Future: Gold at the End of the Rainbow?*, Essex: Pearson Education.

Le Vine, V.T., 1997, 'The Fall and Rise of Constitutionalism in West Africa', *Journal of Modern African Studies*, 35, 2, June.

Lodge, T., 1997, Review of du Toit, *State-Building and Democracy in Southern Africa*, *Journal of Modern African Studies*, 35, 2, June.

Lowe, C., 1999, 'Civil Society, The Domestic Realm, History and Democracy in South Africa', in J. Hyslop (ed) *African Democracy in the Era of Globalisation*, Johannesburg: Witwatersrand University Press.

Luckham, R., 2003, 'Democratic Strategies for Security in Transition and Conflict', in G. Cawthra and R. Luckham (eds) *Governing Insecurity: Democratic Control of Military and Security Establishment in Transitional Democracies*, London: Zed Books.

Luckham, R, Goetz, A. M. and Kaldor, M., 2003, 'Democratic Institutions and Democratic Politics', in S. Bastian and R. Luckham (eds) *Can Democracy Be Designed? The Politics of Institutional Choice in Conflict-Torn Societies*, London: Zed Books.

Marais, H., 2001, *South Africa: Limits to Change: The Political Economy of Transition*, London, New York and Cape Town: Zed Books and Univ. of Cape Town Press.

Nattrass, N. and Seekings, J., 2001, 'Democracy and Distribution in Highly Unequal Economy: The Case of South Africa', *Journal of Modern African Studies*, 39, 3.

Pottie, D. and Hassim, S., 2003, 'The Politics of Institutional Design in the South African Transition', in S. Bastian and R. Luckham (eds) *Can Democracy be Designed? The Politics of Institutional Choice in Conflict-Torn Societies*, London: Zed Books.

Seepe, S., 2000, 'How Mbeki is Hampering the Renaissance', *Mail and Guardian*, June.

Silva, P., 2003, 'Between Autonomy and Subordination: Government-Military Relations in post-Authoritarian Chile', in G. Cawthra and R. Luckham (eds) *Governing Insecurity: Democratic Control of Military and Security Establishment in Transitional Democracies*, London and New York: Zed Books.

Southall, R., 2003, *Democracy in Africa: Moving Beyond a Difficult Legacy*, Cape Town: Human Sciences Research Council.

Swift, R., 2000, 'Democracy: is that all there is?', *New Internationalist Magazine*, 324 June. Accessed online at http://www.newint.org/issue324/keynote.htm.

Tripp, A. M., 2000, 'Political Reform in Tanzania: The Struggle for Associational Autonomy', *Comparative Politics*, January.

Williams, G., 2003, *Fragments of Democracy: Nationalism, Development and the State in Africa*, Cape Town: HSRC.

Williams, P., 2001, Review of Guy Arnold, *The New South Africa* (Basingstoke: Palgrave/Macmillan), in *African, Affairs* 100, 401, October.

3

Legacies and Meanings of the United Democratic Front (UDF) Period for Contemporary South Africa

Raymond Suttner

In essence South Africa is at a crossroads. At one stop some former exiles live in glittering opulence, while at the other the true soldiers of our struggle have been left in bewildering proximity to unendurable poverty. It is antithetical that the former *amaqabane*, or comrades, who are the true (and sadly unsung) liberators of our country are now virtually pariahs in the land they forcibly liberated from the vices of apartheid. While the exiles were fighting imaginary enemies in godforsaken jungles, *amaqabane* were crossing swords—or rather exchanging stones for bullets—with the real enemy, the unforgivable apartheid government, the presumed antagonists of the exiles. In actuality these people, to whom our country is undoubtedly and markedly indebted, have been obliquely driven to the shadows. One such forgotten hero is Motsele Mahapa, [who said]: 'I feel bad that most people who were active in the emancipation of our country are now permanent residents of our deluged prisons, while the so-called exiles are now the heroes of the day'. The irony of it all is that when Umkhonto we Sizwe [the Spear of the Nation, the armed wing of the African National Congress (ANC), colloquially referred to as MK] failed in its ill-fated hit-and-run raids, it consulted the comrades to increase its own backing in the townships—and then, suddenly, *amaqabane* were expendable (Thokozani Mhlongo 2003).

[In the period of Thabo Mbeki's ascendancy] the ideas of the Freedom Charter and the aspirations of the UDF were now buried if not yet dead. The Freedom Charter's principle of non-racialism had begun to go with the return of the exiles in 1990; unlike the UDF, says Max du Preez, the exiles only knew a handful of white comrades (Kenneth Good 2002:161)

But there was always that tension between people who believed the UDF could help the liberation struggle by putting pressure on the government internally and those, especially people in exile, who felt threatened by the UDF (Ryland Fisher 2003).

Why should we mark the anniversary of the UDF—is there a mischievous intent?[1] Are we celebrating a period of existence of a set of organisations because of their instrumental value? Are we marking this period because the UDF and its affiliates contributed substantially towards the liberation of South Africa? Or are we acknowledging their role in bringing the ANC into the mainstream of South African politics, and thus completing tasks set by the ANC? (see Chikane 2003). Or do we see the UDF period representing an alternative to or going beyond the type of democracy and politics that exists today? Does the UDF have a lasting significance, which may or may not be realised within contemporary South African politics? Did the UDF period provide amplifications of our previous understandings of democracy and liberation, and, if so, how and in what way? (see Neocosmos 1998; Cherry 1999, 2000).

Commemorating the anniversary of the UDF may be interpreted as having a mischievous intent. This is because it is often introduced in contemporary discussion in order to contrast how it functioned or allegedly operated with styles of work of the ANC in exile (and, to some extent, the leadership emerging from Robben Island). This feeds into the type of sentiments found in the quotations at the beginning of this chapter. When one commemorates the UDF one is invited to look back to a golden age of popular democracy, which is contrasted with what has happened today, with the alleged exile dominance over the ANC and government (see the title of John Daniel's paper: 'The Mbeki Presidency: Lusaka wins', Daniel 2003; Good 2002; Pallo Jordan interview, 2003, contests, statistically, the notion of exile dominance of ANC and government).

There is some truth and some exaggeration and romanticisation and demonisation in these perceptions

The object of this chapter is to argue for the importance of the period of the UDF, not merely for institutions or constitutional structures of a particular kind, but for what can be drawn from the period. What important practices and values should we try to retain, retrieve or preserve from that phase and take into the present? This is a separate question from whether, and in what ways, the UDF contributed to the pre-eminence of the ANC and its victory.

This is because for all the exaggeration or romanticisation, that moment of the UDF and the 1980s represented something different from what had previously (and has subsequently, for that matter) been experienced in the history of the liberation struggle and was a different experience from that of the ANC in exile.[2] It is also necessary to ask whether some qualities are lacking in the present, which may be remedied by recourse to some of the ideas and experiences of the 1980s, or, alternatively, whether we choose a path of democracy that excludes or already incorporates that experience.

When Jeremy Seekings quotes Walter Sisulu remarking that the UDF placed 'the central question of political power on the agenda…' (2000: 3), the issue is in what way power was raised, and whether it problematised and advanced the question in a manner that had not previously been done. It will be argued that the UDF period introduced democratic possibilities and understandings that may not previously have been articulated within the South African struggle. The legacies and meanings of this period are considered under a number of headings, which are by no means exhaustive and may not rank as the most important, though, in my view, many are. Finally, if the legacy is worth elaboration or has importance, we need to ask how it should influence contemporary politics. That crucial question I leave for future debate (but see Suttner 2004, 2004b).

Mass character and contribution of the UDF period to the demise of apartheid

The period of the UDF represented a mass upsurge on a scale the country had never previously seen, which was probably the decisive element in ensuring that a negotiated settlement became possible. It was, however, part of, and connected to, a wider attack on apartheid, covering a range of fields of activity over a considerable length of time. It involved a broad spectrum of people engaged in a variety of political and wider activities that cumulatively weakened the apartheid regime.

While an insurrectionary climate prevailed in the mid 1980s, the forces of resistance, allied to the ANC, lacked the capacity to overthrow the government. Nevertheless, even at moments of greatest repression, the possibility of governability, sustaining apartheid rule over time, was no longer there. In that sense the periods of ungovernability and people's power, together with international isolation, the attacks by MK, underground ANC propaganda and other activities, created conditions that made the regime's agenda unviable. That both sides were able to prevent the realisation of each other's goals without fully achieving their own, what Antonio Gramsci referred to as a state of politics where 'the siege is a reciprocal one', created conditions that made a negotiated settlement possible (Gramsci 1971: 238-9).

The UDF contribution towards democratic thinking, democratic accountability and notions and practices of popular power

The 1980s introduced modes of practising politics that had never previously been seen in South Africa, that may well condition people's expectations today (cf. Cherry 1999: 404). Here, one thinks of notions such as 'popular democracy', 'people's power', 'self-empowerment', 'the masses driving the process', 'democracy from below', 'and creativity of the masses' (cf. Morobe 1987: 81-95; Neocosmos 1998, 195: 241).

There may have been abuses of various kinds in the period of popular power, but there were nevertheless important contributions and achievements that introduced reinterpretations and new notions into South African democratic discourse. In particular, the period constituted in part a reinterpretation or deepening of the interpretation of the Freedom Charter[3] (cf. Morobe 1987). In many ways this was self-consciously the case, with activists seeing their activity in the street committees or other organs of people's power, as implementation of the first clause of the Freedom Charter, declaring that 'The People Shall Govern!' Thus, in an interview in the mid 1980s Weza Made of Uitenhage remarked:

> Generally, ya, I can say the community is the main source of power, because the state has really lost the control over the people. He has no power over the people in terms of controlling them. This is why the people have formed these area committees, so that they can try to control themselves. What has been preached in the past about the Freedom Charter, even now we are trying to do that practically (Interview, 1986).

The period may also have substantially extended the practice and understanding of non-racialism, non-sexism and other values beyond that of the 1950s, but without removing or raising all of the problems associated with these categories. Before too much is claimed, we should remember that while people at leadership level or those who attended UDF General Councils may have encountered activists from other communities, the vast majority of affiliates may never have met a person from the white or Indian or Coloured community in their political activities. In that sense, while the principle of non-racialism may have been there, the extent of practice will have varied. Likewise, we need to interrogate how deeply values like non-sexism were integrated into peoples' thinking and practice and the related organisational questions and barriers surrounding these issues (cf. Hassim 2003).

Prefigurative democracy

The period represented a notion of 'prefigurative democracy'. By this is meant that people did not understand democracy as being inaugurated on one day, after which all the practices and ideals they cherished would come into effect. They understood that their daily practices were part of the process of building the 'new South Africa'. Means and ends became fused; the democratic means were part of the democratic ends. In fact, what was being done at the time was seen as valuable in itself and not merely valuable in an instrumental sense, contributing towards a distant goal when the (problematic) notion of transfer of power to the people would take place.

Mufson refers to statements and notes of the assassinated UDF and Cradock leader, Matthew Goniwe, emphasising the notion of building the future in immediate practices:

> We want young men and women who are embodiments of the new SA... I f we are instruments of change, we MUST epitomise [the] society we want to bring about. [You] cannot over-drink and hope people will see you as representing a new society. [You] cannot be promiscuous [and] still tell people about [ending the] exploitation of women (Mufson 1990:112, emphasis in original.)

And again, Mosiuoa 'Terror' Lekota, then Publicity Secretary of the UDF said:

> In political struggle...the means must always be the same as the ends...How can one expect a racialistic movement to imbue our society with a non-racial character on the dawn of our freedom day? A political movement cannot bequeath to society a characteristic it does not itself possess. To expect it to do so is like asking a heathen to convert a person to Christianity. The principles of that religion are unknown to the heathen let alone the practice (Anthony W. Marx 1992:124).

Likewise, leading UDF national figure, Murphy Morobe, provided one of the most clearly elaborated outlines of the conception of democracy then prevalent:

> [A] democratic South Africa is one of the aims or goals of our struggle. This can be summed up in the principal slogan of the Freedom Charter: 'The People Shall Govern!' In the second place, democracy is the means by which we conduct the struggle. This refers to the democratic character of our existing mass-based organisations. It is useful to separate these two levels, but obviously they are also connected. By developing active, mass-based democratic organisations and democratic practices within these organisations, we are laying the basis for a future, democratic South Africa.

> The creation of democratic *means* is for us as important as having democratic *goals* as our objective. Too often models of a future democratic South Africa are put forward which bear no relation to existing organisations, practices and traditions of political struggle in this country. What is possible in the future depends on what we are able to create and sustain now. A democratic South Africa will not be fashioned only after transference of political power to the majority has taken place, nor will it be drawn up according to blueprints and plans that are the products of conferences and seminars. The creation of a democratic South Africa can only become a reality with the participation... Our democratic aim ...is control over every aspect of our lives, and not just the right (important as it is) to vote for a central government every four to five years. ...When we say that the people shall govern, we mean at all levels and in all spheres, and we demand that there be real, effective control on a daily basis (Morobe 1987:81-2, emphasis in the original).

The problem with the notion of transfer of power to the people lies partly in its instrumentalism, that, at a particular moment, something called power is handed over, a 'thing' is passed from one set of rulers to another, and after that something completely different is done. Poulantzas has correctly remarked:

> To take or capture state power is not simply to lay hands on part of the state machinery in order to replace it with a second power. Power is not a quantifiable substance held by the state that must be taken out of its hands, but rather a series of relations among the various social classes... The State is neither a thing-instrument that may be taken away, nor a fortress that may be penetrated by means of a wooden horse, nor yet a safe that may be cracked by burglary: it is the heart of the exercise of political power (Poulantzas 2000:257-8. See also Hobsbawm 1982:24 ff., on Antonio Gramsci's focus before and beyond the moment of 'transfer of power').

The instrumental conception of power tends to devalue immediate activity, whose relevance is seen as purely in relation to realising something else—the seizure or transfer of power at some decisive moment in the future. This is a notion that converges with classic Marxist-Leninist texts as well as general conceptions of transition held by most national liberation movements (Lenin 1968, Suttner 2004).[4]

The notion of democracy of the UDF period was more complex, though not always adequately or fully articulated or realised. It did envisage the notion of 'transfer of power', but it simultaneously saw people building democracy at that very moment. It envisaged establishing elements of people's power immediately, transforming relationships of power, between powerful and powerless even before the moment of 'taking state power' when the people would ultimately govern themselves at the level of the central state.

In that sense it involved a conception, which has in practice come to have relevance to the way the democratic transition unfolded, where there has not been one decisive moment of 'transfer' with all else following. Power has been 'transferred' since 1994, but all sorts of institutions and relationships still have to be transformed in order to ensure that peoples' lives are changed.

People understood what they were doing in the 1980s as a moment of self-empowerment, where they did not wait for leaders to tell them what to do, but directly exercised their democratic rights in their political practice. The UDF leadership was present and the ANC, in particular, gave broad strategic direction. But people on the ground were more than mere instruments implementing what others advised or instructed. They were direct actors, who decided what should be done and how and in so doing exercised considerable creativity.

People's power and conditions for its success and failure

The notion of people's power was not unprecedented in South Africa. Govan Mbeki recorded the existence of people's courts in the Pondoland rising of the 1950s and there are no doubt other examples that can be so classified (Mbeki 1984:25). Some people, especially in the Eastern Cape, saw the M-Plan of the 1950s, one of whose components was street-level organisation, as a precedent for the People's Power period (see Cherry 1999:403-4). The M-Plan was developed by the ANC after the Communist Party was declared illegal, on the expectation of its being proscribed. It was a preparation for ANC underground organisation (Suttner 2003).

But the UDF appropriation of the traditions of the 1950s did not always take account of, or was not fully aware of, its contradictory character. Thus, the conception of the M-Plan also entailed strong elements of top down/ transmission of leadership decisions (cf. Suttner 2003:32-134). In contrast, the People's Power period was on the whole a 'bottom up' experience and the notions informing it theoretically were primarily from the grassroots upwards.[5] Yet the power and promise of the UDF period had its ups and downs, moments of great creativity and democratic involvement and also abuse, with 'kangaroo courts' and intolerance of diversity. It is important to identify, insofar as we can, what conditions were most conducive to success, meaning popular democracy without abuse, intolerance and violence, and what conditions most likely to result in the negative features. This is partly related to periodisation of the UDF experience. The times of most successful popular power depended on the intensity of state repression. The lower the intensity the greater the likelihood for successful exercise of popular power. The period of the states of emergency (1985-89, with a short break when it was temporarily lifted in 1986) saw the arrest of almost all the most experienced leaders and a situation where, in many communities, the youth took command. More violence was then practised and less broad community involvement secured (see also Neocosmos 1998:202-210).[6]

People's power was usually most successful where representatives from a wide range of sectors determined action on behalf of and in consultation with the community. This wide representativity was especially important in the enforcement of consumer boycotts. Where this element of broad involvement was lacking, coercion often resulted. Likewise, crime control could work effectively where it enjoyed the greatest community involvement and consent. It could degenerate into violence and abuse where only sections of the community, who were able to exact punishments, took command.

The UDF period saw some examples, in Port Alfred, for instance, where community representatives of a broad character managed important aspects of township life. The fleeing of government officials left a vacuum, which the civic structures filled. The Bantu Administration[7] building was taken over and turned into a much-needed crèche. The same period saw extensive community action, including consumer boycotts enforced without resort to violence (interview with Gugile Nkwinti 1986; see also Mufson 1990).

In Atteridgeville, Uitenhage, Fort Beaufort, Port Elizabeth, Mamelodi at times, Graaf Reinet and other places, community efforts at crime control at a street and block level saw significant results insofar as residents as a whole were involved and the activities were seen as fulfilling a social goal that was regarded as broadly necessary (interviews with Titus Mafolo and Mapheti Leeuw regarding Atteridgeville and Weza Made regarding Uitenhage, 1986). Crime control is often equated with the existence of people's courts. My impression from research in 1985/6 is that most of the more successful examples of popular justice did not entail the existence of courts.

In various parts of the country, as the state of emergency took its toll on experienced leadership, it was easier for the less experienced youth who tended to want quick results, or criminal elements, to assume command. This often led to extensive violence and degeneration of popular organs into vehicles of terror.

The UDF as both an agent of the ANC as well as autonomous actor

The relationship between the ANC and UDF is an important and difficult question to uncover. There are some statements of ANC figures suggesting that the ANC set up the UDF or directed the UDF, as the apartheid state alleged. There is no doubt that the ANC had for some years wanted to see the development of mass organisation within the country, the reoccupation of the leadership space by organisations advancing the broad vision of the Congress movement[8] (cf ANC Green Book 1979). It is clear that establishment of a broad front of popular organisations corresponded in many respects with what was required and recognised by the ANC as necessary to remedy organisational deficiency on the ground (Barrell 1992; ANC 1979). The opening up of 'legal space' in order to pursue mass mobilisation and organisation constituted what the ANC described as one of its 'four pillars' of struggle.[9] But that does not mean the ANC 'set up' the UDF nor that it controlled the UDF and its affiliates. This is well captured in an interview of the late ANC President, Oliver Tambo, originally published in 1984:

> We called for united action to resist …We called for mobilisation of our entire forces. We called for united action, 1982 and 1983. It was necessary that we should meet this new offensive by the enemy as a united democratic force. Nothing else would help. I think our people responded remarkably to this call. The emergence of the UDF was exactly what we were talking about during the year of Unity in Action, 1982. It was what we envisaged in our call in 1983 for United Action. We had called for confrontation with the enemy on all fronts, by all our people in their various organisational formations. The response to this call was the emergence of the UDF.
>
> Question:…The regime says one of the reasons why it is taking action against the UDF leadership is that the UDF is a front of the ANC. Now if we say that the emergence of the UDF and present day mass upsurge is a result of organisation and mobilisation by the ANC, does it follow that the UDF is a creation of the ANC?
>
> Tambo: NO! NO! It does not follow, because the ANC has for a long time now, ever since it was banned, actually called on the people to organise themselves: any organisation, even where it differed with the ANC, provided only it was oriented against the apartheid system, we supported it. So we have encouraged the formation of organisations. These 700 organisations that belong to the UDF were not created by the ANC. But the ANC has called on the people to organise themselves, whether they organise themselves into ping-pong clubs or whatever it is, but we said, organise and direct your attention and activity to freeing yourselves so that you become human beings and citizens of your own country, which you are not! (Tambo 2003).

There is little doubt that members of the ANC underground played a role in UDF organisations and affiliates, but that is not the same as saying the ANC, whether from outside or in the underground, 'ran' the UDF. Yet a reality of the time was that many members of UDF affiliates saw themselves as carrying out the mandates of the ANC. Every night many would tune in at 7 p.m. to listen to Radio Freedom (the ANC station broadcasting from a number of African states. See Interview, for example, with Pharepare [General] Mothupi, Polokwane 2004). Wherever possible they would obtain ANC and SACP literature. Of particular interest was the January 8 statement on the anniversary of the ANC. Here the organisation mapped out a general strategic vision and also specific 'tasks' for various sectors. It might read: 'to the students we say' and address students, suggesting in general terms what they felt were necessary political tasks in the year that lay ahead. Many activists in the UDF would pore over these words and extract meanings for what they should do in their specific sectors and organisations.

But the authors of the January 8 statements did not know the detailed conditions confronted in the various sectors and organisations, and in parts of the country facing distinct problems and possibilities. Consequently, the way this guideline or broad vision was interpreted remained in the hands of the affiliate. It was not ANC headquarters in Lusaka, nor UDF headquarters in Johannesburg that dictated how these 'instructions' or 'the line of march' was interpreted. And many a time the interpretation given on the ground was one that may well have surprised those who made the initial call for particular activities to be engaged in. For example, when the ANC leadership called for the building of elementary organs of people's power, they could not envisage the distinct issues and opportunities in the various parts of South Africa. The building of people's parks, or establishment of street committees, or involvement in various community mediation efforts was the result of initiatives of people on the ground. The local activists generally saw themselves carrying out ANC policy, but the details could only be worked out in the practical conditions faced in specific townships.

But the ANC knew the language that would mobilise people to do things, often better than the UDF leadership. In the mid 1980s, the UDF leadership wanted students to return to schools, shortly after the establishment of the Soweto Students' Crisis committee, which later helped initiate the national body, the NECC (National Education Crisis Committee). A delegation visited Lusaka to seek assistance. The ANC issued a statement exhorting the students to return, saying that the classrooms were their 'trenches'. They did return, albeit not on a long-term basis. One may regret the use of military terms, but that was the language that worked and the ANC had the skill in its communications to know what imagery would be effective with which constituencies.[10]

The UDF and its affiliates popularised the ANC, but it was not an invention of, or set up by, the ANC or a surrogate for the organisation. Govan Mbeki is therefore not sufficiently accurate in his characterisation of the 1980s: '[T]he ANC had captured the political centre stage and *established its hegemony* through structures like the United Democratic Front...' (1996: x, my emphasis). Nor is he correct in referring to the mass uprising of the 1980s as 'directed and coordinated by the ANC underground...' (1996: xi. See also statement of former ANC spokesperson, Tom Sebina, and criticism in Neocosmos 1998: 203).[11] This is not to suggest that the ANC underground was unconnected to the legal struggle, something that is mystified in Seekings's work, repeatedly mentioned without explaining what significance it had (2000:56, 164). MK played a role, for example, in assisting stayaways on occasions by blowing up railway lines, thus making it difficult for those who wanted to go to work to do so. Hassim is not correct, in my view, in counterposing the civics 'political approach' to that of guerrilla warfare (Hassim 2003:48). Many MK interventions were attempts to complement civic grievances, for example, attacks on Bantu Administration buildings or in the case of the attack on the Soekmekaar police station—probably the first of such assaults, was directed against police who had been involved in forced removals (Interview Petros 'Shoes' Mashigo 2003; See also Seidman 2001). And underground propaganda units often issued pamphlets in support of specific community action.

Many underground activists played a role in UDF structures, but that is not the same as 'directing and coordinating' them. That would not have coexisted easily with the culture of UDF, where concepts of internal democracy made it difficult for a small group (which underground units were by definition) to direct an organisation. This is not an attempt to counterpose the democratic qualities of the UDF to inevitably less democratic qualities of the underground. But the different modes of operation and cultures of political work, made it impossible for so large a phenomenon to be directed and coordinated in the way Mbeki suggests. The underground may have had democratic goals, but its mode of organisation had, by definition, to be conspiratorial (see Suttner, unpub, 2004).

It may well be that various underground groups had great influence, just as other powerful personalities carried great weight, but all positions had to be won democratically. This, of course, applied less when there was extreme repression and when the states of emergency were in place. In that situation, internal democracy contracted and those who could adapt best to those conditions undoubtedly had greater influence. Also, practices occurred that were out of line with many of the fundamental tenets of the UDF. But this does not to establish anything about influence of the underground or ANC generally on the UDF. It is not clear who were best able to take advantage of whatever disarray state repression caused. Was it the ANC underground or the 'comtsotsis' (a term used to describe gangsters, known as 'tsotsis', who posed as 'comrades')? It is not clear and may have varied from situation to situation. The relationship between ANC and UDF was complex, for while UDF was not a tool of the ANC, very many of its activists did see themselves as under ANC discipline. Obviously they interpreted this in a variety of ways. But they saw themselves as carrying out broad strategies of the ANC. This self-perception is one of the reasons why the UDF did not consider continuing after the unbanning of previously illegal organisations. There was a tendency on the part of the UDF to see itself as a 'curtain raiser' before the main team arrived on the field, a type of 'B-team mentality'. And it is probably the reality that most members of affiliates of the UDF did see themselves falling under the leadership of Lusaka.

But there were other options, such as the possible continuation of a coordinating body like the UDF enduring, parallel to the ANC, in order to link to a number of sectoral organisations. One of the reasons why this was not considered was that there was a sense that they should return to the 'changing rooms', to make way for the main team. They did not realise that in addition to what the 'A-team' may have done and could still do, *there was something specific that the period of the 1980s had brought into the political arena*. The UDF also coordinated organisations pursuing a wider range of activities than any political organisation could ever do. A political organisation concerns itself with politics, which, however broadly conceived, can never be so wide as to encompass all the activities of sectorally focused organisations.

The UDF saw its own intervention in a very modest light. In the *Eighteenth Brumaire*, Karl Marx remarks on the unwillingness of people who are doing something really new to see or depict it that way. He refers to the tendency to attribute inspiration to those who have gone before them, to dress what they are doing in the garb of those who preceded them:

> The tradition of all the dead generations weighs like a nightmare on the brain of the living. And just when they seem engaged in revolutionising themselves and things, in creating something that has never yet existed, precisely in such periods of revolutionary crisis they anxiously conjure up the spirit of the past to their service and borrow from them names, battle-cries and costumes in order to present the new scene of world history in this time-honored disguise and this borrowed language... (Marx 1984:10).

From the outset, the UDF clothed itself in the Congress garb, especially of the 1950s, and indeed it was part of that tradition. It was part of the ANC in the broad sense. But a former UDF leadership figure, the Rev Frank Chikane (now an ANC leader and Director-General in the office of the President) blurs the importance of the UDF, independent of the ANC connection, when he writes:

> Looking back, the UDF taught us all very profound lessons in leadership. In the first instance, the leadership of the UDF always saw themselves as the interim leaders of the movement in the context of the banning of the peoples' organisations and the imprisonment of our leaders. We saw ourselves very much as 'holding the fort' for the leadership in jail or in exile… The United Democratic Front was indeed a holding operation, albeit a very important one! (Chikane 2003).

While the UDF did hold the fort, it also represented something qualitatively new. The UDF recovered some of the legacy of the 1950s that had been ruptured in the repression of the 1960s, but it went beyond that. A whole generation had grown up without access to literature about the Congress movement. This is not to say that the memory was wiped out, but there was a rupture, organisationally, in terms of symbols and also the free and widespread diffusion of values. The UDF reconnected people to that tradition, but it also went beyond that and beyond anything that had been practised by leadership whether in exile or in prison. It was only people on the ground in the various arenas of struggle who had that opportunity. It does not reflect on the quality of leadership or organisation elsewhere to say that something new was being done which extended the horizons of the liberation movement.

Continuities and differences

The UDF did not constitute a total break with what came before it, nor with organised activity in other places and terrains of struggle. Continuities were there beyond what are recognised in much of the literature, which counterposes the UDF to both exile and the underground. The exile experience is generally characterised as having been top down, centralised, secretive and militaristic (see Daniel 2003; Good 2002). But this may have been more varied than is generally conceded and dependent on whether people were located in military or civilian structures. Also, the exile experience is said, unlike UDF, to have been unconducive to debate. Yet informants from the exile experience argue that debate and political discussion were the stuff of life in the camps (Pallo Jordan interview 2003). Even if valid, the existence of sites of debate and discussion is obviously not the same as suggesting that decision-making was generally 'bottom up'.

On the one hand, then, the exile experience to which UDF is counterposed may not have been sufficiently and accurately characterised. On the side of the UDF there are elements of romanticism and reluctance to acknowledge large degrees of continuity and similarity in elements of both experiences. In the UDF, the range and boundaries of debate tended to expand and contract, according to security or perceived security considerations. But there was also a large measure of intolerance that coexisted with the broad democratic perspectives of the Front. Black Consciousness (BC) activists were often chased off platforms or beaten up and the Northern Transvaal UDF structures were also involved in the burning of 'witches' (cf Delius 1996; van Kessel 2000).

At an organisational and ideological level, there was also a degree of convergence. While exiled organisations may have operated according to democratic centralism, many UDF affiliates (for example, the Soweto Youth Congress) adopted similar guidelines. While people in exile learnt their ideology from Progress Publishers books emanating from Moscow (Serache interview 2002), these same texts circulated widely and were the basis for much political education inside the country. Many of these texts still circulate to this day.

In other respects, the 1980s does not stand on its own, isolated from experiences that went before or were contemporaneous. In particular, the 1976 uprising was a key factor in opening the space leading to the UDF experience. But also the impact of Robben Islanders was crucial in influencing many former BC leaders towards the 'Congress position' (cf. Seekings 2000:31 and interview with Nat Serache, 2002, regarding the role of assassinated former Robben Islander, Joe Gqabi). This was the case both in prison and from the ANC underground, which, contrary to the existing literature, was very much present after the arrest of the top leadership, who were sentenced in the Rivonia trial (see Buntman 2003 for prison accounts and Suttner unpub, 2004, on underground organisation). Indeed, many Robben Islanders came to play key roles within UDF, bridging gaps between generations, traditions and experiences.

Homogeneity and heterogeneity

The UDF always asserted that it was not itself a liberation movement and that the ANC performed that role. It nevertheless formed a part of, and articulated its role as an element of, the broad liberation forces headed by the ANC. This also meant acceptance of what one may describe as a specific 'national liberation model', whereby the national liberation movement is seen as the embodiment of the nation (see further, Suttner 2004). This may also be one of the reasons why the UDF saw its dissolution as inevitable with the arrival of the liberation movement. Acceptance of the 'national liberation model' also had consequences at the level of conceptions of pluralism, homogeneity and heterogeneity. It meant sharing a sense of the liberation movement as the nation, which was one and undivided.

When we assess the stance the UDF took towards various issues we need to put ourselves in the shoes of people active at the time. They faced the possibility or likelihood of arrest, torture, death and victimisation of their families. They faced an enemy that did everything to divide the South African people and black communities. Confronting this, the UDF raised a simple slogan that was the opposite of apartheid: 'UDF unites, apartheid divides'. This tallied with the ANC's notion of building a united, non-racial and non-sexist South Africa (although the latter adjective was then a recent inclusion, very unevenly assimilated). Asserting that unifying vision and notion of a common nationhood was, in a sense, revolutionary. Its realisation demanded the destruction of apartheid, dissolution of bantustans and the removal of a whole array of laws and practices.[12]

In line with this vision, there were strategies and tactics that promoted particular types of alliances, all aimed at uniting as wide a range of people behind a demand for an undivided South Africa, based on democratic values, and narrowing the base of the apartheid regime.[13] Understandable and commendable as this was, it also had limitations. The notion tended to neglect the presence of distinct identities within that unity and gloss over the problems associated with implementing non-racialism, the coexistence of different peoples and cultural groups and belief systems within that unity.

What space would be allowed for asserting difference? In the apartheid period, where difference was stressed by the regime, there was a tendency on the side of the liberation movement to underplay distinct identities. That is why, even today, where South Africa has a constitution that allows and encourages manifestation of a range of different identities, in particular, freedom of sexual orientation, practice within the society may well be lagging behind.

With regard to minority communities, there was a correct rejection by both ANC and UDF of the apartheid regime's insistence on 'group rights', which, in reality, meant minority group *privileges*. But this may have led to a failure to address anxieties of these communities, who feared for their legitimate *rights* as minority peoples. In this context, the dissolution of organisations like the Transvaal and Natal Indian Congresses may have been ill-advised or premature (see Suttner, unpub, 1990). Obviously such a statement—raising the possibility of 'uniracial organisations', may evoke outrage from those who conceive models of organisation in the abstract. Neville Alexander, for example, uses a definitional argument about 'race', which cancels out the implications of the lived reality of distinct communities (see his interview in Frederikse 1990:206). My statement is a practical one related to how best a community can be organised, given the fears and anxieties it may have. If a community requires or desires specific organisation for itself, whether as Indians, Coloureds or whites, it must be considered. It does not necessarily entrench racial stereotypes. Indeed, such organisation may be part of the process of overcoming these.

Contextualising the conditions impacting on debate at the time

The conditions that impacted on the UDF activist self-identification with the ANC are not always factored into evaluations of the debates of the time. When we assess these debates we need to recall that many leaders and activists were trying to propagate ideas of illegal organisations without falling foul of the law. When Seekings (2000) speaks of the open propagation of Marxism, that applied to certain university lecturers but not to those known or suspected of being ANC members and Communists. These risked charges. They had to 'hold the line' but often without recourse to some arguments that could have strengthened their case. There was always a fear and reality of repression and a responsibility not to invite it through careless reference to illegal literature or organisations.

Activists and leaders saw themselves 'holding the line' for the ANC and did not want the regime to drive a wedge between themselves and Lusaka. In general, UDF activists were very cautious about negotiations and maintained a very rigid position. One would see on the back of T-shirts long statements about conditions set for talking—much longer and more onerous than anything set by Lusaka. UDF leaders felt they should take the lead from ANC and not show any wavering, which would allow the enemy to breach their ranks. One of the problems that arose in the post-1990 period is that people inside as well as in MK were not always adequately briefed about various shifts that had been made and took some time to accept that insurrection was no longer on the agenda, but had been displaced by talks.

This context—of fighting the regime—also impacted on the limits of debate. There was no search for truth in the abstract. In debating the Freedom Charter, for example, it was part of a battle for hegemony, asserting the primacy of a tradition. It was in a period where that tradition had been proscribed and was being re-established with frank partisanship, and in the face of hostility from both the left and right (whatever its strengths in terms of gathering of sources that had been neglected, this was obviously the case with Suttner and Cronin 1986). Obviously in that context what one said was not as balanced as it can be now, 20 years later, in a period of tranquillity, when the survival of a tradition is not as urgent or may be secure or, alternatively, endangered in a quite different way.

Connecting the UDF experience to that of the rest of the continent

In an important work, Michael Neocosmos connects the UDF experience to that of the rest of the continent. He draws on Mahmood Mamdani's thesis that the victory of liberation movements in Africa is based on the defeat of popular struggles (Mamdani 1990). Thus, the unbanning of the ANC is interpreted as replicating a pattern where various organs of popular power, representing popular nationalism, are disbanded or collapsed into the ANC. This is a prelude to the ANC representing itself as the repository of the nation. This is the displacement of popular nationalism by 'state nationalism'.

Neocosmos argues, correctly, that the various popular organisations which were affiliated to the UDF played both a sectoral and political role. The post-1990 period saw the dissolution of the UDF. Popular organisations were redefined as playing a sectoral role, leaving politics to the ANC (it has not worked out that way, as the Congress of South African Trade Unions (COSATU), the Congress of Traditional Leaders of South Africa (CONTRALESA) and some other organisations do engage in the political arena on various questions). Neocosmos (1998) sees this purported monopolisation of liberation politics by the ANC as a prelude to a specific statist conception of politics, where the nationalist organisation, soon to control the state, is seen as the vehicle for realising popular political aspirations. Organisations outside the ANC, while independent, are to give politics a wide berth, since that is taken care of by the ANC. There is a great deal to be said for the critique of statism, rejecting the idea that the state should deliver, with the masses being passive onlookers. I agree with Neocosmos that the masses should be decisive in driving processes, and that is something which has not yet been integrated into the democratic transition (I leave aside difficulties there may be in precisely determining modes of implementation).

It is not only an issue for organisations independent of the ANC but also a question of how the ANC relates to its own membership, how branches can have a vibrant role, when their organisation is the dominant factor in government. It relates to what role they play beyond periodic voting. The impression left in Neocosmos's (1998) work is that this is not a crucial question, while that of independent civil society organisations in opposition to the ANC's 'statist project' is. In reality, both are important and the internal character of the ANC is as important for democracy as the existence of viable organisations outside of the ANC and the state. The ANC is a quite different organisation from most or all others on the continent. Many of these are of relatively recent creation or limited lifespan. Consequently, the tradition of mass allegiance to the ANC over many generations and in many forms is something specific that cannot be factored in as if it were something common to the rest of the continent.[14]

But a cult of anti-statism, which Neocosmos (1998) is in danger of falling into, may be as dangerous as 'state worship'. We do need a strong state in South Africa for transformative purposes and we can already see that whatever the deficiencies that have been identified by various writers, it is far from simply being a 'neoliberal' state. There is an uneasy coexistence in state interventions between conservative macroeconomic policies and extensive welfare projects. While these projects have many deficiencies in terms of reach and sustainability, the quality of many peoples' lives has however been transformed. With regard to the previous political role played by civil society organisations, we have seen and Neocosmos (1998) acknowledges that most of these organisations saw themselves 'as ANC' and that is why they were prepared to step back.

The central issue is not whether there is a division of labour between political organisations and social movements/organisations of civil society, but whether this division also encapsulates the type of democracy that the 1980s brought to the fore. That is not achieved nor denied by a division of labour in itself, but by looking at a variety of other factors. These include:

a   What characterises the democratic trajectory envisaged, is representative democracy the only mode of expression for the masses, and, if not, does it include various forms of participatory and popular activity, and, if so, how are these manifested? In my view popular involvement and activity may well be manifested inside the ANC. But this may also find expression in alliance with the ANC, but independent of the organisation, or also in opposition to the ANC and its allies. All of these are possibilities. The weakness of Neocosmos's (1998) approach is that the definition of the civics as having a sectoral sphere of operation is treated as *ipso facto* implying that South African democracy now entails a pure 'good governance'/representative democracy trajectory, to the exclusion of popular self-expression. That is how it has unfolded up till now. But that does not mean it is uncontested nor that the possibility for other forms of democracy are closed.

b   How does the ANC relate to organisations independent of its sway, or even in opposition to itself? The ANC and also the UDF, it should be recalled, are recent converts to pluralism. Consequently, both strands of liberation have tended to view organisations outside their fold as anti-democratic, the word 'democratic' being equated with the main bearer of the national democratic project, the ANC. It is important that the notion of pluralism becomes entrenched in its broadest meanings and understood as conducive to democratic consolidation. Not all interests can or should be represented by the ANC. This is not to suggest, however, as many political scientists claim, that democratic consolidation requires the 'circulation of elites' in the foreseeable future, that is, that the potential defeat of the ANC in the short-term is a precondition for democracy to be firmly established in South Africa (see Suttner 2004b). This notion of democratic consolidation and pluralism needs to include a commitment to the viability of opposition political parties. This is something that many people in South Africa may shrink from because of the contempt they feel for the role of some of these parties. But the reality is that democratic consolidation depends on people voting for these parties rather than disrupting democracy. That is one of the uncomfortable truths that are necessary to accept (cf. Suttner 2004).

The character of South African democracy is not fixed in stone. Nothing has been finally decided. There has yet to be thorough analysis of the type of configuration of forces ranged behind or being assembled behind the ANC-led government. Under apartheid, the ruling bloc consisted of an alliance of classes, drawn from the white community and black collaborators, benefiting from apartheid. There is, thus far, no thorough analysis of the character of forces forming or being drawn into a new ruling bloc. Nor is there clarity regarding the weight each class or class fraction is carrying in decision-making and ultimately in the overall trajectory of South African democracy and transformation.

Conclusion

This chapter has argued that the UDF experience has left a legacy and meaning that is contested. It is a legacy that has been partially embraced in contemporary South Africa. It is one that has sometimes been romanticised or, alternatively, characterised as utopian (e.g. van Kessel 2000:274 regarding popular power). In many peoples' lives it was far from utopian for some period of time. Whether such practices can be permanently sustainable and popular power can coexist with representative democracy in a long-term relationship is unclear. There may not be any precedent internationally.

The chapter has also argued that the UDF experience, while connected to the ANC has elements that relate purely to local initiative, people acting on their own to deal with local problems and implementing popular power in relation to areas of their lives that mattered to them, but may well not have occurred to people in Lusaka or UDF Headquarters. The UDF period introduced some new elements into liberation discourse and experience. But it also contained extensive continuities and converged in its practice and thinking with much that was found in exile and other experiences.

Some important works in recent years have helped contextualise and explain the period and conditions leading to regional and local differences, manifestations of various types of people's power and abuse of power. Much of this writing helps account for factors that UDF leaders were not able to see nor study in the heat of the moment, in a period when decisions had to be made with the information that was at their disposal (see especially Seekings 2000; van Kessel 2000; Lodge and Nasson 1991; Cherry 1999; Neocosmos 1998; Marks 2001; Adler and Steinberg 2000). Apart from published works, there have been a number of theses, covering regional and local developments (see especially Cherry 2000). The period does deserve such investigation and further study, recording what happened, but going beyond that into the theoretical questions, in particular, the questions the UDF period raises for contemporary democracy. Cherry (2000) and Neocosmos (1998), make important beginnings with this theme.

Notes

1. The paper was written in 2003, the twentieth anniversary of the formation of the UDF. Although it has been revised, the spirit in which it was then written, responding to that date, is retained here. The chapter forms part of a wider body of research funded through the Nordic Africa Institute, Uppsala, Sweden.
2. At the same time it will be argued that there are large degrees of convergence between the UDF and the ANC in exile that have not been adequately acknowledged.
3. The Congress of the People adopted the Freedom Charter in 1955, following a broad campaign to elicit the grievances of ordinary people and their vision of a free South Africa (see Suttner and Cronin 1986).
4. Interestingly, the South African Communist Party (SACP), as part of its re-evaluation of Marxism following the collapse of Eastern European socialism, has adopted a slogan that departs from this position: 'Socialism is the future-build it now!'.
5. Michael Neocosmos, personal communication by e-mail, 18.08.2003 asks (in another context), however, whether top-down decisions necessarily preclude democratic possibilities, whether they may not under specific circumstances be an umbrella under which popular struggle develops.
6. The use of violence in this period was complex and related to a range of factors going beyond the question of apartheid and often connected to such issues as inter-generational tensions.
7. Africans were described in various ways at different phases of apartheid. In this period they were called 'Bantu' which literally means people and they were 'administered' through a specific department.
8. The term 'Congress movement' refers to organisations allied to the ANC.
9. The other pillars were international struggle, armed struggle and underground organisation.
10. For examples of the prevalence of military imagery, cf. Marks 2001, where youth

refer to themselves as members of 'detachments'.
11. Paradoxically the same inaccuracy is conveyed for different reasons (in wanting to convey the character of exile culture) by Sakhela Buhlungu when he writes of 'those in exile such as the late president of the ANC, Oliver Tambo, and the late Alfred Nzo who issued *commands* to underground structures and ANC-aligned structures of the Mass Democratic Movement (MDM) as a whole' (2002:182, emphasis mine).
12. The 'bantustans' refer to the areas set aside for occupation by Africans, where they were supposed to realise their political aspirations, some of these areas having a fake independence conferred on them.
13. It should be noted that the UDF did not advance acceptance of the Freedom Charter as a precondition for affiliation. This was in the vain hope of attracting Black Consciousness adherents.
14. I have been warned that CODESRIA scholars resist ideas of South African 'exceptionalism', but am ready to deal with any 'fall out' from this statement.

References

Adler, G. and Steinberg, J., eds, 2000, From Comrades to Citizens. The South African Civics Movement and the Transition to Democracy, Houndmills: Macmillan Press.

ANC, 1979, The Green Book, Report of the Politico-Military Strategy Commission to the ANC National Executive Committee, August 1979. http://www.anc.org.za/ancdocs/history/mk/green-book.html

Barrell, H., 1992, 'The Turn to the Masses: The African National Congress' Strategic Review of 1978-79', *Journal of Southern African Studies*, 18, 1.

Buhlungu, S., 2002, 'From "Madiba magic" to "Mbeki logic": Mbeki and the ANC trade union allies', in S. Jacobs and R. Calland (eds) *Thabo Mbeki's World. The Politics and Ideology of the South African President*, Pietermaritzburg: University of Natal Press.

Buntman, F., 2003, *Robben Island and Prisoner Resistance to Apartheid*, Cambridge: Cambridge University Press.

Cherry, J., 1999, 'Traditions and Transitions. African Political Participation in Port Elizabeth', in J. Hyslop (ed.) *African Democracy in the Era of Globalisation*, Johannesburg: Wits University Press.

Cherry, J., 2000, Kwazakele. The Politics of Transition in South Africa: An Eastern Cape Coast Study, Unpublished Ph.D. thesis, Rhodes University, South Africa.

Chikane, F. Rev., 2003, 'The Origins and Significance of the United Democratic Front (UDF)', in Umrabulo, June http://www.anc.org.za/ancdocs/pubs/umrabulo/umrabulo19/umrabulo.html

Daniel, J., 2003, 'The Mbeki Presidency: Lusaka Wins', *South African Yearbook of International Affairs*, available on www.hsrc.ac.za

Delius, P., 1996, *A Lion Amongst the Cattle. Reconstruction and Resistance in the Northern Transvaal*, Portsmouth, NH, Johannesburg and Oxford: Heinemann, Ravan Press and James Currey.

Fisher, Ryland, 2003, 'UDF Showed Us the Rainbow', *The Star*, 05.03.2003.

Frederikse, J., 1990, *The Unbreakable Thread. Non-Racialism in South Africa*, Johannesburg: Ravan Press.

Good, Kenneth, 2002, *The Liberal Model and Africa. Elites against Democracy*, Houndmills: Palgrave.

Gramsci, Antonio, 1971, *Selections from the Prison Notebooks of Antonio Gramsci*, Edited and translated by Q. Hoare and G. Nowell Smith, London: Lawrence and Wishart.

Hassim, Shireen, 2003, The Limits of Popular Democracy: Women's Organisations, Feminism and the UDF', *Transformation* 51.

Hobsbawm, E. J., 1982, 'Gramsci and Marxist Political Theory', in A. S. Sassoon (ed.) *Approaches to Gramsci*, London: Writers and Readers Publishing Cooperative Society.

Lenin, V.I., 1968, [1918], 'The State and Revolution', in *Selected Works*, Moscow: Progress Publishers.

Lodge, T., et al., eds., 1991, *All, Here, and Now: Black Politics in South Africa in the 1980s*, Cape Town: Ford Foundation and David Philip.

Mamdani, M., 1990, 'State and Civil Society in Contemporary Africa: Reconceptualising the Birth of State Nationalism and the Defeat of Popular Movements', in Africa Development: 15, 3-4.

Marks, M., 2001, *Young Warriors. Youth Politics, Identity and Violence in South Africa*, Johannesburg: Witwatersrand University Press.

Marx, A. W., 1992, *Lessons of Struggle. South African Internal Opposition, 1960-1990*, Cape Town: Oxford University Press.

Marx, K., 1984 [1869], *The Eighteenth Brumaire of Louis Bonaparte*, London: Lawrence & Wishart.

Mbeki, G., 1984 [1964] *South Africa. The Peasants' Revolt*, London: International Defence and Aid Fund for Southern Africa.

Mbeki, G., 1996, *Sunset at Midday. Latshon'ilang'emini!*, Braamfontein: Nolwazi Educational Publishers.

Mhlongo, T., 2003, 'Our Forgotten Heroes. SA's True Liberators Live in Poverty', *Sowetan Sunday World*, 9 March 2003.

Morobe, M., 1987, 'Towards a People's Democracy: The UDF View', *Review of African Political Economy*, 40, 1.

Mufson, S., 1990, *Fighting Years. Black Resistance and the Struggle for a New South Africa*, Boston, Massachusetts: Beacon Press.

Neocosmos, M., 1998, 'From Peoples' Politics to State Politics: Aspects of National Liberation in South Africa', in A. O. Olukoshi, ed., *The Politics of Opposition in South Africa*, Uppsala: Nordic Africa Institute.

Poulantzas, N., 2000 [1978], State, Power, Socialism, London: Verso Books.

Seekings, J., 2000, *The UDF. A History of the United Democratic Front in South Africa 1983-1991*, Cape Town, Oxford and Athens: David Philip, James Currey and Ohio University Press.

Seidman, G., 2001, '"Guerrillas In their Midst": Armed Struggle in The South African Anti-Apartheid Movement', *Mobilization: An International Journal*, 6 (2).

Suttner, R. and Cronin, J., 1986, 30 *Years of the Freedom Charter*, Johannesburg: Ravan Press.

Suttner, R., 1990, Discussion Paper, 'Clarifying our Approach towards Minority Rights', mimeo unpublished.

Suttner, R., 2003, 'The African National Congress (ANC) Underground: From the M-Plan to Rivonia', *South African Historical Journal* 49 November.

Suttner, R., 2004, 'Transformation of Political Parties in Africa' *Transformation* 55.

Suttner, R., 2004a, 'Being a Revolutionary: Reincarnation or Carrying Over Previous Identities? A Review Article', *Social Identities* 10, 3.

Suttner, R., 2004b 'Democratic Transition and Consolidation in South Africa: Advice of 'the Experts', Current Sociology 52, 5.

Suttner, R., 2004c, 'Characterising ANC/SACP Underground Organisation', mimeo.

Suttner, R., 2004d, 'ANC Underground After Rivonia—Dead or Alive?', mimeo.

Tambo, O., 1984, Interview, in Mayibuye, nos 10, 11. 1984, Reprinted in Umrabulo. http://www.anc.org.za/ancdocs/pubs/umrabulo19/umrabulo.html

Van Kessel, I., 2000, 'Beyond Our Wildest Dreams.' The United Democratic Front and the Transformation of South Africa, Charlottesville and London: University Press of Virginia.

Interviews

Weza Made, Johannesburg, 1986.
Pallo Jordan, Cape Town, 2003.
Mapheti Leeuw, Johannesburg, 1986.
Titus Mafolo, Johannesburg, 1986.
Petros 'Shoes' Mashigo, Pretoria, 2003.
Mothupi, Pharepare, Polokwane, 2004.
Gugile Nkwinti, Johannesburg, 1986.
Nat Serache, Johannesburg, 2002.

4

The 1987 Zimbabwe National Unity Accord and its Aftermath: A Case of Peace without Reconciliation?

Terence M. Mashingaidze

Introduction

When Zimbabwe attained independence in 1980, socialism was dominant in the Third World and the ruling party embraced this doctrine as its governmental ideology. Socialism was viewed as the most appropriate method for achieving socio-economic equity, justice and prosperity. The recently ended war had caused massive destruction of infrastructure and the population had swelled beyond the capacity of the existing facilities. In the aftermath of the struggle for independence, the government had to move fast in dealing with the popular demands that informed the struggle. Anyang' Nyong'o (1987:18) aptly noted that:

> It was observed that the appropriate response to popular demands was developed; that development could be planned for; that planning essentially involved the optimum utilisation of available domestic and foreign resources to achieve certain growth targets; and that for the majority of popular masses to benefit, these growth targets had to be in the rural areas, hence rural development.

All sections of society were to contribute to development under the tutelage of the socialist state. The immediate post-colonial era witnessed phenomenal growth. Many schools, clinics, veterinary and crop marketing facilities were constructed, uplifting the standard of living of the general populace. However, in the political arena, the dispensation that emerged had no room for diversity. Zeleza (1997:412-13) observed that:

With the attainment of *uhuru* there was the institutionalisation of the independence contract in which all, the people, the masses, were supposed to pray at the altar of nation building and development, and the articulation of sectional class, social, community, ethnic and gender interests was frowned upon as selfish and subversive.

Herein lies the paradox of post-colonial governance: liberation movements, under whose banner independence was attained, fought for plurality of the political space, but upon assuming the portals of power, sought to obliterate difference. This chapter examines this dynamic in the case of Zimbabwe. In particular it focuses on the Matabeleland crisis and highlights the inadequacies of the Unity Accord established to end the violence. These have spilt over into the present tensions and contradictions within Zimbabwe.

The Matabeleland crisis: 1982–1987

Incapacity to tolerate political difference and/or the lack of tolerance to share political space by the ruling elite marred Africa's post-colonial nation building processes. Zimbabwe's civil war of 1982 to 1987 was an outcome of the homogenous conceptualisation and practice of nation-building in Africa. Close to twenty thousand people perished in what became known as the Matabeleland crisis (see the report by the Catholic Commission for Justice and Alexander, McGregor and Ranger 2000 for a detailed critique on the history of violence in Matabeleland).

The war pitted the newly formed (Zimbabwe African National Union Patriotic Front, ZANU-PF) government against its liberation ally, Zimbabwe African People's Union Patriotic Front (ZAPU-PF). The war was a spill-over from the nationalist politics of the 1960s and 1970s. Nationalism had the ambiguity of being both exclusionary and all-embracing. It subsumed class, ethnic and religious differences, and, at the same time, tried to use these cleavages for its sustenance. Alexander observed that the escalation of violence after the end of the liberation war built on the two guerrilla armies' (Zanla for ZANU and Zipra for ZAPU) regional patterns of recruitment and operation during the 1970s, and the history of animosity and the distrust between the two armies and their political leaders (Alexander, McGregor and Ranger 2000: 181). These patterns left Zipra forces dominated by Ndebele speakers from Matabeleland, while Zanla was predominantly Shona-speaking. Operational areas maintained significance in terms of political loyalties: voting largely, though not completely, followed ethnic and regional divisions, creating the possibility of conflict along these lines (Cliffe, Mpofu and Munslow; cited in Alexander et al 2000: 181). Zipra's capacity for conventional warfare was also a source of friction. Following ZANU-PF's victory in the February 1980 elections, the possibility that the clearly surprised and disappointed ZAPU would use these forces, which were still largely based outside the country, to obtain victory by other means was a source of concern for ZANU-PF. These seeds of distrust and division fell on fertile ground in the early 1980s (Alexander et al 2000:181). When the war ended guerrillas were supposed to move into Assembly Points (APs) for disbanding, demobilisation or integration into the newly created Zimbabwe National Army (ZNA). However, there were incessant, often violent, conflicts between Zanla and Zipra combatants caused by mutual suspicion. This resulted first in the demotion of the ZAPU leader, Joshua Nkomo, serving in the national unity government, from Minister of Home Affairs to Minister Without Portfolio (Alexander et al 2000:181). This angered ZAPU and Zipra cadres. The government secretly initiated the training of the notorious Fifth Brigade by 106 North Korean instructors. In February 1982 the government announced it had discovered vast amounts of arms on properties owned by the ZAPU Company, Nitram, and around Zipra APs. These allegations were used as grounds for confiscating the properties and sacking Nkomo and other ZAPU ministers. Many deserted the army due to fear of persecution and took up arms.

After February 1982, the room for political conciliation disappeared. Prime Minister Robert Mugabe treated the caches as definitive proof that ZAPU had always been planning a coup. It was said that it had held back forces and cached weapons to fight in a final struggle to overthrow a ZANU-PF government if it came to power (Alexander et al 2000:181). Subsequent attacks on the Prime Minister's residence were ascribed to Zipra guerrillas. Joshua Nkomo continued professing his innocence and that of his party, but to no avail.

South Africa, through its policy of destructive engagement with the frontline states, exacerbated the situation. It fomented guerrilla insurgency in the country. South Africa sabotaged Inkomo Barracks in August 1981, and nearly succeeded in liquidating the ZANU-PF leadership. The Zimbabwe Air force was decimated in an attack on the Thornhill airbase in July 1982. In August of the same year, three white soldiers of the South African Defence Forces (SADF) were killed in a clash inside Zimbabwe (Alexander et al 2000:181). At the end of 1982, South Africa launched 'Operation Drama', an effort, which involved recruiting, and arming a Zimbabwean insurgent group dubbed, Super ZAPU. The ZANU-PF government grew increasingly paranoid. All this resulted in ZANU being convinced that the crisis could only be resolved militarily. Former Zipra cadres were persecuted, especially those in the army. Some fled for dear life while those who remained in the army were often demoted. Alexander *et al* (2000:181) note that:

[T]he desertion in 1982 of thousands of armed former Zipras from the Zimbabwe National Army (ZNA) and their persecution at home led to a vast increase of dissident violence in Matabeleland. These dissidents were not the same as those of 1980. Their position was due to the deterioration of relations within the ZNA and targeting of former Zipras outside it, a situation that was to worsen dramatically with the deployment of the notorious Fifth Brigade to Matabeleland North in 1983.

The Fifth Brigade was unlike other units of the ZNA. It was accountable only to the then Prime Minister, and not to the normal military chain of command. It was specifically intended for what were termed 'internal defense purposes' (Alexander et al 2000:181). From its deployment in Matabeleland North in January 1983 until its withdrawal from Matabeleland South in late 1984, the brigade carried out a grotesquely violent campaign. It targeted party chairmen and civil servants, civilians at large, as well as former Zipra combatants, refugees, and anyone suspected of having crossed the border to Botswana in the course of the liberation war. Former Zipra combatants rarely survived encounters with this brigade. Its violence largely shaped the spread and character of dissidency (Alexander et al 2000). The operation to expunge the dissidents was code-named *Gukurahundi* (in Shona, this phrase means the first rains of the year that wash away rubbish). Although the government deployed many sectors of its security apparatus, the Fifth Brigade excelled in repression. Many people were tortured, raped, murdered, maimed in the pursuit of dissident quashing. Many people still bear the mental and physical scars of the war.

There are differing views on the civil war. Although ethnicity was a factor in the war, in terms of its spatial dimensions, expressions and victims, its course did not altogether follow ethnic lines. The dissidents did not enjoy civilian support. Areas that were predominantly Shona were also attacked if they were perceived to be amenable to the dissident cause, especially those that fell under the ZAPU spheres of influence during the liberation struggle. Such areas included Hurungwe and Gokwe. On the part of the former ZAPU cadres who joined dissident ranks, the war of the 1980s had no political leadership, had no civilian and party support, no hope of success but only of survival (Alexander et al 2000:181). No protagonists in the disturbances of the 1980s were immune to tribal animosities. The Fifth Brigade and other state security units targeted largely Ndebeles. On the other, the dissidents attacked Shona speakers, particularly those in the Midlands district of Mberengwa. The Matabeleland inferno ended after the signing of the Unity Accord on 22 December 1987 between Prime Minister Mugabe and the ZAPU leader Joshua Nkomo, who had been persecuted by the ZANU government, and had ultimately gone into exile. A blanket amnesty was given to the dissidents and many surrendered mostly after assurances from their leadership.

A critique of the 1987 Unity Accord

The best way to bring peace and reconciliation in communities is through truth telling and a shared willingness to reconcile by all the major actors in a war. Civil wars and systematic repression need to end and the keyword in post-conflict reconstruction is 'reconciliation'. The government, social organisations, the churches, and the entire population have to come to terms with the past in one way or the other.

All cultural and religious traditions have forms of reconciliation. Each of these traditions also puts forward certain requirements regarding reconciliation. For example, the truth is to be established 'officially', damages are to be paid, the guilty are to be recognised publicly, the victims are to be restored their honour, or the guilty persons are to be submitted to real or symbolic punishment (Gatsheni-Ndlovu 2003). These are also manifest in international law. The preamble to the Universal Declaration of Human Rights states, 'that it is of utmost importance that the human rights are protected by the supremacy of law'. A government is, therefore, obliged to investigate all accusations of violations of human rights, and report the violations from the past (Gatsheni-Ndlovu 2003).

In Rwanda, the government built memorials to remember victims of the genocide and revived the traditional *gacaca* system of justice as a way of healing the nation in the aftermath of the 1994 genocide. Helen Vesperini (2002: 20) noted that:

> [T]he Rwandan government has revamped a traditional style of community justice known as the gacaca court system. The dual aim of the courts is to deal with the backlog of genocide suspects crammed into the country's prison, and heal the deep scars left by the 1994 genocide that killed at least half a million Tutsis and moderate Hutus.

The 1987 Unity Accord ended the war but did not bring peace and reconciliation. It was elitist and embodied a top-down approach to governance. Nkomo and Mugabe signed the Accord and then sold it to the people. The grassroots were never consulted in the peace-making process and no reconciliation efforts were made.

According to Gatsheni-Ndlovu (2003), the foundation of reconciliation is the recognition of suffering. This distinguishes reconciliation from a process which does not go beyond political negotiations and compromises. Recognition of individual suffering may be shaped by extensive official reports with a great deal of attention to individual cases or by measures of compensation and redress which benefit the victims, by remembering the names of the victims, as in religious celebrations, on memorial stones, in literature, etc., or by lasting public recognition of the pain and grief the victims and dependents have to live with. Reconciliation is the first step towards a society which can give a lasting guarantee for dignity and justice. The 1987 Accord resulted in the cessation of hostilities but brought no peace and unity. Victims of the violence have not been compensated. Neither have those who perpetrated the violence been tried nor have they sought the forgiveness of their victims, at least through acknowledging their roles in the crisis. The Zimbabwean Unity Accord is viewed, perceived and analysed in personality terms rather than as a communal and national undertaking. Many saw the passing away of Nkomo, in July 1999, as the death knell of the Accord. Bulawayo Human Rights Lawyer David Coltart (2000) noted that:

> [J]ust as the President Robert Mugabe is the cement that holds ZANU (PF) together, Nkomo was the cement that held PF ZAPU together and those former (PF) ZAPU members who are now ZANU PF. I think there is a possibility that his death will unleash some political battle to get his mantle. It could speed up the disintegration of the party in the region but much will depend on the public who respected him because of his history.

Former ZANU-PF Central Committee member, Norman Mabhena, who noted that after Nkomo the ruling party had no chance of dominating the Matabeleland region echoed the above sentiments by observing that 'there is no way ZANU-PF can rise again in Matabeleland. It won in the last elections (1995/6) because people respected Nkomo' (see *Sunday Mail*, 2 July 2000 and also the *Financial Gazette*, 13 March 2002).

The people of Matabeleland and the Midlands have survived two terrible civil wars in as many decades, and they have received no guarantee that it will not happen again. In spite of apparent state and dissident atrocities there has been no official apology. In fact, the war episode is spoken of in muffled voices by officialdom. The Ndebele ethnic communities in Matabeleland and the Midlands are still hostile towards the ruling ZANU-PF party and its government (Gatsheni-Ndlovu 2003:2). This was indicated by their overwhelming votes for the opposition Movement for Democratic Change (MDC) in the parliamentary and presidential elections of 2000 and 2002. Some of the weaknesses of the Unity Accord are that it was crafted in a *minimalist* way that did not go beyond a power-sharing formula between the leading political elites in ZAPU-PF and ZANU-PF. The dominant post-Unity Accord politics in Matabeleland and the Midlands regions revolved around the issues of marginalisation, state accountability, and quest for an apology, as well as compensation for the victims of the state sanctioned violence of the 1980s. These demands proved that the Unity Accord had a poor post-conflict peace-building framework that encompassed the aspirations and demands of the grassroots (see Gatsheni-Ndlovu 2003:2).

The post-Unity Accord scenario in Zimbabwe did not embrace pre-requisites for reconciliation and durable peace. Lasting peace can be established through a number of mechanisms which include some of the factors raised below.

1. The establishment of all-embracing political system through power-sharing arrangements between erstwhile protagonists. This was partly achieved in Zimbabwe because (PF) ZAPU assumed posts in government and Joshua Nkomo became one of the country's two Vice-Presidents, a post that he held until his death in July 1999. Democratic rebuilding involving eradication of fear among citizens, and enhancing accountability, transparency, legitimacy, human security, and social peace is also necessary.

2. Psychological rebuilding is imperative to communities that have survived the ravages of violence. The CCJP report noted that part of the process of psychological healing for any victim of abuse is being given the opportunity to recount that suffering to a supportive, non-judgmental audience. While the signing of the National Unity Accord was positive for reconciliation, there are many other experiences that the national leadership need to hear and take account of if they wish to prevent similar clashes. The process of opening up involves not just the victims but also the perpetrators of violence. They need an atmosphere of truth telling in order to purge themselves of their memories of events. National exorcism is imperative. In African cultures those who do injustice to others need to compensate their victims in order to avoid the wrath of avenging spirits. It is in this spirit that Truth Commissions have been set up in many parts of the world, notably South Africa and Rwanda.

3. The establishment of effective and impartial systems of justice is crucial to reconciliation. The state should also regard court verdicts in order to establish citizen confidence in the judicial system. In the context of the 1982-1987 crisis the government showed a pathetic disregard of the verdicts of the courts. In 1982, Zipra commanders Lookout Masuku, Dumiso Dabengwa and others were arraigned before the courts for treason and the evidence against them failed to convince a high court judge, but they remained in jail until 1986 (Alexander et al 2000:188).

4. Reconciliation also entails reconstruction and economic development. According to international treaties, victims have a right to material compensation.

Post-colonial Zimbabwe's development paradigm was rural-oriented, and Matabeleland and some parts of the Midlands Provinces did not benefit due to the ongoing disturbances. In this context, after the Unity Accord massive, infrastructural development and rehabilitation should have been undertaken. Unfortunately, not much was done and the people feel alienated from national development processes. This was confirmed in the 2000 Parliamentary elections in which the ruling ZANU-PF was trounced in all but two of the Matabeleland constituencies. One of the ex-Zipra luminaries, Dumiso Dabengwa, a losing ruling party candidate in the elections, observed that:

> [T]he people have rejected us not only as candidates, but also as ruling party ZANU-PF now. The reason is that since the signing of the Unity Accord in December 1987, the people of Bulawayo feel they have not gained anything. The people have been saying what is the use of supporting ZANU-PF and its candidates and that is their message (*Sunday Mail*, 2 July 2000).

The Zimbabwean Unity Accord glossed over truth telling, an integral component of South Africa's Truth and Reconciliation Commission, thereby downplaying its relevance to reconciliation (Gatsheni-Ndlovu 2003:2). The Catholic Commission for Peace and Justice (1997:3) noted that:

> [O]ne of the most painful aspects of the 1980s conflict for its victims is their perception that their plight is unacknowledged. Officially, the state continues to deny any serious culpability for events during that year, and refuses to allow open dialogue on the issue. In effect, there is a significant chunk of Zimbabwean history, which is largely unknown, except to those who experienced it first hand. All Zimbabweans, both present and future, should be allowed access to history.

Memory, history and contemporary politics: Putting the 1980s war into perspective

Zimbabwe is currently in a crisis. Its economy is in a state of paralysis. The political sphere is characterised by violent intolerance. Zimbabwe's deterioration began in 1995. From that point on, fiscal deficits, foreign currency shortages and fuel scarcity became the major characteristics of the Zimbabwean economy. Civic organisations increased in number and began to shape critically society's views. Of major interest in this regard was the emergence of a vibrant civil society, notably the National Constitutional Assembly (NCA), in late 1997, which spearheaded the crusade for a new constitution to replace the anachronistic Lancaster House Constitution of 1979. The government responded by establishing the National Constitutional Commission (NCC). The NCC was mandated to seek people's views and, consequently, formulate a homegrown constitution. However, the NCC's draft constitution was rejected by the people in the February 2000 Referendum. This outcome was due to the opposition campaign against the Commission's Constitution through both the electronic and print media.

Raftopoulos argues that the government began to face intense pressure, starting from the late 1990s, from many quarters calling for socio-economic reform. Much of this agitation began to be articulated through the newly formed neo-liberal oriented MDC:

> [T]his party was an outcome of broad alliance politics, bringing together trade unionists, intellectuals, the urban middle class, rural producers, commercial farmers, and sections of the industrial class. The alliance—based on a widespread disillusionment with the government's economic mismanagement, the demand for constitutional, and criticism of a trans parent land reform process—has brought together many seemingly contradictory interest groups into a conjectural alliance, which faces many tensions over future policies (2001:1).

All this pressure, linked to declining legitimacy, compelled the ruling party to revive its political fortunes through aggressive and violent means. Various interests groups were co-opted by the establishment in an attempt to win back lost political ground. Veterans of the liberation war and unemployed youths were used to aggressively mobilise and co-opt the disenchanted masses back to the ruling party fold. President Mugabe began to use radical rhetoric to condemn the West, the whites and the 'misguided opposition' for being responsible for the country's increasingly poor state. He capitalised on the peasantry's land hunger by attempting to generalise the struggle for land to a continental level and project it into the proposition that the struggle over land was the sole signifier of authentic, liberated nationhood (Raftopoulos 2001:3). With that claim, contradicted as it is by two decades of land reform failure, came something else: a memory of an anti-colonial struggle that only ZANU-PF can invoke, a memory of a time when the party was, in fact, a fish within the sea of the rural masses (Raftopoulos 2001:3).

This revived form of nationalism emerged largely because of the government's failure to improve the citizens' material reality in the 1990s. According to Sklar, 'any generation that fails to cope effectively with problems of society will seek solace in escapist, reactionary, and racialist forms of nationalism, which obscure the cause of its failure and accomplish little lasting value' (cited in Falola 2002:xv). In the Zimbabwean social, political and economic conflagration, the country 'has been divided into two': the rural ZANU-PF.–dominated and the urban MDC-dominated spheres. In the last two elections, the parliamentary elections of 2000 and the presidential elections of 2002, this dichotomy emerged. However, the MDC is extremely popular in the rural provinces of Matabeleland and the Midlands. It scored emphatic victories in the two elections. This is quite different from other Shona-dominated constituencies where ZANU-PF) has apparent hegemony. The popularity of the MDC in these rural areas is because of the people's memory of what the ZANU government did to them in the 1980s and its failure to develop their areas in the years after. This displeasure partly explains the emergence of sectarian and opportunistic parties that have emerged with the aim of riding on the crest of this antagonism. Among these are ZAPU (different from the nationalist one of the 1960s) and the Liberty Party of Zimbabwe, whose policies advocate a federal system of government. They hoped to divide Zimbabwe into five provinces with each having its own regional government, parliament and budget, but occasionally reporting to the central government.

Conclusion

The Zimbabwean government is aware of the grievances of the people of Matabeleland and some parts of the Midlands but there is little it can do considering the poor state of the economy. Again, acknowledging the injustices of the past in the current harsh macroeconomic environment for which it is largely to blame, would further antagonise the people. This means that the culture of silence will continue for some time to come. The government is more concerned with keeping its hold on power than on any meaningful peace-building projects. The ruling party has co-opted many sections of society, youths, women's groups and intellectuals, into the political realm in the past five years in scenes analogous to the 1980s when ZANU-PF was still a hegemonic, commandist-cum-para-militaristic party, with no regard for dissenting ideas. Notably the participation of youth in the Zimbabwean body politic has been viewed with scepticism. Some have castigated the process for creating social and political banditry (see *The Daily News*, 6 September 2003). Youths have been involved in both pre-and post-election violence. Much of the violence in Zimbabwe's highly polarised political terrain is ascribed to the youths. Youths have contributed to the shrinkage of democratic space in the recent past. In an attempt to win support the ZANU-PF, government revived the Youth Service programmes of the 1980s in the form of the National Youth Service. Ostensibly, the National Youth Service was introduced to reorient Zimbabwean youths into patriotic and self-reliant young men and women, but, in reality, was designed to woo the young back into the fold. The compulsory national service programme was introduced in early 2000. This acute desire to keep power at all costs by the ruling party has resulted in violence, intolerance and the victimisation of truth. Such a scenario does not provide an enabling environment for what happened in Matabeleland and the Midlands in the 1980s to be heard.

References

Alexander N. J., McGregor, J. and Ranger, T., 2000, *Violence and Memory: One Hundred Years in the Dark Forests of Matabeleland*, London: James Currey.

Anyang' Nyong'o, P., ed., 1987, *Popular Struggles for Democracy in Africa*, London: Zed Books.

Falola, T., 2002, *African Politics in Post-Imperial Times: The Essays of Richard L Sklar*, New Jersey: Africa World Press.

Financial Gazette, 13 March 2002

Gatsheni-Ndlovu, S., 2003, 'Zimbabwe's Failed Peace Building Projects: An Analysis of Lancaster House Agreement of 1979 and the Unity Accord of 1987', paper presented at the Department of History and Development Studies, Midlands State University, May. Also available at http://home.planet.nl/~loz/maneng77.htm

Sunday Mail, 2 July 2000.

The Catholic Commission for Justice and Peace and The Legal Resources Foundation, 1997, *Breaking the Silence–Building True Peace. A Report on the Disturbances in Matabeleland and the Midlands 1980–1988*.

Raftopoulos, B., 2001, 'The Labour Movement and the Emergence of Opposition Politics in Zimbabwe' in B. Raftopoulos and L.M. Sachikonye (eds) *Striking Back: The Labour Movement and the Post-Colonial State in Zimbabwe, 1980–2000*, Harare: Weaver Press.

The Daily News, 6 September 2003

Vesperin, H., 2002, 'Justice on the Grass', in *BBC Focus on Africa*, January–March.

www.zimbabwesituation.com

Zeleza, T. P., 1997, *Manufacturing African Studies and Crises*, Dakar: CODESRIA.

5

Race and Democracy in South Africa

Cheryl Hendricks

Introduction

Race and racism continue to form a core part of the identification and experiences of South Africans and the structural and ideological manifestations of a racialised order persist. Many South Africans believed that democratic rule would end racism and racialised interactions. Ten years later, these are ongoing. This chapter seeks to explain the persistence of racialisation and racism through an examination of the relationship between race and democracy.

Over the past two decades there has been an abundance of theoretical literature on race and democracy and their linkages to other social categories and periods. For example, there are texts theorising the relations between race and gender, race and reason, race and modernity, race and capitalism and race and enlightenment. Few texts, however, interrogate the nexus between race and democracy, or between race and development for that matter. This is odd for liberation struggles in the Third World, particularly in Africa, were simultaneously about the institutionalisation of democratic rule and the deracialisation of their societies.

South African academic writing on race and racism has largely been descriptive or based on a political economy approach which tends to portray race relations as epiphenomenal (though there are some interesting interventions primarily from the disciplines of psychology and English literature). There is a definite need for a more critical and theoretically informed engagement on race and racism in South Africa. This chapter contributes to such critical engagement by beginning to analyse the relationship between race and democracy in general and to illuminate their interaction in the South African context. The chapter argues that liberal democracy's premise of equal rights-bearing citizens, and the focus on political equality, is problematic when applied to racialised formations such as South Africa. This conceptualisation creates tensions for it neglects, and, thereby, implicitly condones, the reproduction of racially inscribed structural inequalities. This problematic is replicated in the prevalent hegemonic ideologies of non-racialism, nation-building and 'rainbowism'.

On race and democracy

Social science has long accepted that racial identities are social constructs. It has only recently added the rider that this does not imply their irrelevance, for racial categories continue to shape the popular discourse of social relations and have acquired a material reality. Discrimination on the basis of skin colour persists, racial stereotypes remain ubiquitous, race still largely determines life chances in many countries and people are still politically mobilised on the basis of race. Essed (2002) has directed our theoretical lenses on 'everyday racism' for it is everyday encounters that relations of domination and ideologies are reproduced and consolidated. Essed defines racism as 'ideology, structure, and process, in which inequalities inherent in the wider social structure are related, in a deterministic way, to biological and cultural factors attributed to those who are seen as a different 'race' or 'ethnic' group' (2002:185).

In a similar vein, Omi and Winant (2002) coined the phrase 'racial formation' to capture the coherence of the multitude of racial projects (interpretations, representations, efforts to reorganise and redistribute resources along racial lines, and so forth), existent within a bounded space. They contend that:

> a vast web of racial projects mediates between the discursive or representational means in which race is identified and signified on the one hand, and the institutional and organisational forms in which it is routinised and standardised on the other. These projects are at the heart of the racial formation process... [For them] race is now a pre-eminently political phenomenon (Omi and Winant 2002:127-128).

To understand the nature of racism, its effects and the ways in which it has become 'common sense', one therefore has to engage in a context-specific socio-historical analysis. The conceptualisation of a 'racial formation' is used here to foreground the relationship between race and democracy in the South African context.

Goldberg (1990) highlights the continuously changing nature of racist discourse. He asserts that it has become 'more subtle in its modes of expression' but 'more central to the modern self-conception' (Goldberg 1990:ix). If race and racism remain central to conceptions of self and to the ways in which societal structures function, then it becomes necessary to see in which ways liberal democracy (as a form of governance) incorporates or excludes this identity and practice in the organisation of relations and the mediation of competing interests.

Although political scientists studying Africa have been pre-occupied with the study of democracy, the above concerns have not been prominent in their debates. Instead, the debates have centred largely around the preconditions for democracy, its measurement (formal versus substantive), and, currently, the ingredients needed for its consolidation. If democracy was primarily construed as deracialisation of power and sovereignty during the period of decolonisation, it is now typically embedded in a minimalist universalistic rights discourse that emphasises procedures for selecting and alternating the political elite. Checklists for democracy are not concerned with relations between citizens, groups within a society, or relations between countries or continents. However, it is well known that 'racial formations' can continue to thrive in the absence of an overtly discriminatory legislation. Inequalities, based on race, class, ethnicity, gender, and so forth, if not explicitly addressed, co-exist with political equality within a liberal democratic order. When this occurs, the quality of the democratic project is compromised.

Democracy has become synonymous with modernity and liberalism and these have been shown to be intimately intertwined with the development and propagation of racist thinking (Said 1978; Bhabha 1994; Mudimbe 1988; West 2002). Conceptualisations of modernity developed through the colonial encounter and were predicated on the representation of a racialised savage 'Other'. Europe defined its modernity in relation to its depiction of those in its empires (as elaborated by many post-colonial theorists, for example, Pieterse 1992). Goldberg (2000, 2002) and others have elaborated the racist thinking of the 'fathers' of enlightenment and/or liberalism. Liberals could justify colonisation and non-democratic practices that pertained in the colonies by excluding the subjects through their portrayal as 'qualitatively different' (Fitzpatrick 1990:249). Fitzpatrick argues that 'Racism was, in short, basic to the creation of liberalism and the identity of the European' (1990:249). He illustrates how liberal legality purports to be universalistic but is ethnocentric and its practice often has racist outcomes. Goldberg (2002) brings a similar argument to bear on morality.

If racism was intrinsic to the development of modernity and was incorporated into liberal thought, then it is possibly still latent in the theorisation and institutionalisation of liberal democracy, the form of governance associated with it. It is not possible, due to space and time limitations, to tease this out. However, it is important to point out that an ideology/practice may be racist in its original conception, but as it becomes universalised, may be modified and/or subject to indigenisation/domestication. This is why the oppressed people often buy into the modernist project (the essential elements being economic development via industrialisation, nation-state formation, and, more recently, a specific form of state-labelled democracy). They hope to achieve political and socio-economic development in forms appropriate to their local conditions; hence, the necessity for indigenisation of received development ideologies and practices. For this reason, democratisation and Africanisation have been seen as two sides of the same coin within the African context. However, as will be illustrated below in the South African context, the simultaneous implementation of the two processes in 'racial formations' can lead to socio-political tensions.

At this point it will suffice to note that liberal democracy can indeed function in a society that excludes others by virtue of race. This has been shown in the case of the United States and South Africa. Also, many of the explanations provided for the lack of political development in Africa (usually taken to mean the implementation of liberal democracy) have centred on 'culture' which is often a euphemism for race. A 'qualitative difference' between peoples is therefore often still used to frame debates on democracy.

In the last two decades, liberal scholars have been wrestling theoretically with difference in what has become known as the 'communitarian' versus 'libertarian' debate. The question at the heart of the debate is whether liberalism can give due recognition to cultural minorities or whether it is in fact the 'tyranny of the majority'. The 'communitarians' argue that liberalism cannot incorporate collective rights because of its key tenets of individualism and autonomy while 'multiculturalists' (liberals seeking to move beyond the doctrine of individuals as exclusive agents of politics), for example, Kymlicka (1995), contend that liberalism emphasises tolerance as well as autonomy, and is flexible enough to give recognition to minority cultures (through protection of languages, proportional representation, and so on). The 'multiculturalist' strand of liberalism is an example of the modification of theory to deal with the reality of differing cultural groups within a society. This debate is limited in that it primarily deals with minority cultures.

Angela Davis (1997) and Himani Bannerji (2000) provide a critique of multiculturalism arguing that multicultural liberal governments emphasise diversity within the borders of the state without questioning the representation of groups or taking account of power differentials between existing groups. Analysing the Canadian situation, Bannerji remarked: 'The multi-ethnic, multi-national state, with its history of racialised class formation and political ideology, discovering multiculturalism as a way of both hiding and enshrining power relations, provided a naturalised political language even to the others of the Canadian society' (2000:31). She argued that multiculturalism's 'articulating basis' must be 'an antiracist and feminist class politics... that would speak to multiplicities of tradition and power relations between them, marking the internal power-inscribed differences within the space of the nation, as well as in multinationalities' (2000:5). There is an ambiguous relationship between multiculturalism and the nation-building project. Zealous multiculturalism, with its continuous stress on difference, can undermine nation-building—a continuous and contested project whose framework and discourse shift with alterations in the balance of power, but nevertheless necessary in a racially divided context such as South Africa.

It is necessary then to identify more firmly the links between race and democracy, specifically liberal democracy. Liberal democracy, the chapter argues, may not be racist in intent but, if not sufficiently domesticated, can be racist in effect. Liberal democracy does not require a racist discourse to maintain race-based hierarchies. If one merely views liberal democracy as a procedure for the alteration of power it appears to be value-neutral. The tensions arise from its focus on political equality and its disregard for the structured inequalities arising from class, gender, ethnic and racial divisions. In short, liberal democracy does not seek to mediate material inequalities between citizens, rendering equality in 'racial formations' largely abstract. It is in the relations between citizens that liberal democracy's limits in moving beyond race-based inequities, or complicity in maintaining these inequities, are to be discerned. Rights matter most in everyday practices, yet it is here that liberal democratic procedures have the least bearing. If everyone is equal but a pervasive culture still exists, and is acted upon, that stereotypes blacks into categories of inferiority, or if the majority of blacks remain confined to the ghettos, then equality remains fictitious and racialised social orders continue to reproduce themselves at local, national and international levels. Racism is systemic, and an ideology or form of governance that distinguishes between the private and public realm, simply operating in the latter, will, 'irrespective of the attitudes of liberal democrats themselves' (Cunningham 2002:68), perpetuate existent relations of domination. It is precisely for this reason that, in 'racial formations', added measures need to be instituted to correct the entrenched power imbalances so that there is a congruence between political and socio-economic equality.

Race and Democracy in the South African Context

The history of race relations and the ideologies and structures that induced racialised power configurations in South Africa are well documented and analysed (See Dubow 1989, 1995; Goldin 1987; Keegan 1996; Marx 1998). In brief, these 'racial projects' date to the onset of colonialism in South Africa where initially in the structuring of a slave-based society, and later in the subjugation and incorporation of Africans further inland, the basis for race-based hierarchies was entrenched. Liberalism's presence in the Cape, from the nineteenth century, did little to alter the racialised patterns of power. The 'colour-blind' policies introduced in the Cape, after the abolition of slavery, often used in South African historiography for the portrayal of fundamental differences between Anglo and Boer forms of rule, actually illustrate the limitations of this form of legislation within a 'racial formation' for the policies continued to reproduce a social order similar to that of the Boer Republics. Mamdani (1996) has clearly shown that the logic of controlling the native, through a dualism of customary/civic, was manifest everywhere in Africa. What was unique to South Africa, then, was not the method of rule, but the entrenchment of racist practices that accompanied the advent of sovereignty; hence, the term 'internal colonialism'.

The Act of Union in 1910 and the adoption of a policy of segregation were key 'racial projects' consolidating the 'racial formation' of the first four decades of twentieth century South African state building. The creation of the Union was an attempt to unite whites and consolidate their hegemony through the exclusion of Africans from the rights and privileges afforded to citizens of the nation-state. Officialdom was indoctrinated with 'bioculturalist' conceptions of race, aligning 'readings of bodily difference closely with differences of class, lifestyle and general repute' (Posel 2001:53 employing Gilroy's concept), in a way that was certainly not new to the twentieth century. The place of blacks was theorised through a discourse of civility: not only were they too uncivilised to be allowed the rights of citizenship, they were destined by their biological make-up never to be able to acquire those rights. This discourse was used to justify the confinement of blacks to 'pre-modern' forms of rule that were seen as naturally aligning culture and phenotype. It is in this psycho-social context that a democratic order could be established for whites, while excluding the majority of the country's inhabitants.

Dubow has defined segregation as 'a complex amalgam of political, ideological and administrative strategies designed to maintain and entrench white supremacy' (1989:1). These strategies can be conceptualised as 'racial projects', representing blacks as essentialised 'other'. The Mines and Works Act (1911), Native Land Act (1913), Native Affairs Act (1920), Native Urban Areas Act (1920), and a host of other legislations, constituted the foundation for the 'racial formation'. Despite this legislation African urbanisation continued and there were mounting pressures for the extension of democratic rights from organisations such as the African National Congress (ANC) and the African People's Organisation (APO). Though blacks were always viewed as a threat, a people to be contained, the discourse of *swart gevaar* (black danger) echoed loudly in the 1930s. Whites became scared not only that a black physical presence would threaten them politically but also that their very identity would wane through inter-racial social and sexual mixing. Dubow has argued that 'Interracial sex was indeed held to sap the fibre of white civilisation at its most susceptible point by undermining race "pride" and purity' (1995: 180). This demanded that further racial projects be set up to secure white supremacy. The leaders of the ANC and APO, in turn, enamoured of the liberal principle of 'equal rights to all civilised men' challenged the liberal government's own episteme by continuously pointing to their acquisition of the traits of civility. But the markers of civility, in the minds of whites/colonialists, were predicated on race from the start.

In the context of social and economic flux, apartheid became the dominant ideology for maintaining white dominance and 'purity'. Historiographers have been at pains to point out the differences between segregation and apartheid. However, apartheid should be seen as a refinement of the basis of an established 'racial formation' through a series of new laws that sought to clearly demarcate and consolidate the boundaries of groups, both in terms of identity and space. According to Posel:

> Die apartheid-gedagte (the apartheid idea) offered the promise of heightened discipline, regulation and surveillance: boundaries were to be reasserted and spaces reorganised, the movements of people systematised and contained, races rescued from 'impurity', the notion of family rehabilitated and 'the savage discipline of tribal life' restored. At the core of this aspiration to order lay a vigorous and thoroughgoing reassertion of racial difference (2001: 52).

The Population Registration Act (1950) and the Group Areas Act (1950), along with a series of amendments to the Immorality Act and the Mixed Marriages Act, were legal foundations of 'racial projects' designed to create this social order. Race, by this time, had already constituted 'common sense.' Apartheid's novelty was to introduce race as a determining factor of all facets of everyday life. Through lived experiences race became more 'real' for the racial identity was invested with a materiality that simultaneously reinforced people's claims to identification (for continued access to resources or in solidarity/opposition) and gave credence to innate 'differences' (See Hendricks 2004). The political system operating here, though exclusionary, was procedurally democratic for those that it enfranchised. Maré notes:

> The apartheid state inherited the Westminster model of parliamentary representative democracy established in 1910.... The fact is, however, that by the time of the transition, institutions of democratic representation had long been in existence in South Africa, attendant with a long undeniable tradition of democratic participation and representation of interests/even if applied to a specified margin of the population. It was thus why some analysts described South Africa as an 'herrenvolk' democracy... (2003:30-31).

Faced with the entrenchment of race discrimination, the liberation movement adjusted their modus operandi and ideology. A younger generation, inspired by the rising tide of anti-colonialism throughout the continent, embraced a new discourse of African Nationalism. Mandela notes in his autobiography:

> African nationalism was our battle cry, and our creed was the creation of one nation out of many tribes, the overthrow of white supremacy, and the establishment of a truly democratic form of government. Our manifesto stated: 'We believe that the national liberation of Africans will be achieved by Africans themselves...The Congress Youth League must be the brainstrust and power-station of the spirit of African Nationalism' (1994: 87).

The discourse of the African Nationalists in the Youth League had a Pan-African content, stressed national liberation as opposed to reform, and emphasised Africanisation, not non-racialism. This Lembede-inspired ideology was short-lived in the ANC, although it continued to resonate through principles like majority rule and through the formation of the Pan African Congress (PAC).

The events that led to an ideological shift within the ANC, that led to the adoption of a policy of non-racialism are well documented and will not detain us here. The Freedom Charter, adopted in 1955, laid the basis for a policy of non-racialism. The Charter's preamble affirmed the principles that South Africa belongs to all who live in it; that only a democratic state, based on the will of the people, can secure to all their birth right without discrimination on the basis of colour, race, sex or belief. It, furthermore, established the principles that 'the people shall govern', noting that everyone has the right to vote and to take part in the administration of the country; that all national groups shall have equal rights—in the bodies of state, courts, schools, including rights to have their own language protected and develop their own folk culture and customs; and that the land shall be shared among those who work it.

It should be reiterated that non-racialism was not 'an unbreakable thread' within the ANC (as argued by Frederikse 1990 and Walshe 1971). Its adoption as principle was a 1950s phenomenon and really only gained widespread support through its popularisation by the United Democratic Front (UDF) in the 1980s. Previously, the ANC largely conceived of South Africa in the liberal 'race-relations' mode of thought as a multi-racial society that needed to construct harmonious relations between the races. ANC documents and speeches, by leaders of the time, were littered with statements that South Africa consists of four races—at points referred to as nations—Black, White, Indian and Coloured (see the works of Neville Alexander in this regard, 1979, 1986, 2002).

The birth of the UDF, in 1983, was a decisive factor in the move away from a four nations thesis to that of one non-racial nation. Constituted as a 'broad church' of anti-apartheid activists, the UDF saw non-racialism as a method for mobilisation and a principle for governing societal relations. The content of non-racialism has, however, always been subject to debate. For authors such as Taylor (1996), and many within the liberation movement, non-racialism meant that race would no longer play a role in the organisation of society: people would transcend racial identification. But Alexander (2002) and Maré (1999) argue that the ideologues of non-racialism still accepted that there were four races in South Africa and that 'non-racialism will merely mean that such "racial" categories' will not form the basis of discrimination' (Maré 1999:247). Similarly, Marx comments that 'the UDF opposed the physical aspects of national domination and accordingly was concerned less with changing individual consciousness or identity than with mobilising material resources and followers across perceived racial divisions' (1992:16). Shula Marks noted that the discourse largely centred around rights and that it posited that an 'individual's citizenship, legal rights, economic entitlement and life chances should not be decided on the basis of "racial ascription"' (1994:2). There was, therefore, little conceptual difference between non-racialism and multi-racialism. Consequently, identities, during this period, remained racialised and entrenched.

Both the ANC and the UDF favoured a liberal democratic system. They were attracted to the guiding principle of the equality of all citizens and to the electoral procedure of one person one vote that would afford South Africa, through democratic elections, a black majoritarian government. The logic was influenced by Nkrumah's idea of 'seek ye first the political kingdom'. Seekings (2000) has argued that within the 'broad church' of the UDF different constituencies emphasised different aspects of UDF ideology (and one can extend this to the ANC as well). He argues that 'non-black' comrades were attracted to the equal rights aspects, while the township comrades were more animated by the idea of 'people's power', a euphemism for Black Power.

There were, thus, different interpretations of the structural implications of those espousing the ideologies of non-racialism and liberal democracy. For blacks the structural basis of the new state would have to lead to their habitation of the portals of power in all spheres and would have to produce social justice. This view of what a non-racial democracy was supposed to bring about was not necessarily shared across the racial divides. It is this tension that begins to play itself out in the post-apartheid state.

Post-apartheid South Africa

Throughout the latter half of the 1980s the call by the masses was for the establishment of one non-racial, non-sexist, democratic state. This vision became ANC policy during the transition period. Internal dynamics as well as external factors, which have been elaborated on by many authors (See Friedman 1993; Maphai 1994) necessitated that these be the principles governing a future society. It was the only vision that could bring a peaceful resolution to the conflict. The discourses of non-racialism, civic nationalism and multiculturalism were key to enabling the transition for they entitled all to see themselves as citizens of a reconstituted state with all the rights and privileges that universal democratic citizenship confers.

Bates remarked :

> when citizens rebelling in the name of democracy stand on the brink of political victory, then tyrants convert. They seek the protection of the law and the courts, they demand due process, and, hoping to live out their natural lives in comfort and to die peacefully in bed, they propound the inviolability of persons and property. Formerly the most dangerous enemies of liberal government, they become some of its most fervent champions (1999:83-84).

The National Party (NP) could find common ground with the African National Congress in the pursuit of democracy and the creation of a non-racial society, and together form a Government of National Unity. The NP could negotiate the relinquishment of exclusive political power by whites in exchange for democratic governance that assured equal rights and continued access to resources. And, after the 2004 elections, the NNP could dissolve and many of its erstwhile stalwarts cross over to join the ANC. Transformation in South Africa was not to be the 'drive the foreigner out' phenomenon characteristic of the decolonisation of other African countries. Reduced political power did not represent as great a threat as once conjured in the imagination of whites. Through centuries of privilege whites have acquired the 'cultural capital' (to employ Bourdieu's concept) to continue to play a central role within the newly formed democratic state that is premised on the protection of individual rights. Often-heard remarks that they are faring better within the post-apartheid society can be explained in the light of this.

A discourse of 'rainbowism' emerged to symbolise the new state that had been formed. The 'rainbow nation' conceptualisation was constructed to signify a new-found unity, and yet simultaneously recognise difference of both the racial and ethnic variety. Suddenly, all were enjoined not to 'move beyond' previously constructed identities but to celebrate their difference. Gqola has provided an insightful critique of the concept, stating:

> The rainbow is also a reflection, a spectacular visual illusion. Within the boundaries of rainbowism there exists a series of possibilities that (potentially) rupture the ideal. Rainbows are a fantasy, yet they remain symbolic and constitutive of the new 'truths' in a democratic South Africa. Rainbows appear 'mysteriously', they are not dependent on human labour. They are transitory, fleeting and perpetually out of reach... Instead rainbowism is evoked at specific points where a certain kind of non-racialism, though not necessarily anti-racism, needs to be stressed. We are not always rainbow people, only some of the time when the need arises. Belonging to the rainbow implies that the members of the rainbow have equal access to the mythic pot of gold, wealth... social stratification makes nonsense of the argument that we all have access to (economic) resources (2001:99-100).

She further notes that the rainbow nation conceptualisation 'foregrounds difference at precisely the moment in which it trivialises it' (2001:99). Recognition of difference not only requires space for the re-capturing/ reconstruction/celebration and essentialising of cultures but also the means to redress existing inequities between these groups. Though 'commodity spectacle[s]' (signs/symbols) (McClintock 1995) are necessary and quite easily accommodated within liberal democracy, structural changes need to be implemented. The Mandela-led government, pre-occupied with racial reconciliation, was conscious of this need and insisted on Affirmative Action as a means of redress. But it is under the Mbeki-led government that we have seen a more overt attempt to bring about structural change. It is also at this point in the South African democratic experiment that charges of 're-racialisation' have been levelled at the practices of Mbeki's government.

In the Mandela era, the contradiction of the non-racial rainbow nation was exalted: racial reconciliation was emphasised at the expense of broad-based black empowerment. Under Mbeki's leadership, the discourse in South Africa altered and a more concerted effort was made to effect the economic equality of blacks. The 'coming of a new dawn', an African Renaissance both nationally and continentally, was the vision informing Mbeki's presidency. He boldly drew attention to the continued gap between whites and blacks in the economic realm and noted that little progress had been made in consolidating unity. Under his leadership there has also been an inquiry into racism in the media and an international conference on racism.

The Promotion of Equality Act, the Employment Equity Act and a policy of Black Empowerment denote a shift from the more neutral language of employing 'others', characteristic of Affirmative Action, to a racially qualified transformative programme. The Employment Equity Act stipulates monitoring and accountability to ensure black representation and speed up the process of change. Statistics released on Employment Equity indicate that there is need for far more policing of the system. The pace of change has been slow. In the year 2000 to 2001, whites were awarded 91 percent of all top management promotions, 92 percent of senior management promotions and 89 percent in the professional and middle management category (See the Department of Labour's Employment Equity Report 2001). From this report it is clear that 'government thus remains the key area where transformation is taking place while the private sector resembles the patterns of yesteryear' (Hendricks 2003). Black Economic Empowerment programmes have also had a limited impact in creating equality between the races. The benefits have been concentrated among too few blacks, in turn deepening class cleavages among blacks. The UNDP report (2003) is an indictment of the state of transformation in South Africa. The report indicates that the:

> Human Development Index has worsened (from 0.73 in 1994 to 0.067 in 2003), poverty still engulfs 48.5% of the population (21.9 million in 2002), income inequality has increased (from 0.60 in 1995 to 0.63 in 2001), the majority of households have limited access to basic services, and the official unemployment rate has sharply increased to more than 30% in 2003.

These kinds of statistics have been employed by the left to make an argument that the transformation of South Africa has been restricted. Essentially, they argue that the ANC has limited the democratic project to political equality and that it is merely utilising the discourse of African Nationalism and race-based economic policies for a particular class project – the creation of a black bourgeoisie. That a black bourgeoisie has emerged as a consequence of state-led transformation is undeniable. This process of class formation is not a peculiarly African trait. The state has always been the site of accumulation for the bourgeoisie in Third World societies – even the Afrikaner bourgeoisie was promoted in this way. However, the argument by the Left tends to render all change that has occurred as insignificant for the larger black community and, more damning, points to a binary division of a new black bourgeoisie, aligned to a white power structure pitted against the black masses. Things are not this categorical in post-apartheid South Africa. As in the era of apartheid, race and class cannot be neatly separated in the post-apartheid state. Any state intervention to deal with poverty or deprivation must invariably have blacks as the primary beneficiaries because the face of deprivation is not white. Black Economic Empowerment, Affirmative Action, even discourses asserting African Nationalism, are state strategies and ideology to effect change for blacks at large. Any attempt to reduce it simply to a class project is analytically and politically disingenuous, to say the least.

The centre-right and right have become recent converts to the non-racialism paradigm. They, too, critique government's corrective measures as leading to a 're-racialisation' of the society. The arguments revolve around government's use of the same racial categories as in the apartheid past: it is claimed that this reproduces racial difference of otherwise more fluid identities, or is reminiscent of the past when some groups were advantaged, and so forth. Maré notes that the 'unproblematic acceptance of the socially meaningful existence of races, furthermore, closes off the option of different ways of looking at the world and finding more complex and dynamic explanations for social conditions and social relations' (2001: 89). The centre right and right attempt to use the liberal democratic principles of the primacy of the individual and equal rights to counter group-based measures of redress.

As argued in a previous paper, 'to posit South Africa as "re-racialised" presupposes that at some point race had ceased to be a defining factor' and that equity has been reached (Hendricks 2003). Race has not ceased to be a meaningful category and continues to function as the marker of inequity. This is why it continues to structure politics, a factor evident in the recent elections where, despite worsening socio-economic conditions for the poor, the ANC was returned to power with an even greater majority than in 1999.

Political analysts have been concerned about race-based voting patterns, likening voting behaviour to a 'racial census'. They contend that this leads to one-party state dominance, and reinforces racial cleavages, and that racialism prevails and is displayed in the public discourse, the collection of race-based statistics, etc. (see Hendricks 2003). Race-based voting patterns are deemed to lead to the degeneration of democracy itself by limiting competition and the possibility for the alteration of power. In line with this reasoning, Giliomee and Simkins (1999) labelled South Africa an 'awkward democracy'. Within these arguments we see a neat separation between identity and interest where blacks are said to be utilising primordial factors, as opposed to the supposed rational calculations that should inform voting behaviour (See a similar contention raised by Friedman 1999). However, identity and interest, in 'racial formations' especially, are not mutually exclusive. It is a rational calculation to assume that a predominantly black political party which has a history of advocating black empowerment/advancement, and which in very real terms over the last ten years has delivered the basics in addition to the intangible freedoms people now enjoy, is far more likely to deliver on its promises than those political parties previously linked to the apartheid state.

Amidst this lamentation on the recalcitrance of race there are those who argue that non-racialism was not what it seemed and that race-based consciousness could be liberatory. There is also the more obvious critique that race needs to be considered in order to rectify skewed patterns of distribution. Alexander asserts that 'Non-racialism meant that you had to become or be a black Englishman. And this is why I insist on saying that in fact what we did was to de-Africanise our understanding of the liberation struggle. The Eurocentric aspiration was in fact the most salient' (2001: 111). Xolela Mangcu urges us to see race as 'a cultural concept that gave people their identity [instead of] a problematic physiognomic concept, a burden that [has] to be transcended in a broader search for certain universal values such as freedom and justice' (2001: 22). Clearly, the theoretical space is beginning to open up for us to critically engage with issues of racial identity and its place or relationship to democratic governance in South Africa. Racial identification can no longer be dismissed as a false consciousness which, when used in policy formulation, inherently promotes racism, in much the same way as the continued use of gender distinctions (themselves social constructs) is not sexist (See Mosley 1997 in this regard). The continued usage of these categories of identification represents strategic choices so that inequality is not masked by an appeal to an abstract universalism. It is the meaning that we ascribe to or invest in these identities and the relations between their bearers that constitute the problematic—not the identity in and of itself.

Racism certainly still exists in South Africa and its dominant pattern remains that of the apartheid past, although it expresses itself within different forms. Antjie Krog's book, *Change of Tongue*, captures an aspect of this change when it depicts a multi-racial school sporting event. At the event she asks an official 'Why is everybody happy? The reply is "The blacks are happy because it is a black kid beating the whites. The whites are happy because the winning kid is from a white school and is trained by them"'. Later in the text a black school principal notes:

> It doesn't matter how things have changed, before you know it, the whites have manipulated it in their favour. When you say your school does not have a track or long-jump pits or high jump or shot put-equipment, they say you must stop blaming everything on apartheid. When you ask if you can bring your athletes to their school, they say that they must first get permission from the school board, and that only meets next term. And you dare not call them racist, because now they have a few black kids in their school (2003:18).

It is that competition between now supposed equals, when material conditions obviously belie that equality, that promotes racial tension. Those who can afford it send their kids to private schools, or 'historically white schools', not because they necessarily want their kids to be 'Englishmen': these schools remain the sites for class reproduction or class mobility. The hue of the upper classes has certainly diversified, but the hue of the bottom 20 percent remains unchanged. 'Racial projects' are being created in South Africa. Black empowerment is a 'racial project'. But there is a qualitative difference between the advancement of an excluded majority as opposed to a historically (and contemporary) privileged minority. We cannot ignore emerging class differences but also cannot make a claim that this should be our primary focus, to the exclusion of race.

Conclusion

The limits and contradictions of liberal democracy are clear in the South African context. The marker for the consolidation of democracy—the possibility of the alteration of power—will remain weak in the context of continued race-based inequality, for the issues that brought the ANC to power remain relevant. Relations between citizens are important and require a direct group-based focus. However, the policies for the redress of race-based hierarchies will produce the kind of defensive response that has developed where whites and other minorities now ironically employ the liberation movement's discourse of non-racialism to counter ANC-led government's redistributive policies and practices. For liberal democracy to thrive in a 'racial formation' like South Africa, it requires domestication where group-based corrective measures are brought to bear. It requires that we move beyond political equality to create the conditions where all have the ability to realise their potential. It requires the acknowledgement that despite policies of non-racialism and multi-culturalism, the dominant culture will reflect the numerical majority and government policies and practices will be aimed at the welfare of this majority. This is not racist. It represents the normalisation of the society.

References

Alexander, N., 1979, *One Azania, One Nation: The National Question in South Africa*, London: Zed Books, (Writing under pseudonym 'No Sizwe').

Alexander, N., 1986, 'Approaches to the National Question in South Africa', *Transformation*, Vol. 1.

Alexander, N., 2001, 'Panel Discussion', *Transformation*, Vol. 47.

Alexander, N., 2002, *An Ordinary Country: Issues in the Transition from Apartheid to Democracy in South Africa*, Pietermaritzburg: University of Natal Press.

Bates, R., 1999, 'The Economic Basis for Democratisation', in R. Joseph, (ed) *State, Conflict and Democracy in Africa*, Boulder: Lynne Rienner.

Bannerji, H., 2000, *The Dark Side of the Nation: Essays on Multiculturalism, Nationalism and Gender*, Toronto: Canadian Scholars' Press.

Bhabha, H., 1994, *The Location of Culture*, London: Routledge.

Cunningham, F., 2002, *Theories of Democracy: A Critical Introduction*, London and New York: Routledge.

Davis, A., 1997, 'Gender, Class and Multiculturalism: Rethinking "Race" Politics', in A. Gordon and C. Newfield (eds) *Mapping Multi-Culturalism*, Minneapolis: University of Minnesota Press.

Dubow, S., 1989, *Racial Segregation and the Origins of Apartheid in South Africa*, Oxford: Macmillan Press.

Dubow, S., 1995, *Scientific Racism in Modern South Africa*, Cambridge: Cambridge University Press.

Essed, P., 2002, 'Everyday Racism: A New Approach to the Study of Racism' in P. Essed and D.T. Goldberg (eds) *Race: Critical Theories*, Oxford: Blackwell.

Fitzpatrick, P., 1990, 'Racism and the Innocence of Law', in D. T. Goldberg (ed) *Anatomy of Racism*, Minneapolis and Oxford: University of Minnesota Press.

Frederikse, J., 1990, *The Unbreakable Thread: Non-Racialism in South Africa*, Bloomington: Indiana University Press.

Friedman, S., ed., 1993, *The Long Journey: South Africa's Quest for a Negotiated Settlement*, Johannesburg: Ravan Press.

Friedman, S., 1999, 'Agreeing to Differ: African Democracy, its Obstacles and Prospects' *Social Research* Vol. 66/3.

Giliomee, H. and Simkins, C., eds., 1999, *The Awkward Embrace: One Party-Domination and Democracy*, Cape Town: Tafelberg.

Goldberg, D.T., ed., 1990, 'Introduction', *Anatomy of Racism*, Minneapolis and Oxford: University of Minnesota Press.

Goldberg, D.T., 2000, 'Liberalism's Limits: Carlyle and Mill on "The Negro Question"', *Nineteenth-Century Contexts*, Vol. 22, No.1.

Goldberg, D.T., 2002, 'Modernity, Race and Morality', in P. Essed, and D.T. Goldberg (eds) *Critical Race Theories*, Oxford: Blackwell.

Goldin, I., 1987, *Making Race: The Politics and Economics of Coloured Identity in South Africa*, England: Longman.

Gqola, P., 2001, 'Defining People: Analysing Power, Language and Representation in Metaphors of the New South Africa', *Transformation*, Vol. 47.

Hendricks, C., 2003, 'Revisiting Debates on Transformation in South Africa', Unpublished Paper presented at the African Association of Political Scientists Conference, Durban, June.

Hendricks, C., 2004, 'Burdens of the Past, Challenges of the Present: Coloured Identity and the Rainbow Nation', in B. Berman, D. Eyoh and W. Kymlikca (eds) *Ethnicity and Democracy in Africa*, Oxford: James Currey.

Keegan, T., 1996, *Colonial South Africa and the Origins of the Racial Order*, Cape Town: David Philip.

Krog, A., 2003, *A Change of Tongue*, Parklands, South Africa: Random House.

Kymlicka, W., ed., 1995, *The Rights of Minority Cultures*, United States: Oxford University Press.

Mamdani, M., 1996, *Citizen and Subject: Contemporary Africa and the Legacy of Late Colonialism*, Princeton, NJ: Princeton University Press.

Mandela, N., 1994, *Long Walk To Freedom*, Boston: Little Brown and Company.

Mangcu, X., 2001, 'Liberating Race from Apartheid', *Transformation*, Vol. 47.

Maphai, V., 1994, 'The Politics of Transition since 1990: Implications of the stalemate' in V. Maphai, ed., *South Africa: The Challenge of Change*, Harare: SAPES Books.

Maré, G., 1999, 'The Notion of "Nation" and the Practice of "Nation-Building" in Post-Apartheid South Africa', in M. Palmberg (ed) *National Identity and Democracy in South Africa*, Sweden: Nordic Africa Institute.

Maré, G., 2001, 'Race Counts in Contemporary South Africa: An Illusion of Ordinariness', *Transformation*, Vol. 47.

Maré, G., 2003, 'The State of the State: Contestation and Race Re-assertion in a Neoliberal Terrain', in J. Daniel, A. Habib, and R. Southall (eds) *State of the Nation: South Africa 2003-2004*, Cape Town: HSRC Press.

Marks, S., 1994, 'The Tradition of Non-Racism in South Africa', Paper presented at the History Workshop on Democracy: Popular Precedents, Practice, Culture, University of Witwatersrand, July 13-15.

Marx, A., 1992, *Lessons of Struggle: South African Internal Opposition 1960-1990*, Cape Town: Oxford University Press.

Marx, A., 1998, *Making Race and Nation: A Comparison of the United States, South Africa and Brazil*, Cambridge: Cambridge University Press.

McClintock, A., 1995, *Imperial Leather: Race, Gender, and Sexuality in the Colonial Context*, Great Britain: Routledge.

Mosley, A., 1997, 'Are Racial Categories Racist?', *Research in African Literatures*, Vol. 28, No. 4.

Mudimbe, V.Y., 1988, *The Invention of Africa: Gnosis, Philosophy, and the Order of Knowledge*, Bloomington: Indiana University Press.

Omi, M. and Winant, H., 2002, 'Racial Formation', in P. Essed, and D.T. Goldberg (eds) *Critical Race Theories*, Oxford: Blackwell.

Pieterse, J.N., 1992, *White on Black: Images of Africa and Blacks in Western Popular Culture*, New Haven: Yale University Press.

Posel, D., 2001, 'What's in a Name? Racial Categorisations under Apartheid and their Afterlife', *Transformation*, Vol. 4.

Said, E., 1978, *Orientalism*, New York: Pantheon Books.

Seekings, J., 2000, *The UDF: A History of the United Democratic Front in South Africa 1983-1991*, Cape Town: James Philip.

Taylor, R., 1996, '"Race" and the Transition to Democracy in South Africa', *Critical Arts*, Vol. 10. No. 2.

Walshe, P., 1971, *The Rise of African Nationalism in South Africa: The African National Congress 1912-1952*, Berkeley: University of California Press.

West, C., 2002, 'A Genealogy of Modern Racism', reprinted in P. Essed and D.T. Goldberg (eds) *Critical Race Theories*, Oxford: Blackwell.

Republic of South Africa, 2001, *Executive Summary of the Employment Equity Report*. Issued by the Department of Labour, South Africa.

UNDP, 2003, *Human Development Report: The Challenge of Sustainable Development, Unlocking Peoples Creativity*. http://www.undp.org.za/nhd2003.htm.14 June 2004.

6

From Apartheid Social Stratification to Democratic Social Divisions:
Examining the Contradictory Notions of Social Transformation Between Indian and Black South Africans

Lwazi Siyabonga Lushaba

Introduction

Apartheid was a system founded on an unsustainable notion of racial superiority. Racial discrimination was an integral part of its perverted logic. For its continued existence apartheid required not only statutory provisions but also a social structure that would help safeguard white interests by sowing seeds of division among the oppressed. At a politico-legal level, therefore, apartheid was constituted by a set of legal provisions that compartmentalised blacks into distinct ethnic categories while simultaneously creating separate intermediary categories, i.e., Indian and coloured, under the theory of separate development. Though these groups were also considered inferior to whites, they were accorded better treatment than the 'savage' blacks, thus setting them apart from this social group.

Apartheid social stratification, therefore, was a skewed social engineering process, which involved constructing and deconstructing social identities in accordance with the dictates of white racial domination. Differential racialisation was a central aspect of this engineering process. Despite, the inferiority status of all non-whites and their collective classification at certain historical junctures as blacks, political exigencies led to hierarchical modes of self-perception that correlated to that of the prevailing social structure. The identity formation discourse, along with mental constructs through which social relations were to be negotiated, occurred and developed within the strictures of the apartheid epistemology (for an elaboration of this view see various contributions to the volume edited by Erasmus 2001).

Through education and other social policies, group consciousness was imbued with discriminatory concepts that were later to be used by these groups in negotiating their social relations within the inter-subjective space of apartheid coexistence. Images of blacks as culturally inferior, coloureds as alcoholics and violent, and Indians as unreliable and deceptive, were conjured up and signified 'the other'. More importantly, it dictated the nature of social relations between these groups. An asymmetrical apartheid social system of signification therefore emerged in which the intermediary groups were placed below whites and above blacks.

A corollary of this was the racial ordering of opportunities which led to unequal development among the dominated. The form of this unequal development entailed not only access to better infrastructure, social amenities and opportunities for social progress, but also notions of superiority encapsulated in the variables of prestige and honour. Hence, '[G]rowing up coloured meant knowing that you were not only not white, but less than white, not only not black, but better than black' (Erasmus 2001:13). A similar attitude, perhaps in a more pronounced form, was prevalent among Indians. Beyond drawing our attention to this fact, the above quotation also points to a gap in the literature on social relations under apartheid in South Africa. Further research on the nature of inter-group social relations among the dominated is, therefore, necessary to complement the studies that focus mainly on black and white relations.

The notion of being better than blacks common among coloureds is replicated in the notion of 'being' held by Indians (see Reddy 1995; Bhana 1997; Prabhakara 2003). The attitude and behaviour of some Indian leaders towards blacks is reflective of the general group attitude. Bhana affirms this in his observation that 'Gandhi in common with the Indian leaders generally, not only harboured racial prejudice against Africans but considered them inferior' (cited in Prabhakara 2003). Gandhi's objection to sharing the same facilities with 'Kaffirs', as he referred to blacks, in prison evocatively displays this prejudice. Gandhi was not persuaded by the fact that his arrest occasioned by protests against discriminatory laws aimed at non-whites generally was a reason cogent enough to forge a common agenda with all those whose rights were violated by the same laws (particularly blacks). In affirmation of his attitude he wrote, in 1909, about Indians and their view of the black other, 'we may entertain no aversion to "Kaffirs" but we cannot ignore the fact that there is no common ground between them and us in the daily affairs of life' (Reddy 1995:19).

The above depicts the social mantra upon which rested the politico-legal superstructure of apartheid. The interaction between constitutive social and political elements of apartheid together with the contradictions they produced are all summed in what we refer to as apartheid social stratification. The integration of different groups into the apartheid economic system to perform roles determined for them by their social identities was coterminous with the unequal social ranking of non-white groups. This system reinforced, through the award of material benefits, prestige and social honour, the fissures in the apartheid social structure.

This chapter examines these divergent sources of power, prestige and the notions of social relations they entail with the ultimate goal of fashioning an understanding of the multi-faceted task of democratising them. Democratising social relations in post-apartheid South Africa, a task euphemistically referred to as social transformation, logically involves the deconstruction of social relations and stratification ostensibly designed for the purposes of perpetuating apartheid. Put differently, its theory and practice (social transformation) has to be historically located in the apartheid project. As social constructs, South African identities are located in apartheid histories. The historicity of these identities and social relations is not only continuous with the task of transformation in the post-apartheid South Africa, but also provides the historical material for such a project. A dominant view in the literature and public policy discourse in South Africa was that the history of social relations in the apartheid era was purely a history of class (interfaced with race) conflict or economic relations.

Employing a historical analysis of the social relations between Indians and black South Africans, this chapter shows the limitations of the Marxian understanding of apartheid, especially its conception of racial capitalism. The chapter contends that this conceptualisation failed to direct attention to other subtle but equally important aspects of apartheid social stratification. Consequently, it led to a limited notion of social transformation as essentially a democratisation of black and white socio-economic relations. This conceptualisation negates the reality of other historically constructed social categories that are neither black nor white. In a study of coloured identity politics aptly titled 'Coloured by History, Shaped by Place', Erasmus recognised the need for a perspective of social transformation that 'creates a space for voices until recently lost in debates centred around a black and white reductionism'. Quite correctly, she argued that the black and white notion of transformation is a fixated framework that 'too often assumes that someone's politics can be read off the colour of her skin with little attention to her everyday practices' (2001:15).

This chapter will show that, like most other South African identities, an Indian identity is a product of racialised power relations and privilege (apartheid social engineering), loaded with meanings that took their social significance from the apartheid racial discourse. It, furthermore, contends that social transformation is a complex process that extends beyond 'democratising' relations between blacks and whites. The chapter draws on both Marxist and Weberian analysis, believing that, together, they provide a more adequate explanation for the social relations that developed between Indians and Africans. The remaining part of this chapter is divided into four sections. The first section outlines a broader framework for analysing social inequality in South Africa. The second section analyses the historical construction of a distinctly South African Indian identity and the inter-group relations that emerged between it and blacks. The third section highlights a new social transformation challenge, and the fourth concludes the chapter.

Explaining inequality: Between Marx and Weber

The field of political sociology has spawned an extensive literature with divergent perspectives (see Coser 1966). Though they all study the same phenomenon—inequality—they emphasise different aspects and deploy different units of analysis. Structural functionalists are concerned with the problem of integration and equilibrium in society and employ the individual and occupational categories as units of analysis (leading proponents of this school include Warner 1941, 1949, and his associates in the Warner school, Davis and Moore 1945; Parsons 1966, 1970). Marxists and neo-Marxists pay closer attention to material inequality engendered by different class relations to the forces of production, i.e., the social organisation of labour is the principal cause of inequality. Max Weber undercut the long dominance of the Marxian school of thought. In response to Marx, Weber formulated the concept of a status group, thereby pointing to the equal significance of non-economic sources of inequality. This sparked a popular debate between Marxian and Weberian sociology.

The dominant perspective of apartheid, in the 1970s and 1980s, was Marxists. It theorised apartheid South Africa as capitalism interfaced with race or what is fashionably referred to in the literature as 'racial capitalism' (for this perspective see Slovo 1976; Magubane 1979; Marks and Trapido 1987; Adam 1971; Wolpe 1972, 1980 and several issues of the *African Communist*, Journal of the South African Communist Party). Champions of this school interpreted the apartheid social structure in essentially economic terms that defined the black majority as an alienated working class that fulfilled the labour needs of a racialised capitalist system. By implication social relations in this society were a secondary function of relations of production, read as the relations between persons marked off from each other by differential rights and obligations with regard to productive property. We return later to the inadequacies of this perspective but it suffices to point out that it glosses over aspects of inter-group relations that are outside the boundaries of its economically determined social structure. This lacuna observable in the Marxian analysis is addressed in Weber's construct of social stratification which notes that interaction among individuals and groups is also conditioned by cultural, socio-psychological and other non-economic determinants.

Notwithstanding the barrage of criticism that Marxian sociology has been subjected to, its relevance and analytical value has not diminished. We elaborate here on Marx's theory of social inequality bearing in mind Littlejohn's counsel that, 'Marx's theory of social stratification is not something distinct from his theory of society and its development' (1972:11).

For Marx the development of society is a continuous struggle between social forces whose interests are either, secured and identifiable in the current (class society) or in the envisaged epoch (classless society). Qualitative changes that occur after the conflict (class conflict) are located in the economic mode of production. Societies evolve historically in this fashion (his theory of historical materialism). For Marx, capitalism is constituted by two identifiable classes; the dominant (that owns the means of production) and the dominated (working class that only owns their labour). Simply put, every other aspect of their social existence is a function of the relations of production: the economy, therefore, constitutes the base of the political and legal superstructure.

The politico-legal superstructure functions in furtherance of the capitalist economic aim of social production and individual appropriation. In the logic of the Marxist perspective people relate to each other on the basis of their class interests. Effectively, therefore, in a capitalist society people experience social relations as economic relations. Unequal economic relations result in unequal social relations. The following oft-quoted statement found in the preface to *A Critique of Political Economy* captures the essence of Marx's theory of stratification:

> In the social production which men carry on they enter into definite relations that are indispensable and independent of their will; these relations of production correspond to a definite stage of development of their material powers of production. The totality of these relations of production constitutes the economic structure of society – the real foundation, on which a legal and political superstructure arises and to which definite forms

of social consciousness correspond. The mode of production of material life determines the general character of the social, political and spiritual processes of life. It is not the consciousness of men that determines their being, but, on the contrary, their social being that determines their consciousness... With the change of the economic foundation the entire immense superstructure is more or less rapidly transformed. In considering such transformations, the distinction should always be made between the material transformation of the economic conditions of production which can be determined with the precision of natural science, and the legal, political, religious, aesthetic or philosophical forms in which men become conscious of this conflict and fight it out (Quoted in Littlejohn 1972:11-12).

From the above quotation Marx's ideas on social structure can be gleaned. It is, therefore, the existence of classes that signifies social divisions and inequality. Socio-political organisation and the distribution of goods in the superstructure have a causal relationship with economic relations in a particular society, i.e., the social organisation of a society and its social relations are but a manifestation of the economic structure and the relations it embodies (for a detailed analysis see Giddens 1971; Avineri 1968; Turner 1987; Elster 1985).

Marxists studying South Africa used the above framework in their explanation of apartheid. In their view, social relations under apartheid were a consequence of economic relations. This view of apartheid as an interface between capitalism and race continues to inform the crippled notion of transformation in the democratic South Africa. Many of its proponents were linked to the liberation movement and, therefore, developed it as a theory of the South African revolution.

The ideas of apartheid as a racial capitalist system conflated class and race interests. Apartheid was seen as a system designed for white capitalist interests, logically ending in the domination and exploitation of the majority black working class. In strict class terms, the means of production were an exclusive preserve of the white bourgeoisie while blacks were inserted into the apartheid capitalist edifice as providers of labour. The organisation of the superstructure corresponded with the capitalist dictates of wealth accumulation by the minority white bourgeoisie. The state and other political institutions found in the superstructure were but instruments, at the hands of the white owners of the means of production, for black working class domination/oppression.

These scholars were confronted with two challenges: the first was whether it was inherently necessary to politically marginalise the blacks in order to sustain capitalist economic relations? Slovo, a leading revolutionary theorist, explained the link between economic exploitation of the black majority and their political domination as a function of economic interests. He argued that;

> [Y]et for all the overt signs of race as the mechanism of domination, the legal and institutional domination of the white minority over the black majority has its origins in, and is perpetuated by, economic exploitation. This exploitation, in the contemporary period, serves the interests primarily of South Africa's all-white bourgeoisie... Since race discrimination is the mechanism of this exploitation and functional to it, since it is the modus operandi of South African capitalism, the struggle to destroy 'white supremacy' is ultimately bound up with the very destruction of capitalism itself (1976:118).

The second was the presence of different supposedly antagonistic classes within the two racial (and supposedly class) categories. But, blacks, just like whites, were not a homogenous class category.

Though a member of the Marxist school of thought, Wolpe recognised that classes as social categories do not automatically translate into social forces and that they are not constituted only on the basis of relations of production. Although he recognised that political, ideological and social instances also play a significant part in the unification of classes as social forces, he failed to transcend the boundaries of class analysis and continued to consider classes as the basic units of analysis. The dominant/dominated, bourgeoisie/working class and black/ white dichotomy, for him, also remained the fundamental contradiction of the apartheid system.

This was the guiding theory of the revolution and it is from it that the currently prevalent notion of transformation in South Africa is largely drawn. The popular view that the task of transforming the post-apartheid society begins and ends with the democratisation of socio-economic relations between blacks and whites is inextricably linked to the declared goal of national liberation as the elimination of the economic basis of national oppression. This meant democratising the process of accumulation. Liberals and communists within the liberation movement proffered different and, at times, contradictory interpretations of the liberation theory. However, the common denominator between all these interpretations was the inability to transcend the economic realm and recognise apartheid's social relations as power relations founded not only on relations of production but also on non-economic cultural and symbolic values.

It is precisely the privileging of economic factors as the only determinants of the nature of social relations that marks a break between Marx and Weber's notion of social stratification. As we elaborate on the meaning and logic of

Weber's construct of social stratification it becomes abundantly clear that the economic determinism of Marxist sociology is oblivious to cultural, educational and other sources of power that often lead to a society divided not along class lines but along status lines. The ability of the apartheid state to forge out of indentured Indian labourers and from people of diverse ethnic, religious and caste backgrounds a relatively cohesive social group that ironically came to define itself as better civilised than blacks cannot be accounted for within the strictures of the Marxist perspective. Both groups were equally integrated into the apartheid economic system as exploited labour but unequally rewarded socially and symbolically.

Why did Indians then fail to consider the destruction of racial capitalism as an integral part of their liberation if like blacks they can be conceptualised as the dominated working class? What were the sources of their supposed 'superiority' over blacks? How were their interests located in the system of differential racialisation? The search for answers to these questions has to transcend the boundaries of Marxian sociology simply because they are beyond its scope. We extend the search for these answers to Weber's construct of social stratification, though these two perspectives should not be considered mutually exclusive.

At the core of the debate between Weberian and Marxist sociology is whether status groups or classes are the basic forms of division, whether classes or status groups are the primary groups in society, and, lastly, whether economic resources singularly or in concert with other resources determine social inequality. Turner captures this tension when he notes:

> [T]he tensions between Weberian and Marxist sociology are focused on the problem of whether economic classes or status groups are the most significant features of social stratification, and thus around the character of political conflict in modern societies. Whereas classical Marxism anticipated the disappearance of economic classes with the erosion of private property in socialism, Weber anticipated the continuation of status differences and status-group conflicts under both capitalism and socialism (1988:2).

A question that arises and to which we now turn is what is the meaning and logic of a status group and status politics. Status connotes one's position in society. It is how positions are assigned in society and what criteria are used that constitutes the whole gamut of status politics-cum-social stratification. For structural-functionalists, role setting and role performance both determine and justify social stratification. Borrowing from Abercrombie, we define roles as 'bundles of socially-defined attributes and expectations associated with social position' (1984:180). For Weberian sociological analysis status becomes important because status positions in society are hierarchically ranked, not on the basis of economic variables, but, rather, in 'terms of greater or lesser privileges and prestige' (Turner 1988). Furthermore, the bases upon which one's status is determined in society are varied and multi-dimensional, ranging from educational attainment, income, profession, to race, class, ethnicity and gender. It can be concluded then that, on the basis of the above, classes are not the only sites within which inequality is lived and experienced.

Weber draws an important distinction between 'ascribed' status (what in ethnic studies is referred to as the 'givens' of life) and 'achieved' status (a position one attains either through educational qualifications or other competitive means)status. Where status positions are allocated on the basis of ascribed attributes, social mobility in such a society is a near impossibility. The hierarchical apartheid social structure which placed whites at the apex followed by Indians then coloureds and lastly blacks defies the Marxian logic of social stratification (on the basis of one's relations to the means of production). The Marxist perspective fails to disaggregate blacks, Indians and coloureds (actually different groups) whose standing in society differed. It fails to realise that differential racialisation ensured that by virtue of being Indian or coloured and not on the basis of one's relationship to the means of production one was pre-determined to have better life chances than a black person. Weber defined status groups at an individual level as a 'plurality of social actors who within a larger social environment successfully claimed a specific social honour and enjoyed certain social privileges'; while at the group level they could be 'communal groups which have privileged access to scarce resources, especially where these resources entail a cultural, moral or symbolic attribute' (quoted in Turner 1988:6). This conceptual framework lends credence to our conclusion about apartheid social structuration being a function of multiple and varied social, economic and cultural factors.

Weber introduces a further distinction between what he calls subjective and objective status. While the distinction between ascribed and achieved status can be considered as the static side of social difference, the latter distinction constitutes its dynamic side. This draws our attention to the social dynamics or implications of social difference, how it is lived, acted upon and internalised. Findings from identity studies informs us that identities are always defined in relative terms—on the basis of difference or similarity (see Barth 1969; Osaghae 1986). Subjective status means self-definition and self-perception. Common consciousness arises when people share the same self-definition\perception, which, according to Weber, results in a collective culture, lifestyle and community of interests. Objectively or externally defined status refers to how outsiders cognitively interact with the social existence of different groups in relation to theirs. Do they recognise them as different? What this means is that as status groups 'belong to the sphere of social honour and are distinguished in the first place by varying degrees of prestige', those status groups conferred with a lesser degree of prestige should recognise this fact and accord the more prestigious groups necessary respect in whatever way (Littlejohn 1972:23). Mayer is perhaps more explicit: 'prestige is a socio-psychological category; an individual or social group cannot enjoy it unless their prestige claims are recognised by others willing to give them difference. Hence, the existence of status differences depends upon awareness of prestige rankings' (1955:66).

As status groups share the same privileges and lifestyle, they tend to cohere into solidarity communities that strive to protect and advance their interests by exercising status closure or social exclusion. Weberian sociology thus argued, contrary to Marxists thought, that inequality in society could also be a consequence of the unequal distribution of social honour and prestige, and not just material rewards. For Weber, economic wealth is not the only criterion for social power and influence. He found in Chinese society an archetype of societies where prestige flowing from educational and or cultural competition was more significant and enduring than economically derived power.

Weberian sociology is alive to the fact that all socially stratified societies are afflicted by conflict although the nature and mode of this conflict may be disguised, hidden or more subtle in expression. Negative perception about the other and its consideration and treatment as inferior are all subtle forms of this struggle that elude all legal mechanisms, including constitutional measures designed to address them.

Of much more interest to us here are the notions of social relations entailed in the difference between classes and status groups. In Marxist sociology all social relations are reduced to economic relations. The framework does not provide space for the non-economic life attributes, i.e., cultural distinctions, educational qualifications, social and occupational mobility. By emphasising socio-political aspects Weber perceptively recognises all social relations as power relations or better still relations of domination (which do not necessarily have to be exclusively economic).

The history of social relations between blacks and Indians in South Africa illustrates the difference between these two perspectives. The relatively better Indian socio-political and socio-economic standing, according to the adherents of the Marxist school, does not alter the larger apartheid capitalist class structure. So, despite their relatively privileged position occasioned by state-backed social advantages and racial laws, the social position and situation of

Indians remain similar to that of blacks. In that sense, their Indian consciousness (typified by both positive and negative claim to social honour and prestige) was a case of false consciousness. In this regard, Slovo argued that:

> ...the 2 million coloured people and the three-quarter of a million Indians are subjected to similar disabilities as groups even though the degree of discrimination and exploitation is in their case not as far reaching and intense. It is only amongst Indian group (the overwhelming majority of whom are workers) that there has emerged a sizeable group of commercial bourgeoisie which is, nevertheless, barred from using its economic resources to break into the top layer of the capitalist structures. In general, the Coloured and Indian people form a natural ally of the African working class masses even though the ruling class often attempts to use their slightly more favourable position to divert them from full involvement in the struggle for all-round radical change (1976:126).

This contention is symptomatic of economic reductionism typical in Marxist sociology.

Historical evidence suggests that the differences which Slovo describes as 'their slightly more favourable conditions' are in need of further delineation as they shaped and informed social relations between these groups and the black majority. Again, history has shown that the reasons for the 1949 Durban riots (these were violent clashes between blacks and Indians in Durban in which several lives were lost) are located in these 'slightly more favourable conditions' enjoyed by Indians at the expense of blacks (Meer 2002). A further examination of inequalities between Indians and blacks reveal that between these groups there exists significant differences which the Marxian conception of apartheid social relations fails to capture. This leads to an incorrect presupposition that social relations between these groups are economic relations. In strict Marxist terms relations between these two groups would for the lack of a better term be considered intra-working class relations. By extension since intra-class conflict is a near impossibility the 1949 Durban riots cannot be explained using Marxian tools of analysis. This leaves a grey area in the Marxist perspective of apartheid social stratification. That grey area, we argue, can only be illuminated through the logic in Weber's construct of social stratification—inequality is explained by the unequal distribution of cultural, educational, social and symbolic resources (honour/prestige)—status.

If employed simultaneously these two perspectives prove a veritable framework for understanding the dynamics of group identity formation and relations under apartheid. Taking the foregoing as a point of departure, we argue that the Indian identity group should be understood as a status group rather than a class in a Marxist sense. This is not to suggest that in its evolution it was insulated from the effects of the racial economic system. On the contrary, it is racialised capitalism that bestowed it with relatively better social conditions in contrast to blacks. In the next section, we look at how these different sources and forms of social power interacted to produce a distinctly South African Indian identity. We hope to show that it emerged as a direct consequence of apartheid social engineering. Secondly, we attempt to tease out from its historical process of evolution the cultural, social and economic meanings through which this group was to negotiate social relations, particularly with black South Africans.

Colonial and apartheid origins of a South African Indian identity, 1860–1994

Before proceeding, a methodological caveat needs to be made, i.e., an exhaustive history of South African Indians is beyond the scope of this chapter and empirical evidence for our historical analysis is drawn mainly from the politics of the Natal Indian Congress (NIC). The Natal Indian Congress came into existence two decades (1894) before both the South African Indian Congress (SAIC) (1924) and the Transvaal Indian Congress (TIC) (1927), and largely laid the foundation for Indian politics. The dominance of the NIC in Indian politics is partly explained by the fact that Natal had the highest number of Indians who settled there throughout the colonial period. Natal is a representative site of Indian politics in all its ramifications and provides a laboratory for testing theoretical postulations about Indian politics. For recent data on Indian politics we are largely dependent upon events in this province, now known as KwaZulu-Natal.

The arrival of Indians in South Africa was due to the needs of the early colonial economy of Natal, particularly the sugar cane agricultural sector. The local Zulu population in the then Natal, unaccustomed to wage labour, was considered unreliable and alternative sources of labour had to be found, leading to the replication of indentured labour that had earlier been applied in other British colonies, e.g., Mauritius. When Sir George Grey, the then Governor of the Cape Colony and the High Commissioner over British Territories in Southern Africa, visited Natal in 1855 an appeal was made to him by the Natal sugar cane planters to recommend the procurement of labour from India. The Indian government's initial ambivalence towards making available Indian workers was to later change after the British Government committed itself to safeguarding their interests as subjects within the Empire (South Africa, at the time, was part of the expansive British Empire).

By 12 November 1860, the first set of indentured Indian labourers had arrived in South Africa. Bagwandeen reports that '342 persons' came on that date while a further '351' strong group came on the 26th of the same month (1989: 4). This trend was to continue until 1911 when the importation of labour from India was discontinued. A total of 152, 184 indentured Indian labourers had by this time arrived in South Africa (Bhana 1997:2). They came mainly from the poor southern and central provinces of India. These migrant workers had the option of serving two five-year contract terms, and upon completion they were allowed to settle in Natal or return to India. Those who chose to serve two five-year contracts were rewarded with a land allocation if they chose to remain in Natal (this privilege was extended to them only until 1891).

Other than this category, another class of immigrants made up of individuals mainly from the western parts of India came at their own volition and expense. These Indians, who were mainly traders, were referred to as 'free' or 'passenger' Indians and mistakenly called Arabs. Business calculations were behind their immigration to South Africa. With the importation of their indentured compatriots, they saw an uncontested market to be exploited. However, this is not to suggest that they were all rich merchants as some of them did not have the requisite capital to start private businesses and, therefore, ended up in petty trading (Bhana 1997). As shown later in the study, this group considered itself superior in status to indentured labourers. These two broad categories, however, conceal other deep-seated cultural, linguistic, religious, ethnic, and caste differences. Unavailability of reliable data indicating the population numbers along the lines indicated, in earlier years, compel us to use 1956 statistics by which time demographic trends might have changed. Notwithstanding this fact, what is indisputable is that the early Indian community in South Africa was as heterogeneous as the Indian society back in India. Analysing intra-group plurality among Indians, Kuper found that by 1956:

> the Hindus, who constitute over 70 percent, of the total South African Indian population are themselves culturally heterogeneous, with differences particularly marked between the Dravidians (Tamil and Telugu speaking) originally from the South of India and the Aryans (Hindustani and Gujarat) who migrated from the North. The Muslims (approximately 19 percent) and the Christians (approximately 6 percent) are mainly descendents of converts from Hinduism... Apart from religion, differences in wealth, education, sophistication *read as status group differences* are probably greater

within the Indian population than any other ethnic group in South Africa (Kuper 1956:15 *italics mine*).

Kuper concluded that ' in most situations it is misleading to generalise about the Indians' (1956:15). Kuper, however, failed to appreciate that a community of interest had by 1956 crystallised among these desperate varnas, ethnic and religious groups. We return to this point in the next section.

Intra-group differences in early Indian politics

Though Bhana does not provide statistical data, he gives a more graphic sociological depiction of the differences that defined the early Indian community in South Africa. We quote him at length in order to show how deeply divided this community was:

> [I]t is important to recognise that, in addition to the obvious regional and class differences between the two categories of immigrants, there were also cultural, linguistic, and religious differences. Among the immigrants from the Southern part of India were Tamil and Telegu speakers; and those who came from the northern and western parts spoke Bhojpuri and Gujarati respectively. They represented Hinduism, Islam and in much smaller numbers, Christianity. India was overwhelmingly subject to the system of castes; and the immigrants who came to South Africa brought with them this aspect of their cultural legacy. In short, the Indians in Natal were an extremely heterogeneous group; and this was soon to be reflected in the organisations that they created for themselves to fulfil basic needs of identity and sub-group cohesion (1997:4-5).

Despite these differences in status, class, religion or ethnic composition, this section of the South African population soon experienced colonial and apartheid discriminatory policies as one 'political' group. It was the collective experience of domination and being consistently lumped together as an undifferentiated group that laid the basis for what was to later become a recognisably South African Indian identity and social category. In the early years of their settlement Indians responded to discriminatory colonial laws through the NIC. It was a mooted bill that was to be tabled before the Natal colonial legislature that prompted Gandhi to mobilise Indians. On 22 August 1894, leading Indian merchants in Natal met in one of the businessmen's residence and agreed to oppose the bill. That meeting marked the birth of the NIC and of Indian politics in South Africa.

The circumstances of its birth made the organisation *ab initio* a business elite association. Its prohibitive £3 subscription fee excluded the majority of indentured labourers and other petty traders. Consequently, the issues that made it onto the agenda of Indian politics were merchant elite interests. For a considerable number of years the modus operandi of the NIC and other Indian Congresses reflected the elitist nature of its leadership. In resolving the issues that affected them, they submitted petitions and memorials to colonial and imperial offices. They paid agents to lobby prominent individuals and government officials. It is, however, not only their interests that set them apart from those in the lower ranks. Bhana reports that many 'of the NIC's commercial elite were keenly aware of the social distance between them and the indentured Indians, and probably did not think seriously of them as potential political allies' (1997: 21). This division between rich and poor Indians coincided with other social divisions. Most indentured labourers, for example, came from the poor regions populated mainly by people of the lower caste while the merchant elite came from the richer regions of India.

The dominance of Indian politics by the merchant elite came to an unexpected end in 1913 when Gandhi, for reasons of political expediency and self-validation, enlisted the support of indentured Indians for the Satyagraha movement. This action caused discomfort among the merchant elite because it would offend the sensibilities of the white ruling class which they naively thought could be persuaded to accommodate their interests without fundamentally altering the overall colonial/apartheid system. Herein lay the foundation of a view that persisted until 1994, albeit in different forms, that Indian interests were not antithetical to white rule but could be accommodated within it, or better still, that Indian interests were coterminous with white interests.

Though it polarised the Indian community, Gandhi's action, in a paradoxical way, also contributed to the emergence of an inclusive Indian political community. The inclusion of indentured labourers and their interests through fighting for the scrapping of the three pounds tax payable by those who wished to remain in South Africa at the expiration of their contracts helped to unite diverse Indian interests and create a sense of 'Indianess'. This 'Indianess', to a certain extent, came at the expense of black South Africans. In order to validate and position themselves Indians were to relate to blacks not as another dominated group but as the 'Kaffir other' whose condition bore no semblance to their own. Through this act, a line between blacks (and black interests) and Indians (and Indian interests) was drawn. Indians defined their position within the colonial and apartheid space by reassuring whites that 'Indians came from a civilisation that was consistent with all the colonial markers of acceptability. The 'Kaffir' was the real source of white fears' (Bhana 1997:31). This can be seen when Gandhi reportedly told the Rev. S.S. Thema as late as 1939 that '[I]t would be a mistake for Indians to join the Africans politically because they would be pooling together not strength but weakness'(cited in Reddy 1995:25). Intra-group divisions, therefore, became less significant while inter-group difference was exacerbated.

Though the NIC and the other Indian Congresses were secular organisations open to people of different religious, ethnic and varna backgrounds, they failed to undercut the necessity of other narrow sectional ethnic and religious organisations whose existence also perpetuated intra-group difference and consciousness. Differences and socially discriminatory practices typical of Indian society were imported wholesale by these organisations and kept alive through customary, religious or varna practices (e.g., the Arya Pratinidhi Sabha which promoted Hinduism, while cultural markers of ethnicity were maintained through organisations like 'Gujarati Youngmen's Society, Karnatic Music Society, Gyaan Prachar Natak Mundal, and so forth) (see Bhana 1997: 137–138).

Linguistic differences appear to reinforce the notion of superiority of passenger Indians. Those of passenger origins often considered themselves as progenies of a nobler social history than those with a history of indenture. This consideration went beyond the immediate past of leaving India and arriving in South Africa. It had its roots in the Indian socio-political set-up. Again Bhana's account is instructive in this regard:

> [T]he passenger Indians came mainly from western parts of India where Gujarati was spoken, and used the term 'Girmitiyas' to refer dismissively to indentured Indians; in the post-indentured period other terms were used with similar irreverence: 'Culculttias' for Bhojpuri-speakers from the Ganges valley, and 'Madrassis' for Tamil-and Telugu-speakers from the Southern parts of India. Not infrequently, the term 'banias' was reserved for the Gujarati-speaking traders to suggest that they were grasping individuals not to be trusted (1997: 37).

Various other lines of difference existed among Indians in their early years in South Africa that we do not consider here. These were mainly class and\or status (inclusive of varna differences) differences also observable in the patterns of settlement, occupational roles, and material endowment. (For a discussion of these aspects of difference see the volumes by Arkin, et al, 1989; Palmer et al 1956; and Meer 1969) The next section will show that though a homogenous Indian identity was a political imposition, it was also willingly accepted and internalised by the Indian community.

The Politics of Indian Sameness and Black Difference

How intra-group differences became submerged into a cohesive and integrated identity group with a curious notion of superiority over native blacks receives our attention in this section. As an immigrant community, Indians in South Africa faced similar problem of integration and were inclined to look inwards for solace and solidarity. Moreover, colonial and apartheid settlement patterns were deliberately designed to ensure inter-group difference and this resulted in a high level of intra-group consciousness. As early as 1906, long before the apartheid social engineering, there were hostile relations between Indians and blacks. Indians willingly participated in the crushing of the Bambatha rebellion in that same year. Gandhi's racist slurs and those of other Indian leaders further aggravated the already vexed relations between the two groups. Such tendencies were not only a function of colonial and apartheid policies. Indian attitudes towards blacks, early in their history in South Africa, suggest that they arrived already contemptuous of blacks. Any attempt to explain the 'othering' of blacks by Indians, therefore, has to incorporate explanations from theories of race (I am indebted to Professor Mijere for drawing my attention to this fact). This chapter is not able to do so given space constraints. However, those aspects of Indian identity that continue to impact upon the transformation challenge can be accounted for within the analysis of colonial and apartheid structures and the dynamics of differential racialisation imputed a slightly different meaning to the otherwise well-studied variant of Asian racism.

Colonial and apartheid regimes in South Africa employed political, economic, social and symbolic measures to consolidate a distinctly South African Indian identity. Immediately after arrival, Indians began to experience collective political discrimination irrespective of their class, ethnic and religious differences. This collective experience engendered a collective response. The long list of colonial laws that Indians were confronted with and to which they had to respond collectively include the Immigration Registration Act of 1897, the Dealer's License Act of 1897, the Franchise Law Amendment Act of 1896, and Act 17 of 1895. Although these laws appear to have been directed at different sections of the Indian population, they were indicative of the larger political situation under which Indians were going to live. The fact that they were barred from the Free State and that their movement between Natal and Transvaal was severely curtailed indicated to them that their disaggregation by the other laws was a matter of political expedience.

Apartheid defined Indians, as it did with all other groups, as separate and distinct. This it did within the dominant discourse centred on racial categorisation. This dominant racial discourse had as its principal objectives foreclosing the plausibility of a united non-white opposition, and, secondly, ensuring that the logic of separate development found meaning in all aspects of social existence. It is this same logic that leads Reddy to conclude that '[V]ery little under the apartheid system could have made any legislative and administrative sense without a framework of racial and ethnic classification inscribed in the legal order... Apartheid made the "racial group" the determinant of all social interaction'. He goes further to ask rhetorically: '[H]ow else could it have been possible to restrict "racial groups" to particular places of residence, to develop racially defined public services, to allow for the unequal access and provision of pubic goods?' (2001:73). The Population Registration Act of 1950 together with the Group Areas Act, its corollary, gave force and effect to the above logic by classifying all social groups in the country. Accordingly, each individual was defined either as a white, Indian, coloured or an ethnic subject, and entered into the population register as such. One's definition and categorisation was also a determinant of one's life chances. Reddy's contention vividly shows this but perhaps more illuminating of the effects of the racial policy discourse on group notions of identity is the narrow consideration of the Group Areas Act by Indians as nothing more than an assault on their business interests (Bhana 1997; Mesthrie 1989).

The formation of the Department of Indian Affairs in 1961 as well as their incorporation into the tri-cameral parliament in 1984 are representative of the attempts to create and define separate Indian political categories which, in turn, reinforced a distinct Indian identity. Through the Population Registration and Group Areas Acts the apartheid state determined whom one was, his/her residential area, with who he/she could associate and what social services were to be availed to him/her. Social service provisioning was, therefore, not determined according to the acceptable norms of need, population, taxation, etc., but according to the meaning and logic of differential racialisation. The quality of social services availed to different groups under apartheid are a clear denotation of the hierarchical ranking of groups under apartheid into status groups. Statistics that provide a conclusive picture of the difference in ratio of state spending per group are not freely available, and, where available, are subject to dispute. To circumvent the problem of inconclusive statistics on social spending under apartheid we refer to the 1995/1996 data. These statistics indicate the cumulative effect of years of uneven social spending between groups.

Table 1 shows through two indicators of the conditions of living—water and sanitation—the disparities (which are a result of uneven social spending) between groups, particularly the gap between Indians and Africans (blacks). Were we to factor in the number of blacks who own houses, where these amenities can be enjoyed, the picture is bound to become more complicated. Table 2 shows the disparity in educational attainment which is not a function of ability or intelligence but of the racial structuring of opportunity(ies). Again the gap between Indians and blacks is more than fourfold. These patterns are replicated in other sectors, e.g., health and housing.

Table 1: Indicators of Living Conditions

	African	Coloured	Indian	White
Indoor Water				
Urban	56 %	80 %	98 %	99 %
Rural	12 %	44 %	81 %	78 %
Indoor Sanitation				
Urban	42 %	70 %	97 %	99 %
Rural	5 %	38 %	72 %	98 %

Source: Adapted from South Africa Survey 1996/97, pp. 803–804, 806–807, 779.

Table 2: Education of Persons over 20, 1995

	Africans	Coloured	Indian	White	Total
No Education	2,640,000	182,000	34,000	8,000	2,864,000
Some Primary	4,495,000	690,000	84,000	35,000	5,304,000
Some Secondary	7,413,000	1,001,000	448,000	2,632,000	11,494,000
Some Tertiary	822,000	102,000	74,000	952,000	1,950,000
TOTAL	15,370,000	1,975,000	640,000	3,627,000	21,612,000

Source: Central Statistical Services, 1995 October Household Survey.

With a relatively better quality education Indians had a competitive advantage over blacks in the labour market. This skewed education system also ensured that they emerged more confident and assertive in their social relations compared to blacks. In a system that attached importance and value to education as a source not only of livelihood but also of respect, Indians could, and, indeed, laid claim to better social honour and prestige. Closely related to this non-economic determinant of power is a symbolic one that was particularly accessible to Indians in Natal. In almost all the cities, Indians were allowed unrestricted access and use of certain parts of the city. Grey Street and its environs in Durban became their commercial hub, and, in the early days, also doubled as a residential area. The city, a location representative of modernity and civilisation, means that presence in it symbolises one's modernity and civility. Being denied presence in the location of modernity meant blacks were inferior while it symbolically validated the superiority of Indian culture and identity.

The majority of Indians who came to South Africa as indentured labourers were later absorbed into the secondary industry as semi-skilled labourers: public sector labour needs could no longer be satiated by the limited white labour. Table 3 partly shows how mobile Indians were within the apartheid occupational structure. The apartheid economy not only accorded Indians greater occupational mobility but also, even if within the constraints of white capitalism, permitted the emergence of a small merchant and commercial class among them. This is how they were invariably made an accomplice in the domination and exploitation of the black majority. The effects of white and Indian economic dominance over blacks is well summed up in Hamburg's contention that:

> [P]overty is partly a matter of income and partly a matter of human dignity. It is one thing to have a very low income but to be treated with respect by your compatriots; it is quite another matter to have a very low income and be harshly depreciated by more powerful compatriots. Let us speak then of human impoverishment: low income plus harsh disrespect... To speak of impoverishment in this sense is to speak of human degradation so profound as to undermine any reasonable and decent standard of human life (cited in Lushaba 1998:54).

Table 3: Distribution of Race Groups by Selected Occupational Levels, 1995 (in %)

	African	**Coloured**	**Indian**	**White**
Senior Management	2.9	2.0	10.7	14.6
Professional	2.0	1.7	6.7	8.4
Technician/related	9.6	6.6	11.9	18.5
Clerical	7.8	10.8	20.9	22.5
Service	11.2	11.6	13.3	10.6
Craft	10.2	14.3	16.0	15.0
Operators	14.0	12.3	12.7	3.8
Elementary Occupation	40.1	38.8	6.0	1.6

Source: Adapted from Central Statistical Services, 1995 October Household Survey.

Taken singly or collectively, the above factors, over time, shaped a distinctly South Africa Indian identity group and armed it with what Hendricks (in this volume and following Bourdieu) calls 'cultural capital', a combination of all forms of advantage in a competitive capitalist economy. In effect, apartheid invested the Indian identity with both material and symbolic benefits and helped to make the identity attractive. While material benefits ensured instrumental loyalty to this group identity, symbolic validation rationalised its intrinsic value resulting in unalloyed loyalty. The socio-economic situation of Indians by the 1980s can be summarily presented as that of social progress. Almost all classes and status groups within the Indian community had experienced upward social and economic mobility. A curious contrast exists between Indians and Coloureds in this respect. Among Coloureds, particularly those who were politically active, there existed a consciousness of the fact that their identity was, to a certain extent, an apartheid construct that had to be deconstructed or discarded if complete liberation was to be realised (a leading proponent and adherent of this view was Neville Alexander).

That a distinctly South African Indian identity developed at the apron strings of apartheid is by now a fairly established fact. What still needs to be answered is how it related to other social categories particularly blacks? Indian social structure is identifiable with the varna/caste system, which, like race under apartheid, determines one's life chances. Evidence suggests that by the 1980s, Indians, irrespective of their caste backgrounds, had opportunities to progress with serious consequences for social organisation. This, coupled with the influence of western education, led to English becoming a lingua franca, especially for Natal Indians, thus obliterating linguistic differences. The emergence in 1921 of the Colonial Born and Settler Indian Association (CBSIA), mainly constituted by the first generation of South African Indians who did not trace their origins beyond the South African borders, with an inward looking political approach, was in sharp contrast with what Bhana (1997) calls the politics of 'Imperial Brotherhood' prevalent until the early 1920s. The last distinguishing fact, for us, is not peculiar to South African Indians but characteristic of all other migrant communities. As people settle in a new place stories are created and told about it, a new history about the group then emerges. A new history of Indian South Africans emerged within the colonial and apartheid milieu, completely different from that of Indians in India.

We conclude this section by briefly looking at how Indians related to blacks while establishing our claim that largely the same processes that were responsible for the emergence of a distinctly South African Indian identity determined the nature of these relations. The relatively better conditions under which Indians experienced domination, particularly under apartheid, interspersed with accommodation politics of the merchant class which dominated Indian political organisations until the late 1930s set an Indian political agenda that consciously differentiated them from the larger liberation politics of the black majority. For them the total dismantling of apartheid was not the fundamental goal of their struggle. Were their interests to be accommodated by the white oligarchy their struggle would have accomplished its mission at that material point in time. Apartheid, for this group, was not recognised for what it was—an amoral and despicable system of racial domination—but was thought of as a system that deprived them socio-economic progress and prosperity.

Radicals that moved into leadership positions within the Indian Congresses fostered a new form of politics unprecedented in the history of South African Indian activism. Contrary to Gandhi's advice they expanded the domain of Indian politics by going into an alliance with other non-European organisations, particularly the African National Congress(ANC), and agreed on a need for collaborative politics. Superficial observation has led to the incorrect conclusion that this broadening of the front can be dubbed a success. We argue conversely that its success only went as far as the recognition of the fact that apartheid domination was an evil against all non-whites that had to be fought collectively. In the realm of practice, this realisation was defeated by the extent to which Indianess had been entrenched and become a prism through which this community read political developments in the country.

Their ambivalence towards the 1950 Defiance Campaign—a collaborative programme—starkly demonstrates the fact that Indians generally considered 'collaborating with blacks a pulling together not of strength but of weakness'. Essentially to them collaborating would have suggested to the government that they should be treated in the same way as blacks, or, rather, that their interests were commensurate with those of the black majority. This, for them, was an eventuality far from what they wished for. Again, here, Bhana's observation on the Indian response to collaborative politics is apt:

> [T]he Indian participation in the passive resistance campaign of 1946-48, was substantial and even enthusiastic in the beginning. In contrast, the response to the congressional alliance was guarded. The alliance signalled a kind of multi-racial vision as articulated in the Freedom Charter that left many Indians ambivalent. The Indian congressional leadership, by its own admission, failed to prepare—*that is to disabuse their constituency of the thinking that their interests are not commensurate or are anti-thetical to those of the black majority*—the ground adequately among its constituents. The doubts about

how multi-racialism would impact upon them in their daily lives persisted (1997:87–88, italics mine).

Marginal integration into the apartheid economy and bureaucracy of Indians with its concomitant status-enhancing effect happened alongside deep immiseration of the black majority, leading to a resentment of this group by blacks generally. An extensive study of the consciousness that emerged among blacks is necessary in order to counter-balance the many uni-dimensional studies of social relations between these groups. However, a few preliminary remarks are possible to make here. Reference to Indians as traitors and exploiters of black labour led to their categorisation in the black consciousness as part of the enemy and as targets of the informal insurgency as black political organisations conceptualised them differently. In black street argot, it became a progressive act to steal from an Indian's shop or business, or to even assault an Indian. During the 1980s, an era of civil disobedience, Indian business interests were identified as targets. Derogatory references to Indians as *'amakula, os'tsharo, mamu'* (derogatory referents) became part of popular public speech among youth comrades, and, interestingly, those who worked for Indian establishments were harbingers of more deep-seated anger and resentment.

That the 1949 Durban riots came at a time when the alliance between black and Indian organisations was already in existence suggests that though state complicity in fanning anti-Indian sentiments among blacks cannot be ignored, there were deep-rooted or underlying feelings of anger that needed to be addressed. Institutionalised inequality, the relative affluence of Indians, displayed in the midst of abject black poverty, the presence in the city constructed as a space of modernity and progress, all led to a resentment of this group by blacks who saw them as doing very little to challenge the state precisely because of the status the system accorded them. All these together led to a conflict between these groups that bore little semblance to class conflict but rather had every mark of conflict between status groups known in Weberian terms as 'the politics of resentment' (Turner 1988). These vexed social relations have implications for the post-apartheid South Africa. A need to transcend apartheid social relations is a social transformation imperative that cannot be overemphasised. What then is supposed to be the nature of democratic social divisions and how can they be attained? We ponder briefly over these questions in the next section.

The challenge of social transformation

Taking the foregoing as a point of departure, it is possible to conclude that South African Indians and the larger social relations that were entailed in the apartheid social stratification cannot be adequately analysed from a Marxist perspective. Apartheid group identities, as the analysis has shown, do not fit neatly into the class categories. Although non-whites were all discriminated against, Indians and Coloureds were better treated, had better social services, were more upwardly mobile and were marginally integrated into the political system.

Domination and exclusion of black South Africans minimised the competition for better opportunities, employment and upward mobility that Indians were to enjoy. Their sense of self was developed at the apron strings of apartheid. What implications does this then have for the post-apartheid social transformation challenge? Marxists would argue that socialising the means of production resolves all contradictions that apartheid spawned. Fragments of evidence from the post-apartheid South Africa seem to validate Weber's proposition that social divisions remain a reality even after socialising the means of production. Alexander has argued quite correctly that:

> it can be said with a huge degree of certainty that even if the proportion of real as opposed to token black ownership of the economy were to rise substantially over the next twenty years or so, this will not automatically translate into any radical improvement in social relations. That is to say, a reduction in racial and social prejudice and a concomitant strengthening of our sense of national unity are by no means mechanical functions of changes in economic or class relations (2001: 483).

Accepting this argument only exposes one weakness in the materialist notion of transformation, that social relations are not a mechanical result of economic processes. The second weakness in the materialist notion of transformation is that it understands domination as having been experienced uniformly by all non-whites. If this perspective were to correctly conceptualise the variations in the experience of domination, it would then be better placed to appreciate the existence of contradictory notions of transformation—particularly between Indian and black South Africans—and therefore expand its transformation framework beyond democratising black and white socio-economic relations to include engendering democratic social relations.

Democratic social relations cannot be legislated into existence neither can the old apartheid begotten relations be legislated out of the public consciousness. Social relations between Indians and blacks are characterised by resentment, despite the efforts at equalisation of opportunities. The transformation challenge, therefore, has to be extended to the realm of identity politics. One such attempt was through the notion of a 'Rainbow Nation' associated with the first democratic president of South Africa, Nelson Mandela. The limits of this approach have been the subject of much academic criticism and, therefore, we need not restate the arguments against it here (for such criticisms see Gqola 2001; Alexander 2001; Mamdani 2001). What is worth stating here is that this perspective only focuses on the positive aspects that are to be celebrated while it hides the underbelly of difference.

The weakness of the previous attempts at democratising social relations in the post-apartheid era can be seen in the salience of apartheid-engineered social relations, particularly between Indian and black South Africans, albeit in a different, subtle and disguised form. Empirically these social relations are encompassed in the contradictory notions of transformation between the two social groups. According to the *South African Pocket Oxford Dictionary*, to transform means to, 'make a thorough or dramatic change in the form, appearance, character, etc' (1994: 1030). Our observations of Indian political, social and economic attitudes in KwaZulu-Natal do not suggest that this group is given to the idea of a thorough, dramatic and complete change of the apartheid begotten political, social and economic relations. This can also be seen in what we refer to as a 'minimalist' notion of transformation that they hold.

Though it may not be entirely correct to argue that the Indian voting patterns in both the 1994 and 1999 elections conclusively show a convergence of white and Indian political interests, it is a sign that the apartheid-sown distrust for black majority rule still resonates in their consciousness (for a different view on the Indian vote see Habib and Naidu 1999). Perhaps the statement by a conservative Indian leader in 1938 that Indians 'do not desire to alter the political complexion of this country' and further that 'there is a community of interest between Europeans and Indians in trade, industry, professions, farming and in every phase of life' has become prophetic (cited in Bhana 1997). What most arguments, in our estimates, about the political alignment of interests between Indians and whites miss is the fact that the generality of the Indian population has never pretended to be fighting for a complete destruction of the structures of white domination.

Today some Indians still show little inhibition in their consideration and treatment of blacks as inferior, in itself a part of the white structuration of political dominance. The respect they extend to other social groups other than blacks is conspicuously absent when their everyday interactions with blacks are considered. Two examples from the author's field notes will perhaps help demonstrate the point. Indians own most of the shops, a fact of apartheid history on its own, in and around Esplanade and Russell Streets in Durban, a residential part of the city now largely populated by blacks. On this particular Indian-owned shop in a ten-floor building on Russell Street, the author noticed a public announcement which reads: 'COMPLAINTS DEPARTMENT IS

ON THE 50th FLOOR'. The author curiously asked what necessitated such a notice. A young Indian boy behind the counter answered quite contemptuously : '[Y]ou blacks (pointing directly at the author's forehead) complain a lot. There is no time for complaints here (pointing suggestively to the confines of the shop). If you are not satisfied you leave'.

The second interesting observation was at the University of Natal (Durban) where the author was conducting library research. After receiving our orders (this author and a research assistant) in a student cafeteria we looked around for an empty table but instead found one meant for four with two Indians comfortably settled on it. Immediately after we placed ourselves in their midst they stood and left the table. It was through my discussion with an old colleague now working in the university and careful observations over a period of time that I was able to understand the offence we had committed. The campus is *de facto* compartmentalised into racial and group zones. The trend is that once a part of campus (including hostels, recreational facilities and areas) has become too 'black' for comfort, Indians and whites migrate to 'safer' zones which they define as theirs through occupation and frequent visits. This, of course, is a trend replicated in the larger society.

Exigencies of transformation require that both public and private institutions should reflect the demographics of the country and report progress to that end to the Ministry of Labour. White business interests that have not yet reconciled themselves with the eventuality of apartheid's collapse and that seek to perpetuate it in subtler ways have found willing accomplices among Indians whose minimalist notion of transformation is in consonance with their agenda. As most laws pertaining to the transformation process define Indians as blacks, it has become politically expedient for these white business interests to promote Indians ahead of blacks simply because, for them, transformation ends with their occupation of these positions and not fundamental change in the overall institutional setting of white privilege, i.e., ownership, equity, corporate and institutional culture, etc. It is perhaps this situation that agitated the political editor of the *Sunday Times* to ask in the title of one editorial, 'Why have all our managers become Indian?'

Closely connected to this is another form of economic racism. As white business seeks to perpetuate another form of racism, economic racism, by moving out of the cities that have become too 'black' for comfort to the shopping malls located in the suburbs beyond the reach of the poor black majority, Indians are replacing them as proxies, perpetuating apartheid in the form of Indian complicity in black labour exploitation. Not only are Indians replacing whites in the city centres as proxies, but they are also extending their own economic presence into the space left behind by retreating white business interests, a process aided by their comparative advantage over blacks in terms of access to capital, business expertise, etc. As a result, perceptions of Indian economic dominance are beginning to emerge among blacks.

The picture painted above brings Indians through their minimalist notions of transformation into direct confrontation with blacks to whom transformation entails a complete dismantling of white domination, including the relative dominance of Indians over them—hence the 'maximalist' notion of transformation. It is this notion of transformation that was being expressed in Mbongeni Ngema's composition lamenting the negative attitude towards the economic dominance of Indians over blacks in KwaZulu-Natal. The popular public reception of the song by blacks is enough proof for a need to expand the sites of transformation to those areas not covered by the crippled materialist notion currently dominant in the public policy discourse. Such a transformation challenge has to include the democratisation of social relations between apartheid created social groups. For Erasmus (2001) this challenge requires an admission of complicity on the part of those groups that were brought in as junior partners in the apartheid social system. This does not seem to be happening, especially among Indians in KwaZulu-Natal. The post-apartheid notion of transformation has failed to democratise social relations simply because it sees only in black and white. But, just as the motto of an Indian radio station, Radio Lotus, declares; 'not everything is black and white'.

Conclusion

Let us conclude this discussion by stating that the purpose of the above argument is not to deny that Indians a played a significant role in the struggle against apartheid. There is an endless list of Indians who formed part of the liberation movement and NIC and TIC were instrumental in the struggle against apartheid. They, however, receive little of our attention simply because they did not alter the larger outlook and pattern of Indian politics. They mostly represented views of a minority that could not be accommodated in the mainstream conservative Indian politics.

Let us sum the essence of this discussion in the following five propositions: (1) Indians under apartheid should be conceptualised not as a class but a status group; (2) a distinctly South African Indian Identity developed inseparably from apartheid; (3) social relations between Indian and black South Africans were characterised by contempt and resentment; (4) notions of transformation held by these groups are continuous with their position under apartheid; (5) for the post-apartheid South Africa to move beyond apartheid social stratification, the social transformation agenda should include the democratisation of social relations.

References

Adam, H., 1971, *Modernising Racial Domination: South Africa's Political Dynamics*, Berkeley: University of California Press.

Abercrombie, N. et al., 1984, *The Penguin Dictionary of Sociology*, Harmondsworth: Penguin Books.

Alexander, N., 2001, 'Prospects for a Non-racial Future in South Africa', in C. Hamilton, L. Huntley, N. Alexander, A.S.A. Guimarães, and W. James (eds) *Beyond Racism: Race and Inequality in Brazil, South Africa and the United States*, Colorado: Lynne Rienner Publishers.

Arkin, A.J., Magyar, K. P., Pillay, G. J., eds., 1989, *The Indian South Africans: A Contemporary Profile*, South Africa: Owen Burgess Publishers.

Avineri, S., 1968, *The Social and Political Thought of Karl Marx*, Cambridge: CUP.

Bagwandeen, D., 1989, 'Historical Perspectives', in A.J. Arkin, K.P. Magyar and G.J. Pillay (eds) *The Indian South Africans: A Contemporary Profile*, Pinetown: Owen Burgess Publishers.

Barth, F., 1969, *Ethnic Groups and Boundaries*, Boston: Little Brown and Company.

Bendix, R. and Lipset, S.M., 1966, 'The Field of Political Sociology', in L.A. Coser (ed.) *Political Sociology*, USA: Harper Torchbooks.

Bhana, S., 1997, *Gandhi's Legacy, The Natal Indian Congress 1894–1994*, Pinetown: University of Natal Press.

Bhana, S. and Bridglal, P., eds., 1984, *A Documentary History of Indian South Africans*, Cape Town: David Philip.

Coser, L.A., ed., 1966, *Political Sociology*, USA: Harper Torchbooks.

Davis, K. and Moore, W. E., 1945, 'Some Principles of Stratification', *American Sociological Review*, Vol. 10.

Erasmus, Z., 2001, 'Re-imagining Coloured Identities in Post-Apartheid South Africa', in Z. Erasmus (ed.) *Coloured by History Shaped by Place: New Perspectives on Coloured Identities*, Cape Town: Cape Town, Kwela Books.

Elster, J., 1985, *Making Sense of Marx*, Cambridge: Cambridge University Press.

Giddens, A., 1971, *Capitalism and Modern Social Theory: An Analysis of the Writings of Marx, Durkheim and Weber*, Cambridge: Cambridge University Press.

Gqola, P., 2001, 'Defining People: Analysing Power, Language and Representation in Metaphors of the New South Africa', *Transformation* Vol. 47.

Habib, A. and Naidu, S., 1999, 'Election '99: was there a "Coloured" and "Indian" Vote?', *Politikon*, Vol. 26 No. 24.

Hamilton, C., Huntley, L., Alexander, N., Guimarães, A. S. A., James, W. (eds) *Beyond Racism: Race and Inequality in Brazil, South Africa and the United States*, Colorado: Lynne Rienner Publishers.

Haralambos, M. and Heald, R.M., 1980, *Sociology: Themes and Perspectives*, Oxford: OUP.

Kuper, H., 1956, 'The South African Indian Family' in M. Palmer et al (eds.) *The Indian as a South African*, Johannesburg: South African Institute of Race Relations.

Littlejohn, J., 1972, *Social Stratification*, London: George Allen and Unwin.

Lushaba, L., 1998, 'The National Question in South Africa: Rainbow Nation, Challenges and Prospects', unpublished B.A. (Hons) thesis, University of Transkei, South Africa.

Magubane, B. M., 1979, *The Political Economy of Race and Class in South Africa*, New York: Monthly Review Press.

Mamdani, M., 2001, 'A Response to Nevile Alexander', in C.V. Hamilton et al (eds) *Beyond Racism: Race and Inequality in Brazil, South Africa and the United States*, Colorado: Lynne Rienner Publishers.

Martin, D-C., 1998, 'What is in the Name Coloured?', *Social Identities*, Vol. 4, No.3.

Marks, S. and Trapido, S., eds., 1987, *The Politics of Race, Class and Nationalism in Twentieth-Century South Africa*, London and New York: Longman.

Mayer, K. B., 1955, *Class and Society*, New York: Random House.

Meer, I.C., 2002, *Ismail Meer: A Fortunate Man*, Cape Town: Zebra Press.

Mesthrie, U.S., 1989, 'Indian National Honour versus Trader Ideology: Three Unsuccessful attempts at Passive Resistance in the Transvaal, 1932, 1939 and 1941', *South African Historical Journal*, Vol. 21.

Osaghae, E.E., 1986, 'On the Concept of the Ethnic Group in Africa: A Nigerian Case', *Plural Societies*, XVI.

Palmer, M., Kuper, H., Naidoo, B.A., Lazarus, A.D, Cooppan, S., 1956, *The Indian as a South African*, Johannesburg: South African Institute of Race Relations.

Parsons, T., 1966, 'A Revised Analytical Approach to the Theory of Social Stratification', in R. Bendix and S.M. Lipset (eds) *Class, Status and Power, Social Stratification in a Comparative Perspective*, New York: Free Press.

Parsons, T., 1970, 'Equality and Inequality in Modern Society, or Social Stratification Revisited' in E.O. Laumann (ed) *Social Stratification: Research and Theory for the 70s*, Indianapolis: The Bobbs-Merril Co.

Prabhakara, M.S., 2003, 'A Cautionary Tale', *Indian Economist and Political Weekly*, May.

Reddy, E.S., 1995, *Gandiji: Vision of a free South Africa*, New Delhi:Sanchar Pub. House.

Reddy, T., 2001, 'The Politics of Naming: The Construction of Coloured Subjects in South Africa', in Z. Erasmus (ed) *Coloured by History Shaped by Place*, Cape Town: Kwela Books.

Slovo, J., 1976, 'South Africa – No Middle Road', in B. Davidson, J. Slovo, A.R. Wilkinson (eds) *Southern Africa: The New Politics of Revolution*, Harmondsworth: Penguin Books.

Turner, B.S., 1988, *Status*, Minnesota: University of Minnesota Press.

Warner, W.L., 1949, 'A Methodology for the Study of Social Class' in M. Fortes (ed) *Social Structure*, New York: Basic Books.

Warner, W.L. and Lunt, P.S., 1941, *The Social Life of a Modern Society*, New Haven: Yale University Press.

Wolpe, H., 1972, 'Capitalism and Cheap Labour Power in South Africa', *Economy and Society* Vol. 1 No. 4.

Wolpe, H., 1980, 'Towards an Analysis of the South African State', *International Journal of the Sociology of Law*, No. 8.

7

Negotiating Nationalism: Women's Narratives of Forced Displacement

Ingrid Palmary

Introduction
This chapter is based on interviews with women from the Great Lakes region (predominantly from the Democratic Republic of Congo, Rwanda, Uganda and Burundi) who were asylum seekers living in Johannesburg, South Africa.[1] My analysis reads these narratives as a reflection of the ways in which women asylum seekers (re)construct their sense of self through engagement with broader social and political discourses on forced migration and national identification. The reading is framed strongly within the boundaries of the popular discourse on asylum policy and legislation. This popular discourse involves clear distinctions between the sides of the conflict, and each woman places herself within one of these clear categories. It is the narrative of a stable, coherent self, free from contradiction: one largely required by the asylum process. I will argue that it is also a narrative that distinguishes clearly between public (political) and the private (personal) acts of violence—a mythical division inherent to nationalist rhetoric.[2]

Another subtext within these narratives, however, shows the multiplicity of identity and how shifting social conditions generate and are themselves redefined by these identities. This paper explores these sub-texts in relation to the ways in which women have been positioned within national discourses (and related discourses on asylum) both internationally and in South Africa. This discussion is intended to frame a particular reading of these women's explanations of how the war affected them and other women and how it continues to affect services offered to forcibly displaced women.

Women, nationalism and forced displacement

The notion that history is dynamic and changing is not new (see for example, Venn 1984). Recently, a great deal of attention has been paid to the ways in which historical events are viewed through the lens of present-day events and experiences, which result in shifting meaning and significance being attached to them (e.g., Corry and Terre Blanche 2000; Gavey 2002). From this perspective, historical events are discursively constructed through a process of bringing some aspects of social reality into sight whilst concealing others (see Parker 1992, 2002). National identity is rooted in these processes of reconstructing history and plays a role in the versions of history that become available as well as being shaped by such histories.

Nations, and national identity, are systems of cultural representation whereby people come to identify with an imaginary, extended community. They are historically produced practices through which social difference is invented and performed (McKlintock 1990; Ranger 1983). The invention and enactment of nationalist mythology requires elaborate systems for the identification of categories of people and the maintenance of 'pure' identity (see for example, Malkki 1995). Thus systems of identifying those inside and outside the system of identification are developed as an imaginary but powerful belief in a shared and common identity.

One of the central ways in which national rhetoric is maintained is through the control of reproduction and the entrenchment of gender relations. National discourse has rested on an artificial construction of a public/private divide in which gender relations are placed in opposition to one another with women being remembered and celebrated for their nurturing and care-giving (i.e., private) roles. They are frequently celebrated as the ones responsible for transmitting values and cultural norms through their role in the socialisation of children. As emblems of national identity, women's bodies are the site for the creation and nurturing of values specific to the national project (Bhaba and Shutter 1994). It is ironic that, in spite of this, sexual violence in times of armed conflict has often been seen as a 'private' crime and, therefore, not as legitimate grounds for asylum applications for women (see, for example, Spijkerboer 2001). In addition, constructed histories of common descent have resulted in the sometimes violent control over women's bodies as witnessed in the use of rape as a strategy of war and the symbolic destruction of women's reproductive systems (Malkki 1995).

The control of sexual and familial relationships is central to the nationalist project and was key to the experiences of the women interviewed in this research. Elsewhere (Palmary 2003) I have argued that one of the consequences, of this rigid and mythical association of women with the private sphere is that their political involvement, as well as the torture and violence (such as rape and sexual violence) that they suffer, is often not recognised as political at all, rather, it is seen as inter-personal violence or individual crime. This division between 'private crimes' and 'political wars' is one that has been challenged more broadly by Simpson (2002, 2003) in his analysis of the South African Truth and Reconciliation Commission. It is, however, also relevant to this specific case. Nationalism, and the conflict that it facilitates, is legitimised by the artificial representation of women as rooted in the private sphere. Thus, resistance to the recognition of women's political activity can be understood because of its potential to erode the legitimacy of conflict, that is, the protection of the 'women and children' (Yuval-Davis 1990). This is a rhetoric that permits war precisely because of the representation of women as frail, passive and embedded in the private sphere. This representation is what Jackson (in Dowler 1998) refers to as misogyny in the guise of chivalry.

However, nationalisms are seldom uncontested and national identity has, in many instances, been a site of contestation and resistance. As noted by Henriques et al. (2002: 428), 'Power is always exercised in relation to resistance, though a question is left about the equality of forces'. Along these lines, women have attempted to create counter-narratives that challenge these nationalist representations and create new possibilities for women to reframe their experiences and challenge dominant discourses. Most commonly, this has involved re-writing women's activities into history and highlighting their political accomplishments (see for example, Thurshen and Twagiramariya 1998; Fenster 1998). However, because of the centrality of women in justifying conflict, women's transgression of the gender norms created and reproduced through nationalist discourse has often been met with severe penalties and violent repression. One respondent in this research explained how men who had been involved in fighting the war could remarry and create a new life after the conflict. Women who had been involved in violence, she said, would not be desirable as a wife. Similarly, other authors have also noted (e.g., Dowler 1998) how women who have been involved in armed conflict are seen as tainted, rather than being celebrated as heroes like their male counterparts.

Africa has seen a surge of nationalisms and counter-nationalisms. The power of national identities can be seen in the conflicts in which many African countries are embroiled and is rooted in a long history of nation building practices which deserve far more attention than I am able to give it here. By way of example, however, one can consider how, in South Africa, during apartheid, concepts of 'nation' and national difference were evoked to justify racist practices. Using the social sciences, and popular discourses, notions of 'ethnic nationalism' were used to justify racial inequality and oppression

(Tapscott 1995). Based on the argument that South Africa was made up of different 'nations', systems for maintaining separate identity through the control of gendered relationships (such as the South African Immorality Act of 1950 under apartheid) were created. Following the collapse of the apartheid state, we have, perhaps ironically, not seen an awareness of the dangers of national identities but a new national project which encourages unity and pride through state sponsored programmes such as the 'proudly South African' campaign and the 'come home' campaign designed to encourage (white) South African's abroad to return to South Africa (http://home-affairs.pwv.gov.za). A full analysis of the ways in which this new 'rainbow nationalism' continues to be based in an artificially gendered public/private divide is beyond the scope of this chapter. Suffice it to say that we continue to see the familiar mix of romanticising and celebrating women's involvement in the private sphere whilst writing out of history their activities in the public realm. Already, research has begun to show how this new rainbow nationalism in South Africa is implicated in the quite frightening levels of xenophobia we are currently grappling with (for more on this see Harris 2001, Sinclair 1999). This brings me back to the familiar mantra of Ann McKlintock (1990:409) that 'all nationalisms are gendered, all are invented and all are dangerous'.

What this brief sketch of the literature from Africa and abroad has highlighted is that one cannot begin to consider the ways in which people negotiate, adopt and resist national and ethnic identities without considering how these identities are saturated in the construction of gendered identities. This construction of women in times of war, as both the moral imperative for war as well as the keepers of values and norms central to national identity, has impacted on the services offered to women who have fled war and framed the ways in which women make meaning of their war-time experiences. This is not to suggest that women simply adopt such nationalist rhetoric. Rather, the meaning they make of their history will be framed within the context of these powerful social and political discourses and will continually be negotiated, framed and re-framed in relation to them. Thus, discourses make available positions for people to take up (Henriques et al 2002). This chapter is, therefore, an attempt to consider how women make sense of the events leading up to their forced displacement to South Africa within the context of South African and their own nationalist rhetoric.

Negotiating national, racial and gender identities

If we understand nationalisms to function in the manner described above, then it is unsurprising that women's narratives of the events leading to their displacement are continually negotiated within the framework of gendered familial relationships as it is these relationships that underlie the conflict. The women's narratives were shaped by nationalist rhetoric which emphasise the separation of private lives (in which most of their narratives were located) and public wars (which they saw themselves as largely removed from). The most common situation in the interviews for this research was for women to describe their experience of the war, or the event that caused them to flee, in terms of the political activities of a male partner or relative. However, descriptions of their own levels of agency and activism varied. In many ways, given the extent to which nationalist rhetoric is rooted in inherently gendered familial ties, it is unsurprising that women should emphasise these ties in describing their displacement. In addition, early narratives about reasons for fleeing to South Africa tended not to express any identification with the identities underlying the conflict in the Great Lakes. Many of the women simply described the war as 'governments not seeing eye to eye' or as a fight between two countries. They tended to describe the war as 'somebody else's' conflict and portrayed their own activities as personal rather than political.

Each woman emphasised parts of her story that fitted within the asylum principles and all emphatically began with the assertion that the war made them leave. In response to the question 'Why did you come to South Africa', each woman emphasised that it was the war: 'So far as she's concerned it was the war; So I went because of the war; She came to South Africa firstly because of the war and secondly the volcano, the earthquake'. Even in the instance where there was a volcanic eruption (in Goma in 2002) the war is stated as the most important reason for this woman's displacement. This can be read within the current xenophobic climate in South Africa where it is popularly believed that many asylum seekers are actually 'economic refugees' seeking better employment opportunities. For example, in a recent meeting with the Australian High Commissioner for Refugee Affairs, the South African Minister of Home Affairs stated that:

> During the 50th anniversary of the 1951 Geneva Convention on Refugee Affairs, I raised the issue that even though in a very small manner as compared with other countries of the world, South Africa is confronted with the constant abuse of its system of refugee protection. Almost 80 percent of the applications we process are unfounded. This means that we employ most of the scarce resources we have available for refugee protection to process the applications of those who seek to abuse the system (Buthelezi 2003).

Of course, all the women discussed the fact that they were suffering economic hardship, unemployment and lack of basic services. However, these were narratives that were far more difficult to access which is likely to be related to the ways in which 'economic refugee' and 'illegal immigrant' or 'unfounded application' have come to be interchangeable in the context of South African immigration. Furthermore, in asylum legislation and procedures it is commonly assumed that political violence can be separated from crime, economic hardship or family instability and that people make decisions to flee based on a single, clear-cut persecution as a result of neatly defined political acts. This has particular consequences for the women in this research whose political activity engaged with the ways in which gender oppression manifests itself in times of war and so blurred the boundaries between family and war. However, recognition of activism that challenges gender norms inherent to nationalist, ethnic and racist projects has not often been recognised as political by state structures and within the state apparatus for processing asylum claims. Based on the literature described above, it could be argued that states have a vested interest in portraying gender relations as apolitical (and women as politically passive) if they are to justify ongoing conflict and nation building projects.

However, the range of national identities that women expressed was rather more complex than these early narratives suggested. Few women could specify their national identity and few national identities could be sustained in the face of complex social situations. For example, one woman who identified herself as Congolese stated, 'During the war [of 1976] my parents went to Uganda. That's where we're grown up, in Uganda. In 1994, we were still in Uganda. That's when the war started, so my husband was in Rwanda and I was in Uganda. In 1995, after the war, that's when I went back to Rwanda'. Ethnic identity (in this case either Hutu or Tutsi) was confounded with national identity in complex and sometimes contradictory ways. Malkki (1995), in her study of Hutu refugees in Tanzania, found that urban based refugees expressed far more complex and multiple identities than those based in refugee camps. She argues that this was a 'pragmatics of identity' where different labels allowed for different access to social networks and services. Although this was clearly the case for women in this study, their experiences of the war and violence was still often rooted in their nationality and the contestation of this nationality was, at times, the key to survival. National identity was sometimes described as a historically located and essentialist notion of what it meant to belong to a particular group, and, at other times, a pragmatic portrayal of one aspect of oneself over another.

This suggests that in spite of the narratives that appear to reflect very clearly the kinds of re-produced nationalist discourses described above, there were frequent contradictions in these constructions, and it is perhaps these that are most interesting in a study of how women frame their displacement.

Several women in the project described themselves as being of mixed parentage. One woman (who emphasised her mixed parentage based on national identity, that is, she saw herself as mixed Rwandan and Congolese) had lived all her life in the Democratic Republic of Congo. She also identified herself as Tutsi and her husband as Hutu and felt her persecution was equally a reflection of her Tutsi identity. She describes the extent to which the nationalist project interfered with her own identity.

> After everything had quietened down [having been released from detention where she was tortured] she was back at work. She was in work again and again last October they came to her work to interrogate her again. And still by the Secret Police who arrested her [previously]. So they took her to UNHCR and from there they went to [names a non-governmental organisation]. So when she got there other Rwandese, who she didn't really know, were already there. And the former Interior Minister of Congo [DRC] was present. So the minister, you know, made a speech and told them that we're going to take pictures of each of you and these pictures, you'll be surprised one day because we'll take you from here to your country. We'll take you back to your country. So she asked him the question 'Our home? Where?' And then the other people you know, the other Rwandese told her, 'well, back to our home in Rwanda'. And then she said, 'No, she's not Rwandese, she's Congolese'. And then she went to see [names a UNHCR official], and she told her she wasn't Rwandese, she had all her documents with her to prove that and this lady told her 'the decision doesn't come from me it comes from government'. They took pictures of her and after that she went back to work.

It was in response to her forced 'repatriation' that this woman arranged with a client of hers to take her out of the DRC to Zambia following which she came to South Africa. This extract shows the artificial intersection between national and ethnic identities with Tutsi being seen as Rwandans and forced removal being framed as a 'return home'. Similar to projects across South Africa, and, indeed, the continent, projects of national and ethnic 'purification' often justify imposed social engineering in the name of respect for culture. Mamdani (2001) notes how traditionally, a woman and by implication any children, would take on the ethnic identity of her husband when she marries. However, in this instance, she strongly resists this and identifies herself as Tutsi. In spite of this, she describes her daughter as a Hutu even though this is an identity that her daughter finds extremely distressing. She says: 'No, mum, I can't believe it, no. The Hutus kill, they don't care'. This woman resists the kinds of gendered norms which are central to the nationalisms on which the war is based by refusing to take her husbands identity. Thus, her resistance to cultural norms of marriage is itself a resistance to the war and was the reason for her persecution. Challenging the validity of identities imposed through nationalist projects is thus profoundly political as the moral imperative for the war is created through regulating patriarchal family structures in such a way that social divisions (such as Rwandese/Congolese, Hutu/Tutsi) are created. This extract also shows, however, that service providers have often failed to challenge the mythical nature of nationalism and have accepted such identities, thereby reproducing them in their own work. The assumptions about women's political activity and what gets defined as political activity structures the kinds of services that are provided and to whom.

This is of course not unique to women's experiences in their countries of origin. The intersection of gender, 'race' and ethnicity also need to be analysed in the South African context to show how it affects refugee women. For example, when this same woman reached South Africa with her daughter, the reception officer at the Department of Home Affairs refused to register the child as hers because she said she was too dark-skinned to belong to this woman. As with her experiences in the Great Lakes conflict, the identities underlying the conflict in South Africa are rooted in gendered familial relationships and the boundaries of the social groups are maintained through enforcing family norms. Thus, we need to consider that nationalism, ethnicity and racism take particular forms for women whose bodies and actions are often manipulated in the attempts to maintain group boundaries. Because of the ways in which national identity is rooted in gender relations their political engagement can be expected to emphasise the gendered nature of 'racial' and ethnic divisions.

However, the negotiation of multiple identities, although often implicit, can also be very conscious, particularly in a conflict situation where particular identities may serve a protective function. That is, not only do women continually resist imposed identities but they also highlight some aspects of identity over others based on the social circumstances they live in. For example, in the earlier extract, the woman could have taken her husband's identity in order to avoid forced removal from the Democratic Republic of Congo. Indeed many women did this. In a discussion about the ways in which women have identified with or dissociated from the war, one respondent had this to say:

> Mostly men [are involved in the conflict and in politics], but some women, you know, participate actively. It's just starting, but a few women, especially the smart ones take part. Yeah, a few women participate in the war. They— not actively, but yeah they do in some ways. But as far as politics is concerned, it's just started. Some women, the smart ones are trying to participate, get

involved in politics. Most of the women back home are not active in anything. They are just housewives. They just take care of the children, stay home and take care of the family. [Begins speaking in French] What she wants to add is that even when the war started, even women who weren't very active in politics—once you say just a few words about politics or the rebels or, you know, something against the rebels you can easily get killed because people will label you as a politician, so they will kidnap you—even the children as well, the same thing... you have to be very prudent.

In this case, acting within and embracing the kinds of gendered identities celebrated within nationalist discourses acts to protect women's safety. Thus, negotiating between identities is not simply a matter of convenience but also survival. The best possibilities for survival are to be 'just a housewife'. This narrative is not unlike that described by Malkki (1995: 168) when she notes that Hutu urban refugees in Tanzania 'manage one or more adoptive identities or labels that were already given and rendered workable by the lived-in settings in and around town'. Thus, women shifted between identifying themselves as 'simply a housewife' or as politically engaged and active depending on the context in which they found themselves and the consequences of this representation. That women would overtly choose to represent themselves as politically inactive in order to avoid persecution further highlights the centrality of gender norms for legitimating war and how much of a threat challenging these norms would be to the nationalist project. Women's resistance to the conflict and the identities that it imposes is inherently gendered due to the specific representations of women in times of war and the reliance on nationalism to control women's bodies. In spite of this, countries around the world have been reluctant to recognise gender as a basis for persecution. In some cases (see Spijkerboer 2001) it is argued that this would result in too many applications, whereas in others it is because of a failure to consider the ways in which war is gendered and how this impacts on women's engagement in the conflict and their victimisation. Gendered oppression, even in the context of war, is seen as a cultural norm rather than a central mechanism by which war is legitimated.

In addition to negotiating multiple identities in order to survive and to resist certain gendered positions, women continually negotiated such identities when accessing services in South Africa. Among the women who were of mixed parentage it was felt that this mixed identity impacted on the services they could access in South Africa. In an informal discussion with one of the women in the projects she described her experience. The field-notes that describe this conversation are as follows:

> She has been to [the agency] and was forced to tell them about her mixed Rwandan and Congolese parentage [as this is the reason she is seeking asylum]. Since then she has been suspicious that this is why they are not giving her financial assistance. She believes that other asylum seekers have been given money for rent on several occasions but with her they told her that they only gave once. She also knows that the official she spoke to told other people about her mixed parentage because when speaking to another person in the agency, he make remarks about 'you Rwandese', in spite of her having presented herself as Congolese. The person who made such remarks is himself Congolese. This is perhaps how conflict, or at least prejudice is displaced across contexts.

The irony in this narrative is that the basis for asylum claim (her persecution based on her mixed parentage) is the same reason for being denied services designed for asylum seekers. This does raise a question about whether and how conflicts from particular regions may be displaced in the contexts in which forced migrants live. Although the context may not be conducive to the emergence of violence in the same way as it has emerged in the refugee producing country, especially among city-based forced migrants, clearly prejudice remains. Some analysis of how this may intersect with local prejudice (such as manifestations of racism in South Africa) may be important to predict such conflict.

Some conclusions

It has already been described how positioning oneself within stereotypical gender identities can be essential to survival whilst resistance to the kinds of gendered norms that legitimate conflict have been a central form of women's political resistance. I have also suggested that service providers have, at times, failed to challenge the stereotypical representations of women as rooted in the private sphere. Refugee women are often represented by service providers as particularly steeped in their gendered activities and norms. We regularly celebrate women's role as caregiver and mother, an approach often encouraged by women's organisations. Refugee women in particular are positioned as 'natural caregivers', good mothers and domesticated (see Malkki 1995; Zabaleta 2003). However, as such images and rhetoric are taken up and become normalised, they serve to marginalise the other competing positions that women occupy and they begin to influence both programme funding and service delivery. The emphasis on African refugees as mothers can be seen in the vast amounts of funding dedicated to the reproductive health of refugee women. Jolly (2003), in her analysis of sexuality in development programmes, notes how, in development discourses in the North, issues of sexuality emphasise reproduction, disease and violence whereas programmes in the North tend to emphasise love, desire and pleasure.

One of the primary consequences of failing to challenge these representations of women rooted in the private sphere is that their resistance has seldom been recognised as political as seen in the refusal to accept gender based violence as sufficient grounds for asylum (see for example Spijkerboer 2003). By failing to challenge the ways in which nationalisms have artificially relied on such gender stereotyping, the political actions of women have remained largely unrecognised as have the forms of persecution that they face.

Notes

1. Some interviews were translated from French and extracts from these appear in the third person. Some of the women had been waiting for up to two years for a decision on their application for asylum. I would like to thank Erica Burma and Dr Daniela Casselli for their helpful comments on this paper and their ongoing support on the project as whole.
2. This narrative may well have emerged even more dominantly given that I was a relative stranger and because the women are likely to have been unsure of my ability to influence decisions on asylum, in spite of my assurances that I was affiliated to an independent NGO.

References

Bhaba, J., and Shutter, B. 1994, *Women's Movement: Women under Immigration, Nationality and Refugee Law*, London: Trentham books.

Buthelezi, M., 2003, 'Meeting with the Australian Representative of the United Nations High Commission For Refugees', Pretoria, 05/06/2003.

Corry, W. and TerreBlanche, M., 2000, '"Where Does the Blood Come From?" True Stories and Real Selves at the TRC Hearings', *Psychology in Society (PINS)*, Vol 26.

Dowler, L., 1998, '"And They Think I'm Just a Nice Old Lady": Women and War in Belfast, Northern Ireland', *Gender, Place and Culture*, Vol. 5, No. 2.

Fenster, T., 1998, 'Ethnicity, Citizenship, Planning and Gender: The Case of Ethiopian Migrant Women in Israel', *Gender, Place and Culture*, Vol. 5, No. 2.

Gavey, N., 2002, 'To and Beyond the Discursive Constitution of Subjectivity', *Feminism and Psychology*, Vol. 12, No. 4.

Henriques, J., et al., 2002, 'Selections from Changing the Subject: Psychology, Social Regulation and Subjectivity', *Feminism and Psychology*, Vol. 12, No. 4.

Jolly, S., 2003, 'Gender Myths and Feminist Fables: Repositioning Gender in Development Policy and Practice', Paper prepared for the International workshop Feminist Fables and Gender Myths: Repositioning Gender in Development Policy and Practice, Institute of Development Studies, Sussex, 2-4 July.

Malkki, L. H., 1995, *Purity and Exile: Violence, Memory and National Cosmology among Hutu Refugees in Tanzania*, London: University of Chicago Press.

Mamdani, M., 2001, *When Victims Become Killers: Colonialism, Nativism and the Genocide in Rwanda*, Princeton: Princeton University Press.

McKlintock, A., 1990, 'No Longer a Future Heaven: Gender race and nationalism', in L. McDowell and J. P. Sharp (eds) *Space, Gender, Knowledge: Feminist Readings*, London: Arnold.

Palmary, I., 2003, 'Nationalism and Asylum: Implications for Women', *Agenda*, Vol. 55.

Parker, I., 1992, *Discourse Dynamics*, London: Routledge.

Parker, I., 2002, *Critical Discursive Psychology*, Basingstoke: Palgrave.

Ranger, T., 1983, 'The Invention of Tradition in Colonial Africa', in E. Hobsbawm and T. Ranger (eds) *The Invention of Tradition*, Cambridge: Cambridge University Press.

Simpson, G., 2002, '"Uncivil Society"—Challenges for Reconciliation and Justice in South Africa After the Truth and Reconciliation Commission', Johannesburg: CSVR. [Available online: http://www.csvr.org.za].

Simpson, G., 2003, *A Snake Gives Birth to a Snake: Crime and Violence in the South African Transition to Democracy*, Paper presented at internal CSVR seminar.

Sinclaire, M., 1999, 'I Know a Place that Is Softer than this...: Emerging Migrant Communities in South Africa', *International Migration*, Vol. 37, No. 2.

Spijkerboer, T., 2001, *Gender and Refugee Status*, Dartmouth: Ashgate.

Tapscott, C., 1995, 'Changing Discourses of Development in South Africa', in J. Crush (ed), *Power of Development*, London: Routledge.

Thurshen, M. and Twagiramariya, C., 1998, *What Women Do in Wartime: Gender and Conflict in Africa*, London: Zed Books.

Venn, C., 1984, 'The subject of psychology', in J, Henriques, W. Hollway, C. Urwin, C. Venn and V. Walkerdine (eds) *Changing the Subject: Psychology, Social Regulation and Subjectivity*, London: Metheun.

Yuval-Davis, N., 1990, 'Gender and Nation', in L. McDowell and J. P. Sharp (eds) *Space, Gender, Knowledge: Feminist Readings*, London: Arnold.

Zabaleta, M. R., 2003, 'Exile', *Feminist Review*, Vol. 73.

8

Wilgespruit Fellowship Centre: Part of Our Struggle for Freedom[1]

Monique Vanek

Introduction

Wilgespruit Fellowship Centre (WFC) was established in 1949 by a group of six men, made up of educationalists and Christian Ministers, known as the 'Wilgespruit Brotherhood' (SACC 1973:86). The Centre was intended to provide a place where different racial groups and denominations could freely meet in South Africa, as such a place did not exist on a permanent basis (Mabille 1998:7). The WFC aimed in the main to promote ecumenicalism—a belief in the spiritual unity that opposed the Nationalist belief in racial segregation and the idea that only the Afrikaners had inherited the kingdom of God (Ibid:7).Secondly, the WFC espoused 'multiracialism'—the free encounter of different racial groups and denominations, where people could begin to see each other's humanity. Through promoting ecumenicalism and multiracialism the Centre played a role in the liberation of South Africa. However, these objectives were set against a backdrop of racial segregation that was institutionalised in the constitution, in the South African parliament, in political practice, and in the minds of the ruling minority (Human Rights Commission 1989). This made it difficult for WFC to operate as a multiracial and ecumenical centre.

Wilgespruit's role in South Africa's freedom struggle

In order to fulfil its aims of operating as an ecumenical and multiracial organisation, Dale White, the warden at WFC, developed a number of programmes to help Christians who were struggling and to alert people and churches to them so that WFC could go out to people in need, and deal with racial segregation(Foster 1972). These programmes included the Youth

Ecumenical Services (YES), which focused on black youth; the Urban Industrial Mission (UIM), which was established in 1966, at the request of the South African Council of Churches (SACC) to focus on achieving the greater involvement of all people in issues relating to community and industry despite the disparities created by racial discrimination;[2] and the Domestic Workers Project (DWP), which was launched in 1970 to focus on assisting domestic workers by teaching them to read and write. In addition to the above programmes, WFC also made available its multiracial conference facilities to organisations, such as the University Christian Movement (UCM), the South African Students' Organisation (SASO), and the National Union of South African Students (NUSAS), who each in their own way opposed apartheid.

WFC also provided all these organisations with T-group training through its Personal Relations Organisational and Development (PROD) programmes, which led to its near closure. The churches established PROD in 1967 for secular purposes. During this year WFC began focusing on developing the needs of student leadership following requests from university student organisations, such as NUSAS and the UCM, for leadership and organisational training. In 1969 PROD courses became part of the many projects offered at WFC.

PROD aimed at enabling persons and organisations to take control of their own direction and decisions.[3] It sought to enable individuals to gain a greater understanding of their human nature and live fuller lives, so that people would not be constantly bound by fear of themselves or others.[4] This was necessary as racial segregation in South Africa was hegemonic. PROD also planned to break down artificial barriers between races and religions that had developed in the country.

According to Horst Kleinschmidt, who was on the NUSAS Executive from 1968 to 1969 and Vice-President during 1970, NUSAS's need for T-group training was spurred by several factors. These included the precarious situation in which NUSAS found itself in the late 1960s. Further, the resistance to apartheid had been dealt a heavy blow, which meant that those at university did not get to meet the previous generation of anti-apartheid activists.[5] Coupled with this, there was the breakaway of South African Students' Organisation (SASO) and the emergence of the Black Consciousness Movement, which aimed at 'consciousness-raising' of the individual rather than 'mobilisation' and political party adherence.[6] This initiative in part reflected trends in the US in the late 1960s.[7] All these factors combined made the work that Wilgespruit was offering in T-group training ideal, because whites in NUSAS felt the need to undo their own inherent racist beliefs, which they felt T-Groups could assist in.[8] Moreover, Wilgespruit Fellowship Centre was one of the few places in South Africa at that time 'where people could meet on a non-racial basis'.[9]

At Wilgespruit PROD courses generally lasted a week. Participants would spend time in a small room with two staff members and 10–12 strangers, who were heterogeneous in job roles, age, sex, and background. There was no leader to tell them what to do, neither was there any particular structure to the group. Participants were left to decide the course of events and create their own social groups, although they were given some theoretical framework from which to work during the sessions.[10] These courses provided many anti-apartheid activists with a way of seeing the humanity in people of different racial groups. It was a powerful experience precisely because a person's habitual way of relating to people and perceiving people was challenged.[11] Generally when people encounter each other they adopt a mask and move away when things get uncomfortable.[12] One could not do so in a T-group session. People were forced to confront their own responses to others and deal with them.[13] Moreover, according to Angela Cobbett, who was a member of the Black Sash, PROD courses revealed new dimensions in the self and others.[14]

PROD also played a role in the Black Consciousness Movement (BCM) and the formation of SASO. These courses gave Steve Bantu Biko the inspiration to form an organisation like SASO. He was led to question his position as a black person in South African society and to examine 'who defines your identity'. During PROD courses he realised that 'people tell me who I am, who I can marry, who I can mix with, where I can live, what my education level has to be and here we are as black people accepting this, I think we need to redefine our own identities'.[15]

The PROD programme came under attack from the media, which was linked to the apartheid government, when in July 1970, *Die Afrikaner*, which was owned by Albert Hertzog, a vindictive racist, ran a series of articles about the WFC. In these articles WFC was accused of being a '*linkse broeines*' (a leftist hotbed) and the central point of the liberal onslaught against South Africa by psychological means. It also accused WFC of being involved in brainwashing techniques, which were being used for the furtherance of a liberal worldview.

Then, in 1971, the *Vaderland* and *Hoofstad* published a condensed version of the original series from the *Afrikaner*. In the *Vaderland*'s[16] condensed version it was argued that the main opposition to the government in South Africa had united in developing a plan to bring about a socialist revolution, by using sensitivity training which was being transmitted through PROD.[17] In addition, it alleged that PROD was responsible for the break up of marriages among those attending T-group training.

SACC responds to WFC

Following these reports, WFC was attacked by the South African Council of Churches (SACC). Consternation over WFC's radical programmes was expressed at its annual conference in 1969. The SACC sent a committee to investigate the happenings at Wilgespruit. Then in 1970 the SACC held an evaluation consultation in which all churches related to Wilgespruit participated. As a result of this consultation, Wilgespruit increased the representation of the churches and donor members on its management committee and gave the SACC automatic representation on its executive committees (SACC 1973).

In 1971, during a weekend of evaluation by several of the trustees following further reports in *Die Vaderland* that WFC was responsible for marriage break-ups, the SACC again reviewed its position on Wilgespruit and expressed concern over the direction Wilgespruit was taking. It also expressed a vote of no confidence in the management of Wilgespruit and suggested that Wilgespruit put its house in order, after which the SACC would reassess its vote of no confidence.[18]

In 1973, the SACC was forced to respond to the WFC after it was investigated by government, through the Schlebusch Commission. The Schlebusch Commission was appointed by the Nationalist government on 4 July 1972, to investigate the UCM, NUSAS, the South African Institute of Race Relations (SAIRR), and the Christian Institute (CI)—all regarded in government circles as potentially subversive left-wing organisations. The commission was made up of six National Party (NP) (MPs) and four United Party (UP) MPs. The government decided to investigate WFC following the completion of the Schlebusch Commission's inquiry into NUSAS in February 1973, during which certain of those questioned gave evidence that they had received T-group training at Wilgespruit. The Schlebusch Commission viewed this training as becoming of the political indoctrination that took place at NUSAS seminars. When NUSAS members told the Schlebusch Commission that they had received T-group training from Wilgespruit, the government suspected it had found the source of left-wing propaganda. Moreover, Wilgespruit was a member of the SAIRR and of the CI, personnel of whom were giving leadership training to the UCM, 'so they said uh ha, we've got the nub of who they are; the great spies'.[19] The government was also unhappy with the fact that WFC assisted SASO in the establishment of the Black People's Convention (BPC) and gave training to a number of black trade unionist leaders in the 1970s, such as Drake Koka[20] of the Black Allied Workers' Union (BAWU), which was formed by the BPC. Further, WFC in collaboration with the BAWU also founded the Black Youth Workers' Council in 1973 to discuss the rights of workers.[21]

As a result of the Schlebusch inquiry, the WFC was required to supply documents showing details of all courses, conferences, seminars, or similar meetings that took place at or outside of Wilgespruit, and in which members of staff were involved from 1969–1972. It was also asked to supply the names of all persons who attended or took part in these activities. The Commission also requested the submission of documents which would provide evidence of the ownership of the farm on which WFC was located. The annual financial statements for the years 1969–1971 of the owners of the property and those who occupied it were also requested. All these documents were subsequently supplied to the Schlebusch Commission, but out of 151 events involving 7,244 participants, from January 1969 to October 1972, of which details were given to the Schlebusch Commission, it decided to focus its inquiry on two activities held by the Centre.[22]

Of the two, one of these was the UCM sexual liturgy, which was held from the 10–16 July 1970 at the WFC's Chapel. The sexual liturgy or 'Encounter 70' was held at the request of the churches, who were concerned about sexual immorality among the youth who were sleeping with each other and maybe even across the colour line.[23] The liturgy attempted to 'use all the symbols in the bible, or what the bible says about sex, so that people would know if I'm a Christian this is what is being said about sexual behaviour'.[24] The liturgy was made up of three parts, two of which were designed by Basil Moore and Colin Collins (who were both associated with UCM) and known as the 'virgins liturgy', and the other was left open to the participants to decide on. A hundred and twenty people attended the liturgy, including observers from Malawi, Great Britain, Finland, and West Germany, and for the first two days two staff members of Wilgespruit were present and a number of voluntary consultants.

The other event discussed in the Schlebusch Commission Report was the T-Group, which was held by PROD in June 1972 at the Centre. It was one of 38 PROD activities held from January 1969 to October 1972, involving 30 of the 790 participants of PROD activities. One of the 30 people who took part gave evidence on that particular session.[25] Several Wilgespruit employees were subpoenaed to testify at the Schlebusch Commission, which was held behind closed doors (Thomas 1979).

In the Schlebusch Commission's *Third Interim Report*, which was tabled in Parliament on 24 April 1973—and widely publicised in the April 1973 issues of the *Rand Daily Mail, The Star, The Sunday Express, Sunday Times, The Sunday*

Tribune, The Natal Mercury, The Argus, Die Vaderland, and *Rapport*—Wilgespruit Fellowship Centre, was accused of:

- Brainwashing several young South Africans, by subjecting participants 'unknowingly to psychological and quasi psychological processes';
- Luring these young South Africans to the Centre by claiming to be linked to the church 'in a Christian ecumenical way';
- Allowing persons to run T–group training programmes who did not have sufficient skills to operate such courses;
- Causing two mental breakdowns during its sensitivity courses;
- Overloading the daily timetables of those attending T-group training in an attempt to exhaust participants mentally and physically;
- Allowing people like Eoin O' Leary, who made use of excessively foul language during T-group sessions and was a heavy smoker and drunkard, to run PROD courses;
- Deriving most of its income from overseas donors;
- Attempting to bring about social and political change within South Africa.
- Having politically active employees, like Maphiri Masekela, in other organisations like SASO, in which she made use of hate speech against whites;
- Hosting religious services such as Encounter 70, which was conducted by the UCM from 10–16 July 1970 and PROD courses, in which crude sexuality and eroticism were mixed with blasphemy; and
- Allowing uninhibited behaviour, such as smoking dagga whilst PROD courses were being held.

The Interim Report exonerated the SACC from any involvement or knowledge about the happenings of Wilgespruit. The Prime Minister of South Africa responded to the Report by declaring WFC a 'den of iniquity' which he ordered the SACC to clean up within three weeks, or government would do so itself. This attack by the apartheid government on WFC was a defining moment in South African history. It showed to what extent the apartheid government was prepared to go to preserve 'a life-style for the whole country which it regard(ed) as essential to maintaining a certain kind of political order' (Holiday 1973). It also demonstrated the extent to which the apartheid government was prepared to go to maintain apartheid. It would do anything to stamp out all opposition and the 'seeds' of resistance, as they saw it,[26] even if it meant accusing a particular organisation of sexual indecency.

Further, the attack led to an outcry within certain circles who felt the government was taking the role of a peeping Tom, since the Commission was expected to investigate state security but by its investigation into WFC it was looking into public morals. The events that were taking place at WFC as stated in the *Third Interim Report* also had another side to them. They caused outrage among certain strata of society, who saw the activities of the Centre as an indication of the demise of social morals and the rise of permissiveness within society.

Church and state relationship redefined

The attack by government on WFC in 1973 also initiated a new round in the relationship between the church and the state, raising issues about what form this relationship should take. It caused the SACC to confront the state instead of supporting it, because the issue of Wilgespruit was broader than a single investigation into a Christian centre. The whole event 'epitomised the struggle in South Africa between two radically different world views. Clerics, parliamentarians and others rushed into a fray, and the salvoes and rhetoric reverberated across the political and ideological battle lines' (Thomas 1979: 84).

The SACC was forced to confront the state because it was the trustee of the Wilgespruit property and, therefore, it was ultimately responsible for the events that took place there. Further, the ecumenical web had become so closely woven by then that it was inconceivable that an attack on the Centre should not involve the SACC.[27] The SACC responded to the Report and government's demand that the SACC clean up the 'den of iniquity', by declaring its full support for the Centre. It also found government's request to clean up the Centre in three weeks impossible in such a short space of time. As a result, it sent representatives[28] to ask the government for more time to discuss the Wilgespruit affair. The government agreed to give the SACC more time provided that the SACC could show that it was serious about doing something about the PROD programme, such as firing and publicly disgracing the Director of PROD, Eoin O'Leary.[29] On 30 April 1973 the Wilgespruit Management Committee together with the SACC met to discuss these issues.

At that meeting certain of those present from Wilgespruit, told the SACC that Eoin O'Leary had done nothing wrong.[30] Further, they noted that if the SACC, as a representative of the church, fired him it would find itself in great trouble in the future. Once it had given in to the government, a precedent would be set. As a result, the next time the government targeted someone it would be impossible for the SACC to resist.[31] After several hours of discussion the SACC and Wilgespruit decided to suspend the PROD programme, rather than fire O' Leary, set up its own commission of inquiry, and to wait for the government's response. A few days later the government gave the SACC more time to deal with the Centre and approved the idea that WFC and the SACC set up its own commission to investigate the validity of the accusations made in the Schlebusch Commission's report on Wilgespruit.

Six representatives from WFC and six from the SACC were appointed to the committee,[32] and J.R. Dendy-Young,[33] a former Chief Justice of Botswana, became its chairman.

The Joint/Dendy Young Commission as it was called aimed at:

- Looking at Wilgespruit's continuing relationship with the church;
- Investigating the correctness of certain allegations made by the Schlebusch Commission's Third Interim Report;
- Investigating all aspects of PROD; and
- Making suitable recommendations to the SACC's Executive Committee and WFC's management committee.

The Joint/Dendy Young Commission cleared Wilgespruit of most of the allegations laid against it by the Schlebusch Commission such as the claim that PROD programmes were politically subversive, that brainwashing of participants took place, and that WFC was unchristian.

The Joint Commission also questioned the validity and accuracy of some of the information given to the committee by witnesses and put the blame for Encounter 70 solely on the UCM, whilst suggesting that Wilgespruit only provided the facilities for it to take place. To rectify the situation at Wilgespruit the Joint Commission recommended that Eoin O'Leary cut back on his drinking habits, whilst conducting PROD sessions, and that an administrator be appointed as soon as possible. The Commission also recommended that a summit meeting be held in November 1973 to discuss ways of increasing the churches' involvement in Wilgespruit, that Wilgespruit's management committee consider lifting the suspension on PROD as soon as possible, that sensitivity training be restricted to Christian education and social service groups, and an association be set up to make sure that sensitivity-trainers were adequately trained to conduct PROD courses and that a code of ethics should be drafted. Further recommendations involved the management structure at Wilgespruit and its constitution and relationship with the SACC.

One unintended consequence of the Joint Committee was that it brought to the surface the internal difficulties of operating a multiracial ecumenical centre. This was explicitly demonstrated by the refusal of black staff at WFC to testify at the Joint Committee hearings. It was also displayed by black staff declaring that the white staff were incapable of 'divorcing themselves from a way of life they have known since birth'. Black staff at the Centre declared, in a *Drum* magazine article, that the multiracial dream at Wilgespruit had failed.[34]

Fear of closure and further events

As a result of the above events, WFC ended 1973 with a feeling of uncertainty about its future. In order to deal with this uncertainty it agreed to pay all employees three months salary if they were dismissed, banned or arbitrary action was taken against them.[35] Despite the fear of imminent closure hanging over the heads of WFC staff and the management committee, WFC had to go on and deal with one of the most destructive attacks yet on its multiracial and ecumenical nature—that of its black staff.

WFC made an effort to deal with the *Drum* Report, to which the black staff had contributed, by discussing it at the executive committee meeting on 5 November 1973. At this meeting the white/black tensions were carefully assessed and a request was made to the black staff responsible for the *Drum* Report to elucidate a memorandum which they had presented to the executive, management and staff on this issue. This was done at a management committee meeting held on 13 November 1973, at which the black staff involved in supplying information to *Drum*, tabled and read out a memorandum with six recommendations on the issue. Also, Dale White (who by that time had become the Director of WFC) and Tish White (who was responsible for the day-to-day running of the centre) made clear their response to the *Drum* article.

In order to rectify the situation between white and black staff, the black staff suggested that blacks find their way to a 'Black establishment and Black destiny' and 'that black programmes be transferred to a centre of their own', where they would be managed by a black committee, for which WFC would administer the funds, until blacks were in a position to do so themselves.[36]

At this same meeting Rakgobane Mohlathe and Maphiri Masekela were asked to meet with Dale White and R. Falkenberg and any other members available, to spell out the implications of their recommendations. It was also decided that since the WFC 'was a multiracial venture for the mutual benefit of all groups involved'; black staff should work within the framework currently established; 'and expressed the expectation that publicity would be activated to show WFC's multiracial character is still both valuable and viable'.[37]

In 1974, in response to the *Drum* article and recommendations made by the black staff in their memorandum, the WFC's management committee decided to increase the number of blacks on this committee, 'so that they could advise the black programmes on the relevance of their activities to the total community needs' and be given the ability to make suggestions to the management committee.[38] Moreover, as requested by the black staff after several consultations, some misunderstandings were ironed out and it was acknowledged that the difficulties between blacks and whites were a crucial problem in South Africa and would have to be constantly monitored.

WFC holds a summit meeting

On 26 November 1973, in response to the suggestions made by the Joint Committee, a summit meeting was held at Wilgespruit. Representatives from the churches, SACC's executive and WFC's management committee were present. This meeting concurred with much of the suggestions of the Joint Committee Report. For example, it suggested that WFC continue its educational programme to the Church and that The Association for Consultants and Trainers (TACT) be established to accredit persons involved in experience-based education. It also suggested that the constitution be changed to allow for the SACC to appoint a representative to serve directly on the management committee of Wilgespruit, and that the church should be given more participation and involvement in the affairs of the centre.

To bring about these changes, which required the constitution to be changed and areas of responsibility to be clarified and located, a sub-committee was appointed. The committee had representatives from the churches, the SACC (the trustees), and WFC management committee.[39] But despite these recommendations at the summit meeting, which seemed to give Wilgespruit the opportunity to act unhindered, WFC was not able to recover its former vitality.

Wilgespruit winds down

On 30 November 1973 Eoin O'Leary resigned from WFC and stopped participating in the Centre's activities. A few months later he was deported to Ireland. According to Horst Kleinschmidt, the departure and deportation of O'Leary led to the WFC losing some of its energy as 'he was more political —with some links to the past political struggle', whereas the others at Wilgespruit 'were more "liberal" and contented themselves with the overall broad influence that the centre made on our society in general'.[40]

The Domestic Workers' Project was transferred to the SACC in 1974, and in March 1974 Youth Ecumenical Services (YES) was unbundled by Michael Maasdorp, the Chairman of WFC at that time. It became independent and was run by Rakgobane Mothlathe. PROD, which was reinstated on 6 August 1973, was left to gradually wind down. By August 1974, due to the unbundling of WFC, the staff was cut to five permanent and four part-time members.[41] Then, in October 1974, the SACC made clear to WFC that the Industrial Mission Programme needed to be separated from the Centre and that UIM was to take on its own identity. The winding down of several of WFC's programmes and its paralysis from 1973–1975 led to a decline in the numbers using the centre. Fears of imminent closure of the centre persisted.

In April 1975, in response to this fear, the executive committee considered selling the property, or building up a residential community with or without the conference facilities; developing the centre to meet the needs of an expanded UIM, or working with adolescent drop outs and runaways.[42] Wilgespruit decided to undertake the latter two initiatives.

WFC rejuvenates itself

In 1976, in response to the request made by the SACC in 1974, that WFC separate the Industrial Mission Programme from the centre and that UIM take on its own identity, UIM began to operate as AIM, promoting the Urban Industrial Mission in the South African context. It aimed at teaching people to love each other and use things, rather than love things and use people.[43] AIM's focus was on industry, and it looked at the quality of work and the plight of people at work. It also looked at how work could be a fulfilment, as a 'co-creation with God, that whatever people did in industry, could actually be perceived and viewed as an extension of God at work.[44]

The Agency aimed at exploring two of the most important aspects of industrialised South Africa: migrant workers and how the 'Industrial system affects race relations, attitudes and behaviour between workers of different racial groups, and what the role' of the churches should be in this respect.[45] It also hoped to provide advice for church and industry on how to establish contact between them.

In an effort to deal with migrant workers, in 1976, AIM ran a project for 23 theological students, in which they were involved in researching various aspects of the migrant labour system. Some were employed on the mines, which resulted in the publication of *Another Blanket* (1977) and *South Africa Today: A Good Host Country for Migrant Workers*, whilst others were responsible for investigating recruiting methods and the situation of migrant families. Moronthsi Matsobane, who was a field officer in this programme, felt these programmes were vital for the Theology Students, as it would ensure that their sermons were relevant to those they preached to:

> their sermons could relate to the experiences of those people, they need to go through that experience themselves, then they can talk from experience and not talk from second hand experience, from reading and that thing. You need to go through a journey... So as at Wilgespruit we needed to live the experience of those people, to begin to understand what really happens there. We had to be those people to understand them. We had to understand how different it is to leave your own family, to go to a foreign country that you do not know, to go through that period of you being taken before you really get accepted and what it was like to be underground. That you had to

go through a period where thirty, forty, a hundred men are put, stripped naked and put in one room and a person goes and looks at their private parts like that, who claims to be a doctor and declares them medically fit.[46]

Another Blanket were a seminal piece of work in which the plight and culture of Basotho migrants were highlighted. Several of the suggestions on how to improve the miners' lives were adopted by some mining houses.[47]

In fulfilling its second main focus, AIM established the race relations project to investigate and research race relations out so that Christians could be provided with new and practical methods in industry, and begin the process of change necessary for growth of all groups in South Africa.[48] In May 1977 AIM was commissioned by five local congregations in Soweto and later by the SACC Division of Mission Evangelism to investigate the growing unemployment among blacks, as no factual information on the causes and number of those unemployed was available. In response to this request, AIM conducted a survey on unemployment. Consultations with experts in economics and with the churches were held and questionnaires were disseminated to black unemployed people in Johannesburg, Durban, Pietermaritzburg. It was extended to the rural areas of the Northern Transvaal and KwaZulu in Natal.

From this research it was found that unemployment affected all age groups, both men and women, urban and rural people and that the cause for unemployment was structural.[49] The findings of this research were published in *Unemployment: A Black Picture* (June 1978). In response to these findings a decision was taken to launch a nationwide church programme on unemployment, involving education, remedial and training activities, and closer collaboration between groups and churches and further discussions on how to deal with unemployment. In fulfilment of this decision, the WFC focused on educating the unemployed, in areas like Soweto and establishing rural co-operatives, because in many of the questionnaires filled out people responded by saying that they would like to be involved in self help projects, rather than receiving gifts of food and soap.[50]

AIM also hosted workshops, attempted to provide skills for self employment through its candle making project (Ukukhanya), the Ukukhanya Soweto Style furniture project, the SHADE co-operative, and by offering career guidance workshops for school leavers, in collaboration with St Paul's Church, Jabavu, Soweto. It also intended to assist black school leavers who were racially discriminated against in the workplace after leaving school. Former teachers who had resigned from Bantu Education, such as Griffiths Zabala, headed several of these self-employment schemes. In addition, AIM began training black trade unionists for the day when black trade unions would be legalised (Dugard and Dean 1981). When the first legal strike by black workers, in South Africa, broke out at Armourplate Safety Glass, Wilgespruit donated money to them through the Urban Training project.[51]

A new constitution and the establishment of Self-Help Associates for Development Economics (SHADE)

By 1978, after spending five years reviewing the constitution, it was finally changed. A notable alteration in the new constitution was the removal of the term ecumenical from many of the aims and objectives. Ostensibly, this step suggested that the WFC was moving away from its initial objective of being an ecumenical centre. Since churches were given more representation in the new constitution this was not the case.

The new constitution brought a new surge of optimism into WFC, which was further encouraged by the increase in the numbers visiting the centre after 1977. This new optimism saw AIM develop new programmes, such as SHADE, which forged close links with the Coady International Institute of St Francis Xavier University, Antigonish, Nova Scotia. The Coady International Institution agreed to provide a five-year educational programmes in co-operative methods and self-help projects with the aim of building up students to enable local personnel to take over the complete management of self-help projects.[52]

SHADE also focused on dealing with the desperate situation of women in rural areas, who were left to fend for themselves while their husbands went to work in the urban areas. It worked together with Catholic missions which had set up self-help groups and communities, 'who were making crafts and things that they could sell to generate an income'.[53] It aimed at teaching these women how to sell and market their crafts, and, later on, it developed into teaching business skills. Under its auspices it also established the Bags and Belts project, Thwasana Co-operative Farm project, the St Mary's Hospital Credit Union and Vegetable Garden.

Conclusion

WFC provided an alternative way of living in a society in which segregation and racial discrimination were rife in every aspect of life. 'It was a real kind of contradiction to the government's way of doing things and nothing they did actually made it go away'.[54] It gave people an opportunity to live in an institution which was working for change, an institution where blacks, whites, Indians, and coloureds could work and meet together, even though there were disparities that existed between them.[55] It gave people who were prepared to be part of WFC an opportunity to explore other levels of their lives and relationships.

According to Sarah Weber it provided a place:

> where people could encounter each other as human beings and get a sense of each other's humanity and it was something that began to create a value system, that people were able to test. I think there were a lot of people, you know, who came to Wilgespruit with an intellectual kind of rational conviction, about things being wrong and needed to do something else because they were morally wrong, but I think what Wilgespruit provided for people was the experience to go with the rational connection, that there was another possibility, that it actually was possible to make different choices and to found them incredibly rewarding and it was an opportunity to really encounter each others' humanity across the black/white divide and I really do think that it was the crucible, that was the container, that was the vessel, where the real contribution actually was made... [56]

And further,

> [I]t was a pre-cursor to a multi-racial society that whites needed to confront their history and personal feelings. WFC did this well. The road to Golgotha was the journey that was opened – often also to older people. As a means to struggle for freedom, this goal was rather too limited for many of us after a while. Also in the end WFC did not "make" many activist leaders. Rather it produced, what I would like to believe, a number of good people who had a better grasp of the history of colonialism and apartheid and what it had done to the majority of the population'.[57]

Through its PROD programmes it helped people to come to terms with their identity. PROD courses also provided 'deeper and more profound ways towards self-awareness. Some of this inevitably challenged social custom. So it was also a discovery into sexuality, discovery for gay people, many other taboos in our up-bringing were challenged'.[58] Even though WFC provided an alternative to what apartheid advocated it was by no means perfect. There were tensions across the colour line, and between staff, the management and the executive committee. The self-help schemes provided by AIM did not always work, because not all people wanted to be self-employed. Some wanted a job where someone else would run the organisation and pay out an income, rather than being an owner of a particular venture.[59] WFC, was also viewed by some like Horst Kleinschmidt as 'a cul-de-sac for anyone to stay there. Some made it their 'religion' and in a way it provided security, because it stopped you from getting into the real opposition to apartheid with personal consequences far more severe than Schlebusch'.[60]

This chapter has charted a critical period in the existence of WFC during the 1960s and 1970s. It has shown the external and internal difficulties faced by organisations attempting to defy the state by offering an alternative to apartheid. But despite these difficulties, unlike many liberal interracial organisations like the Liberal Party, it was able to survive, because it organised its programmes around the needs of society, changed its identity and reinvented itself. Part of this research has shown how impossible and impractical it was for the church to remain independent from the state during the apartheid period. Another dimension was to show the role that WFC played in opposition politics, especially the student left in the late 1960s and early 1970s. In so doing, I have shown how the WFC played a part, which has seldom been explored, in the demise of apartheid.

Notes

1. This chapter is based on my Honours dissertation presented to the University of the Witwatersrand in 2002.
2. WFC Annual Report, UIM 1973, p. 1.
3. WFC Annual Report, PROD Programmes, 1973, p.1.
4. Letter to the Commission of Inquiry, WFC, Roodepoort Transvaal from Paul Sammerfeld, 8 June 1973.
5. Interview with Horst Kleinschmidt via e-mail, 25 November 2001.
6. Ibid.
7. Ibid.
8. Ibid.
9. Ibid.
10. 'The Training Group as a place of learning', Document 18.16 submitted to the Dendy Young Committee, 1973.
11. Interview with Sarah Webster, 17 September 2001, at Grassroots Village Walk. Sarah was one of the participants in the June 1972 T-Group.
12. Ibid.
13. Ibid.
14. *Sunday Express*, 29 April 1973 p.2.
15. Interview with Tish White, 20 November 2001, at Wilgespruit Fellowship Centre.
16. *Die Vaderland* was a loyal National Party mouthpiece.
17. *Die Vaderland*, 'Baasplan onthul vir sosiale revolusie in S.A.', 18 November 1971.
18. Letter to Dale White from John Rees, 23 March 1971.
19. Interview with Tish White, 20 November 20.
20. Drake Koka also worked for WFC in 1972 and was appointed the Interim General-Secretary of BPC.
21. WFC Annual Report for the year 1973, YES.
22. 'Wilgespruit Fellowship Centre Draft', The Commission of Enquiry into four organisations, *Third Interim Report* (Schlebusch Commission), p.3.
23. Tish White, 20 November 2001.

24. Ibid.
25. *Sunday Times*, 29 April 1973, op. cit.
26. Interview with Horst Kleinschmidt, op cit.
27 Ibid. p.84
28. The representatives were John Rees (the General Secretary of the SACC at that time), Rev August W. Habelgaarn (the President of the SACC in 1973) and Archbishop of Cape Town, Robert Selby-Taylor.
29. Interview with Tish White, op cit.
30. Ibid.
31. Ibid.
32. One of those selected to be on the Committee from Wilgespruit was the Rev Dale White, but after some Committee members expressed their concern about the Director of Wilgespruit being on the Committee he was asked to quit, which he subsequently did. 'Director quits investigation', *The Star*, 8 June 1973,.
33. Finding an independent judge to sit on the Joint Committee proved to be an absolute nightmare for the SACC and Wilgespruit. However, the day before the Commission was due to start and all hope seemed to be lost, Dendy Young agreed to sit on the Committee. Interview with Tish White, op. cit.
34. 'Wilgespruit: A Multi-race dream fails' (1973) *Drum*, November, p. 20.
35. WFC: Executive Committee Meeting. Prod Programmes and Recommendations, 5 November 1973.
36. Ibid. p.2.
37. Minutes of the Wilgespruit Management Committee, held at Pharmacy House at 5.30 pm on 13 November 1973.
38. WFC: Annual Report for the year 1973. Annual Meeting of members, Chairman's Report, 22 June 1974. (Theo Derkx, December 1973), p.1.
39. The Sub-committee consisted of three representatives: the Rev. Joseph Wing, for the churches, the Rev Michael Maasdorp, representing WFC, and John Rees, representing the SACC. The representation of John Rees on the sub-committee for the SACC, had to be changed in 1977 because of his resignation.
40. Interview with Horst Kleinschmidt, op. cit.
41. Minutes of WFC Management Committee, held at Diakonia House at 5.30 pm on 26 August 1974.
42. Minutes of a meeting of the Executive Committee held at Diakonia House, Jorrison Street, Braamfontein, at 5.30 pm, 14 April 1975 and Gilbert, W. 1975, op cit.
43. Maasdorp, M. 'Chairman's Report in Annual Report', June 1974 to June 1975', WFC.
44. Interview with Morontshi Dan Matsobane, 34 Hamilton Street, Arcadia, Pretoria (Pensions), 12 December 2001.
45. White, D. WFC Executive Committee Meetings, Minutes. 1975/76, March 1976.
46. Moronthsi Matsobane, op cit.
47. WFC: Annual Report for 1976: Chairman's Report (Canon Michael Carmichael) p.2.
48. WFC: Report to Management Committee on AIM: Progress Report for 1975 and continuation in 1976.

49. White, D. Report Evaluation and Forward Plans 1976-1979. AIM, September 1979, p.5.
50. Ibid. p.5
51. Letter to the Secretary of WFC from J. L. Nthebe, Secretary of Glass and Allied Workers Union of South Africa, 14 March 1977.
52. WFC. Annual Meeting of Members, Chairman's (Canon M. Carmichael) Report for 1978, 31 December 1978.
53. Interview with Sarah Webster, op cit.
54. Ibid.
55. Interview with Lindy Myeza, Methodist Church, Cape Town, December 2001.
56. Interview with Sarah Webster, op cit.
57. Interview with Horst Kleinschmidt, op cit.
58. Interview with Horst Kleinschmidt, op cit.
59. Interview with Tish White, 20 November 2001, op cit.
60. Interview with Horst Kleinschmidt, op cit.

References

Blaxall, A., 1956, 'The Significance of Wilgespruit', *The South African Outlook*, No. 86, October

Borer, T. A., 1998, *Challenging the State: Churches as Political Actors in South Africa 1980-1994*, Notre Dame, Indiana: University of Notre Dame Press.

Carmichael, C. M., Wilgespruit Fellowship Centre. 31 December 1978. Annual Meeting of Members, *Chairman's Report for 1978*.

Document 64, Minutes: of a Joint Committee held on 12 June 1973 submitted to the Joint Committee.

Drum Reporter, 1973, 'Wilgespruit: A Multi-race Dream Fails', *Drum*, November

Dugard, J. and Dean, W. H. B., 1981, 'The Just Legal order', in S.T. Van der Horst and J. Reid (eds) *Race Discrimination in South Africa: An Overview*, Cape Town: David Philip.

Foster, K. WFC Annual Report, 1972, Chairman's Report, p.1.

Foster, K. *Wilgespruit Fellowship Centre Annual Report*, 1972, Chairman's Report.

Holiday, A., 1973. 'Anxious time for a church family', *Rand Daily Mail*, April.

Human Rights Commission et al., 1989, *Human Rights and Repression in South Africa: The Apartheid Machine Grinds On*, Johannesburg, Human Rights Commission, SACC and SACBC.

Maasdorp, M. 'Chairman's Report' in *Annual Report*, June 1974 to June 1975. WFC.

Mabille, G. 1988. 'The founding of Wilgespruit Fellowship Centre: Reflections on the first ten years 1948-1957', Roodepoort, Wilgespruit Fellowship Centre. p.7.

Mabille, G., 1988, *The founding of Wilgespruit Fellowship Centre: Reflections on the First Ten Years 1948-1957*, Roodepoort: Wilgespruit Fellowship Centre.

Minutes of a meeting of the Executive Committee held at Diakonia House, Jorrison Street, Braamfontein, April 14, 1975, at 5.30 pm.

Minutes of the Executive Committee of SACC. March 16-17, 1972.

Minutes of the Wilgespruit Management Committee, held at Pharmacy House at 5.30 pm on November 13, 1973.

Minutes of Wilgespruit Fellowship Centre Management Committee, held at Diakonia House at 5.30 pm on August 26, 1974.

Other Documents

South African Council of Churches, 1973, 'Outlook on the Month Wilgespruit', *South African Outlook*, 103:73, 86, May.

South African Council of Churches, 1973, 'Outlook on the Month, Wilgespruit', *South African Outlook*, May 103:73, 86.

The Durban Parliament, 1st session 1973: 15th sitting, Monday 14 May 1973 at 7.45 pm, No. 3 Committee Room, City Hall.

The Training Group as a Place of Learning, Document 18.16 submitted to the Dendy Young Committee, 1973.

Thomas, D., 1979, *Councils in the Ecumenical Movement South Africa 1904-75*, Johannesburg: South African Council of Churches.

Thomas, D., 1979, *Councils in the Ecumenical Movement South Africa 1904–75*, Johannesburg: South African Council of Churches, p.84.

White, J. St. D & L. December 1973. *Points Raised by the Drum Article*, November 8, 1973.

Wilgespruit Ecumenicist Fellowship Centre. *Report to the Executive Committee*.

Wilgespruit Fellowship Centre Annual Meeting of Members, June 22, 1974, 'Chairman's Report'.

Wilgespruit Fellowship Centre. 1973. Draft. The Commission of Enquiry into four organisations. *Third Interim Report* (Schlebusch Commission).

Wilgespruit Fellowship Centre. Annual Report for 1976: Chairman's Report (Canon Michael Carmichael) p.2.

Wilgespruit Fellowship Centre. Annual Report for the year 1973, Youth Ecumenical Services.

Wilgespruit Fellowship Centre. Annual Report for the year 1973. Annual Meeting of members, 22 June 1974. Chairman's Report (Theo Derkx, December 1973).

Wilgespruit Fellowship Centre. Executive Committee Meeting 1970-1971.

Wilgespruit Fellowship Centre. Report to Management Committee on AIM: Progress Report for 1975 and continuation in 1976.

Letters

To Dale White from John Rees, 23 March 1971.

To the Secretary of WFC from J.L. Nthebe, Secretary of Glass and Allied Workers Union of South Africa, 14 March 1977.

To the Commission of Inquiry, WFC, Roodepoort Transvaal from Paul Sammerfeld, 8 June 1973.

Pamphlets

Human Rights Commission et al., 1989, *Human Rights and Repression in South Africa: The Apartheid Machine Grinds On*, Johannesburg, Human Rights Commission, SACC and SACBC.

EcuNews Bulletin, 12/27, 1 May 1973

Interviews

Interview with Horst Kleinschmidt via e-mail, Sunday 25 November 2001.
Interview with Lindy Myeza, Methodist Church, Cape Town, December 2001.
Interview with Morontshi Dan Matsobane, Pretoria, 12 December 2001.
Interview with Sarah Webster, Grassroots Village Walk, 17 September 2001
Interview with Tish White, Wilgespruit Fellowship Centre, 20 November 2001.

Newspapers

The Argus, April 1973.
Die Afrikaner, July 1970
***Die Burger, 1973.
***The Cape Times, 1973
The Natal Mercury, April 1973.
***National Affairs, 1973.
***Progress, 1973.
Rand Daily Mail, 16 April 1973.
Rapport, April 1973.
The Star, 8 June 1973.
Sunday Express, 29 April 1973.
Sunday Times, 29 April 1973.
Sunday Tribune, April 1973.
Die Vaderland, 18 November 1971 & April 1973.

9

Curfew and the 'Man in the Middle' in Zimbabwe's War of Liberation with Special Reference to the Eastern Areas of Zimbabwe, 1977–1980

Munyaradzi Mushonga

Introduction

This chapter examines one of the many tactics used by minority regimes in southern Africa to delay the process of democratisation in the region, that of curfew. It does so by discussing the application and enforcement of the curfew laws during Zimbabwe's war of liberation with particular reference to the eastern areas of the country from 1977 to 1980. The central argument is that security forces and officers of the minority regime wantonly abused the curfew laws by turning them into a kind of licence to kill the ordinary and unarmed civilians, the so-called 'man in the middle,'[1] with impunity, as the examples and the case studies below demonstrate.

The idea behind the curfew laws was to assist the security forces in dealing with people causing trouble in the rural areas. Unfortunately, the security forces took advantage of the unwritten part of the law and sentenced people to death as they had orders to shoot curfew breakers on sight if they did not respond to an order to stop. We argue that, on the contrary, curfew laws did not protect ordinary people, nor did they effectively deal with the guerrilla threat. Instead, the curfew laws, both written and unwritten, simply gave the security forces and officers of the regime the licence to kill civilians with impunity and to met out any kind of punishment they deemed necessary. Consequently, the civilians found themseves placed between two diametrically opposed demands of the contending forces: the Rhodesian security forces, on the one hand, and the guerrillas, on the other.. Through the Marange, Makoni and Mutasa case studies we show the extent and nature of suffering by men, women and children who, through the curfew, were confined to their homes for a considerable period.

The bulk of the evidence for this research was drawn from parliamentary debates relating to 'curfews and the reporting of terrorists'[2] under the Law and Order Maintenance Act (1974), and from oral testimonies captured during field research in October 1999 and January 2003.[3] The discussion is divided into three parts. The first section provides a brief chronological outline of curfew declaration in Zimbabwe, the second and third sections discuss the curfew laws and show that instead of combating terrorism, security forces indiscriminately killed civilians, with impunity.

Curfew in context

Curfew generally refers to a time after which people must stay indoors and is usually enforced during wartime situations. According to *Webster's Third New International Dictionary* (1986), curfew refers to an order or regulation enjoining withdrawal of persons from streets, or closing of business establishments or places of assembly at a stated hour, usually, though not exclusively, in the evening. This is what the Rhodesian authorities did in most parts of the country in a move they thought would stamp out the guerrilla threat in the affected areas. It would appear the Rhodesians adopted this concept from Malaya from where they had copied the 'protected village' concept.[4] Just like people in the no-go areas, those in the protected villages were also liable to curfew, which ran from 6 p.m. to 6 a.m.[5] The Rhodesian army had either closely studied or actually fought in the Malaya counter-insurgency operations in the 1950s. It is also possible that the idea of curfew was borrowed from Greece, as one MP told the Rhodesian Parliament in 1978 that curfew was nothing new by explaining how the British had tried to use it in Greece and that the moment curfew was on, 'it assisted the military forces to come to terms with people that were causing the trouble'.[6] The MP, however, acknowledged that curfew caused a lot of hardships on the people of Athens at the time, just as it did for the people of Marange, Makoni and Mutasa, and also for all those whose areas were under curfew.

In Zimbabwe, the declaration of curfew is traceable to 1974 when in January, the Smith regime declared a curfew in certain Tribal Trust Lands (TTLs) and African Purchase Areas (APAs) in the north-east of the country. In 1975, the curfew was extended to the entire length of Zimbabwe's borders with Mozambique, Botswana and Zambia.[7] All this was done under the Emergency Regulation Powers (Law and Order (Maintenance) Act (1960) as a measure, among other repressive legislation, to try to contain the escalating war, and possibly crush, once and for all, African nationalism. Under this law, certain areas adjoining the border were declared 'No-Go' areas within which any unauthorised person was likely to be taken for a guerrilla and shot on sight, regardless of the time of day or night.[8] Then, in April 1977, the curfew regulations applying to the Chipinga and Melsetter areas were amended to prohibit the movement of all vehicles between sunset and sunrise. It was in January 1978 that the people of Marange and Mukuni African Purchase Area were told to observe curfew running from 6 p.m. to 12 o'clock the next day.[9] It should be noted that Marange was one of the few places where curfew ran from 6 p.m. to 12 noon the next day (See poster below). In Centenary, Mrewa, Mtoko, Mt Darwin, Mudzi and Rushinga areas, the curfew operated from between 5 and 6 p.m. to between 6 and 7 a.m.[10] Interestingly, for Manicaland and, presumably, the whole country, the curfew was only applied to the then TTLs and APAs, and not to the European farming areas, notwithstanding that there were guerrilla activities in these areas as well. One African Member of Parliament wondered whether Europeans did not break the curfew, as he never heard of a European who was ever killed or lost his life as a result of breaking curfew laws, making it abundantly clear that curfew laws were aimed only at one section of the community.[11] But, MP Goddard was quick to counter this, by pointing out that the curfew could only be applied to such areas where the 'terrorist' presence warranted it, but '... because of the fact that European farming areas are better managed and better policed by the people living there, it is not necessary to have a curfew'.[12]

By the end of 1978, the dusk-to-dawn curfew, which covered large parts of the country, was further extended into the urban areas. The Smith regime announced that a 70 km belt of white farmland along the northern and eastern edges of Salisbury (Harare) outer suburbs, separating the city from the TTLs of Chinhamora, Musana and Chikwaka were liable to the curfew.[13] By about the same time, the curfew was also in force in some African townships of Bulawayo.[14] In the same year in September, the Smith regime proclaimed martial law and, by 1979, the whole country was subject to it. According to the authorities, martial law was supposed to lead to tougher and stronger measures against enemies of the state, with the ultimate aim of liquidating the internal organisations associated with 'terrorism'.

Curfew Breakers: Killing with impunity or combating terrorism?

This section provides a general survey of the application of curfew laws in the various parts of the country and concludes that security forces and other officers of the state killed ordinary civilians with impunity. This is particularly

Poster Distributed by District Commissioner, February, 1978

TO THE PEOPLE OF MARANKE TRIBAL TRUST LAND AND MUKUNI AFRICAN PURCHASE AREA

FOR A VERY LONG TIME YOU HAVE CONTINUED TO FEED, SHELTER AND ASSIST THE COMMUNIST TERRORISTS TO CARRY OUT THEIR EVIL DEEDS. YOU HAVE DISREGARDED PREVIOUS GOVERNMENT WARNINGS OF THE BITTER TIMES THAT WILL FALL UPON OUR LAND IF YOU ALLOW THESE COMMUNIST TERRORISTS TO CARRY ON DECEIVING YOU.

THE SECURITY FORCES DO NOT WANT TO ALLOW YOU TO BE DECEIVED BY THESE PEOPLE ANY LONGER.

YOU ARE NOW WARNED THAT AS FROM DAWN ON THE 20TH JANUARY 1978 THE FOLLOWING RESTRICTIONS WILL BE IMPOSED UPON ALL OF YOU AND YOUR TTL AND PURCHASE LAND.

1. HUMAN CURFEW FROM LAST LIGHT TO 12 O'CLOCK DAILY.
2. CATTLE, YOKED OXEN, GOATS AND SHEEP CURFEW FROM LAST LIGHT TO 12 O'CLOCK DAILY.
3. NO VEHICLES INCLUDING BICYCLES AND BUSES TO RUN EITHER THE TTL OR THE APA.
4. NO PERSON WILL EITHER GO ON OR NEAR ANY HIGH GROUND OR THEY WILL BE SHOT.
5. ALL DOGS TO BE TIED UP TO 24 HOURS EACH DAY OR THEY WILL BE SHOT.
6. CATTLE, SHEEP AND GOATS, AFTER 12 O'CLOCK, ARE TO BE HERDED BY ADULTS.
7. NO JUVENILES (TO THE AGE OF 16 YEARS) WILL BE ALLOWED OUT OF THE KRAAL AREA AT ANY TIME EITHER DAY OR NIGHT, OR THEY WILL BE SHOT.
8. NO SCHOOLS WILL BE OPEN.
9. ALL STORES AND GRINDING MILLS WILL BE CLOSED.

ONLY IF YOU CO-OPERATE AND ASSIST THE SECURITY FORCES IN ELIMINATING THE COMMUNIST TERRORISTS WILL ANY CONSIDERATION BE GIVEN TO LIFTING SOME OR ALL OF THE ABOVE RESTRICTIONS. THE SECURITY FORCES HAVE ALREADY TOLD THE COMMUNIST TERRORISTS THAT THEY ARE FREE TO GIVE THEMSELVES UP AND THEIR LIFE WILL NOT BE ENDANGERED.

YOU CAN ASSIST THE COMMUNIST TERRORISTS CAN THEN RETURN TO THEIR ANCESTRAL LANDS AND YOU HAVE PEACE.

Source: Frederikse, J. 1982, *None But Ourselves: Masses vs Media in the Making of Zimbabwe*, Otazi & *Anvil* Press, Harare, p.88.

so given that, under The Indemnity and Compensation Act (1975), civil or criminal proceedings could not be instituted or continued in any court of law against anyone who was believed to have acted in 'good faith' and for purposes of, or, in connection with, the suppression of terrorism.[15] This Act was also a licence to kill, maim and torture with the guarantee that almost anything was legal as long as it was done in 'good faith'. The Act actually gave protection in advance to acts of the executive and its officials and was, therefore, made to apply retrospectively from 1 December 1972. But under Chapter 65, Section 51, Law and Order (Maintenance) Act (1974), it was mandatory for all people to report as soon as possible and reasonably practical and, in any event, within 72 hours, any information people had concerning the presence of 'guerrillas'. The law read, in part: Any person who:

1. On or after the 16th February, 1973, harbours, conceals or assists in any manner whatsoever any person whom he knows or has reason to believe to be a person who is about to commit or has committed or attempted to commit an offence... or,

2. having harboured, concealed, or assisted any person such as is referred to in paragraph (a) ... wilfully omits or refuses after that date to disclose to a police officer any information it is in his power to give in relation to any such person; or

3. being aware, on or after the 16th February 1973, that a person such as is referred to in paragraph (a) is in Rhodesia, fails as soon as is reasonably practicable and in any case within seventy-two hours of that date... to report... any such person;

shall be guilty of an offence and liable to be sentenced to death or to imprisonment for life.[16]

It is undeniable that while some people in the operational zones supported and protected guerrillas willingly, others did so under duress. For the colonial authorities, the ordinary civilians were not only supporting the guerrillas, but were also protecting and harbouring them. The Law and Order Maintenance Act (1974), chapter 65, section 51, officials believed, would therefore help them prosecute people withholding relevant information particularly concerning the whereabouts of guerrillas. But it is Section 53 subsection (1), (2) and (3) of the same law, which directly dealt with curfew and which is quoted here in full to show the dichotomy between the law and its practical application by officers of the state. It read:

1. [W]henever public disorder occurs or is apprehended, a regulating authority may, by order direct that, subject to any exemptions for which provision

may be made by order, no person in the area or in a specific part of the area in respect of which such authority is appointed shall, between such hours as may be specified in the order, be out of doors except with the written permission of such authority.

2. any person who is found out of doors between the hours specified in an order made in terms of such subsection (1) without the written permission of the regulating authority shall be guilty of an offence and liable, on a first conviction, to a *fine not exceeding one hundred dollars or to imprisonment for a period not exceeding six months and, on a subsequent conviction to imprisonment for a period not exceeding one year* [my own emphasis].

3. an order made in terms of this section shall be published by notice distributed among the public or affixed upon public buildings in the area to which the order applies.[17]

This was the law in theory but, in practice, there was the unwritten part of it, which allowed security forces to sentence people to death on sight. This unwritten law carried a maximum death penalty since the security forces had orders to shoot curfew breakers on sight if they did not respond to an order to stop.

This was the unwritten part of the law, which was widely applied throughout the country in areas under curfew regulations. For example, between March 1975 and February 1976, twelve Africans were officially reported shot dead while breaking curfew.[18] However, it is important to note that the number of people shot during the same period could run into treble figures. This is because the authorities had the tendency to play down casualty figures, not only of civilians, but also those of the security forces, while at the same time inflating guerrilla casualty figures upwards. The security forces used this unwritten law to sentence people to death in the war zones rather than through the courts of law.

In practical terms, therefore, the curfew did not safeguard the ordinary person. If one looks at casualty rates in the TTLs and APAs, as MP, Maposa, pointed out, it was neither guerrillas nor the security forces who suffered, but ordinary people.[19] The curfew, therefore, did not protect ordinary people, neither did it effectively deal with the guerrilla threat. Instead it gave the security forces the licence to kill civilians with impunity. For example, in May 1977 in the Buhera TTL at Kandeya School, security forces flew four helicopters and one spotting plane and started firing at the school children and their teachers for allegedly failing to report the presence of guerrillas. In the process, one teacher and three school children were killed while several were injured.[20] In Chendambuya in the Makoni area, a Grade 7 boy, Simon Mututeku, was brought back dead after being taken for questioning by the security forces.[21]

The official report said that he was killed for breaking curfew. In the same area, a couple was shot when they went to assist their neighbour whose child was seriously ill.[22] Again, one woman was shot and seriously injured in the Zimunya TTL while working in her tomato garden. In Marange, a Mrs Tarondwa was shot dead for breaking curfew with the same fate befalling a businessman, a Mr Zvinoera, for breaking the curfew by just a few minutes.[23] Another two Africans were shot dead in Mzarabani Protected Village for breaking curfew.[24]

At the same time, state officials could mete out any punishment they deemed fit on people who were allegedly harbouring or suspected to be harbouring guerrillas. For example, the people of Chiweshe were punished by closing down, among other things, facilities such as schools, shops, stores, mills, clinics, and beer-halls under the threat of 'tell us what you know about the guerrillas or else these facilities remain closed'. Then in July 1974, the entire population of Chiweshe, about 44,000, were put into 21 protected villages as further punishment. The same strategy was applied in Mrewa. Another example of collective punishment was that meted out to the people of Madziwa in 1974, when about 255 Africans were evicted as punishment for supporting and assisting guerrillas and taken to Beit Bridge. All their cattle were sold, while their crops and huts were destroyed.[25] In Buhera, a Mr John Zvoushe had his twelve cattle shot dead for failing to report the presence of guerrillas while a certain Machinya was rendered sterile after a severe beating for allegedly feeding guerrillas.[26] In Marange, a headman and a headboy had their nine sheep and five goats shot dead for failure to report the presence of guerrillas.[27] Apart from these routine punishments, and long prison terms, the government also promised substantial rewards to be paid to any person for 'true' information given to the security forces or any authorities on the whereabouts of 'guerrillas,' their helpers and their weapons.[28]

The above examples show that the ordinary person was in a very difficult position. He/she was caught between the wire and the wall. On the one hand, the ordinary civilian was ordered to provide food and to supply materials to the guerrillas, and, on the other hand, was required to report the presence of guerrillas to the police. While white MPs actually thought that the African people were to blame for not reporting the presence of guerrillas, African MPs wondered what happened to civilians who gave information under duress. Goddard, a white MP could not agree with those MPs who argued that it was the people's fear of guerrilla reprisals that accounted for their failure to report guerrilla presence. As far as he was concerned, the people were protecting guerrillas and the curfew law was, therefore, there to prosecute those withholding the relevant information. Thus, the demands of the security forces, on the one hand, and those of the guerrillas, on the other, left the 'man in the middle' in a serious dilemma. One inhabitant of Chiweshe area in Mashonaland west aptly summed up this dilemma pointing out that, 'If we report to the police, the "guerrillas" kill us. If we do not report, the police torture us. Even if we do report to the police, we are beaten all the same and accused of trying to lead soldiers into a trap. We just do not know what to do'.[29] Even the Minister of Combined Operations admitted that it was an unfortunate aspect of all wars that innocent civilians had to suffer in bearing the burden of conditions that make war necessary, although, he was quick to shift blame to 'those terrorists, to their leaders, to these heads of African Governments and to the Communists...' whom he said were all supposed to share in the infamy of terrorism.[30]

MP Zawaira also told Parliament that the vulnerable position of the 'man in the middle' tended to ignore the fact that the civilian was not armed. He explained;

> And here you will find people who are armed coming into the TTL village with deadly weapons asking you to cook food for them, and where is the co-operation when a man pointing a loaded gun at my head, and he is saying 'cook....' Where does this element of co-operation come in? If it happened that Europeans... were to... go to the TTLs... they would cook faster than we do.[31]

When R. Sadomba, MP for Nemakonde, asked the Minister of Defence, P.K. Van de Byl, to apply strict discipline to his soldiers who shot curfew breakers indiscriminately, he drew the wrath of the Minister who responded in no uncertain terms, 'I have no intention of attempting to do anything about this and as far as I am concerned, the more curfew breakers that are shot the better, and the sooner it is realised everywhere the better. We are fighting a war and this is not some gentle exercise, which we are doing for the fun of it'.[32]

This response was not only a clear testimony of the atrocities his forces were committing, but also a vindication of them. Notwithstanding this arrogance, black parliamentarians continued to demand that the House deplore the laws governing curfew in the light of the continued indiscriminate shooting of people. On 22 February 1978, MP Mabika, together with MP Nyandoro, tabled a motion asking the House to deplore the laws and regulations relating to the curfew and the failure to report the presence of guerrillas. MP Mabika asked Parliament for certain amendments to be made to the curfew laws. He demanded:

> We feel that... adjustments or amendments may be made whereby... each particular case should be reviewed or examined by the security forces

> concerned and, in certain circumstances, it will be better if this particular law is waived slightly in which it will be better to punish or arrest the curfew-breaker concerned instead of shooting him right away. We find in this country – and in other countries – that a person who commits murder is brought before the courts of law. We feel that it will be justifiable for the people breaking curfew laws on a circumstantial basis to be arrested, charged, or brought before the courts of law.[33]

Unfortunately, these calls counted for nothing as the security forces continued to kill with impunity. Yet, something must be said about the contradictions within the curfew laws. For example, while making it mandatory to report the presence of guerrillas, distance was never taken into consideration. The people of Marange, for instance, stayed 39 km from the nearest police camp at Odzi, while those in Makoni and Mutasa stayed even further away. In the absence of buses and bicycles, it is hard to imagine how this distance could be covered, therefore, making it impossible to report within the stipulated period. Moreover, one may ask, how was one supposed to go and make a report without breaking the curfew and without risking being shot? Again, curfew laws and regulations did not guarantee the safety of disabled people—blind, deaf or otherwise, let alone the elderly. It was in the light of some of these inconsistencies that many MPs from the opposition, mainly black parliamentarians, called for realistic legislation, which did not create criminals, but which allowed people to observe the law.

It must also be mentioned here that the struggle to win the 'hearts and minds' of the 'man in the middle' is at the centre of every struggle. In Rhodesia's war, just like in any other war, the 'man in the middle' was the jewel of both the guerrillas and the government. From the revolutionaries' perspective, the war was being fought on behalf of the people, and, therefore, that expected all African people to support the war. It was in this context that the guerrillas saw all those who did not lend the necessary support as 'enemies of the people' and lackeys of the regime who, therefore, deserved to be attacked, whether armed or not. This explains why the guerrillas, just like the security forces, sometimes used force, punishment and terror tactics in order to force people to render them the necessary support. While the intention was to subvert the confidence of the people in the regime and, hopefully, hasten its collapse, the guerrillas also worsened the suffering of the people. MP Mabika pointed out that 'they too [the guerrillas] are not guiltless of the blood, nor the misery that has been the lot of so many of our innocent civilians'.[34]

On the other hand, the incumbent regime held unrealistic views concerning the role the people must play in eliminating terrorism. The regime expected everyone to be law-abiding and that all had a legal obligation to assist in combating terrorism. If by commission or omission, they failed to in this duty, or if they actually appeared to support the 'rebels', then they were also treated as terrorists, thus becoming real objects of counter-insurgent attack, as the examples cited here have shown. Thus, it is no wonder why the security forces killed civilians with impunity and in the name of combating terrorism.

Curfew laws and the people of Marange, Makoni and Mutasa

Drawing largely from the oral testimonies collected from eastern Zimbabwe, this section discusses how the ordinary person, 'the man in the middle', understood and experienced the curfew in these administrative districts.[35] It discusses the practical experiences of the curfew by the people of Marange, Makoni and Mutasa districts particularly between 1977 and 1980. And again it can be shown that through human and livestock casualty figures, that security forces continued to kill with impunity. This part of the paper also discusses the various implications and consequences of the curfew. Of course, this section does not pretend to cover the three districts in equal breadth and neither does it claim to do the same even for a single district.[36]

As already mentioned, in Marange, the curfew was declared in February 1978 through a poster distributed by the Marange District Commissioner. The poster stated, among other things, the imposition of restrictive conditions. These included the human curfew from dusk to 12 o'clock daily, cattle, yoked oxen, goats and sheep curfew from last dusk to 12 o'clock daily, closure of all stores, schools and grinding mills, a ban on all vehicles, bicycles and buses in the area. Dogs were to remain tied for 24 hours each day. Furthermore, no person was allowed to go on or near high ground, and only adults were allowed to herd cattle, with all children below 16 years banned from going out of their village area at any time, day or night.[37] Anyone who violated these 'regulations' was shot on sight and without warning, and yet the law allowed for a maximum prison sentence not exceeding six months, and on a subsequent conviction, to imprisonment for a period not exceeding one year.

In Makoni and Mutasa, no official declaration was made either through a circular or poster, as the law required, yet the people of these two districts were supposed to observe the curfew from 6 p.m. to 10 a.m.[38] In fact, District Commissioners differed in the manner in which they enforced the curfew. In some areas, curfew times were from 6 p.m. to 6 a.m., in others, it was from 6 p.m. to 9 a.m., while in yet others; it was from 6 p.m. to 11 a.m. It was, therefore, the prerogative of the District Commissioner to spell out curfew times in his area. But as already mentioned, the people of Marange and Mushawasha observed the longest known curfew in the country. One of the interviewees from Marange, Mrs. Chikambiro Marange, had the following to say about the curfew in her area: 'it was a terrible time indeed. We were told that we were restricted to just the cleared areas around our homes *(chivanze)*, at any time before 12 o'clock. We were also told that we could not graze our cattle before 12 noon, neither could we go to the fields before that time'.[39]

While most people interviewed could remember very well when curfew was declared, 1977 in Makoni and Mutasa, and 1978 in Marange, they tended to vary in their understanding of the intentions of the curfew declaration. The curfew imposed upon the people of Marange, Makoni and Mutasa and their livestock was a form of 'house arrest'. For the people of Marange, it lasted 18 hours (6 p.m.–12 noon the following day), while for those of Makoni and Mutasa, it lasted about 16 hours (6 p.m.–10 a.m. the following day). The official intention of curfew declaration, as already stated, was to assist the military forces to deal with the people that were causing trouble and, in the process, helping or protecting the rural population. In Mrs Chikambiro's view, this is the reason why the security forces shot on sight any person who dared move a few metres from his/her homestead outside the regulated time. They (security forces) also moved from house to house, in search of 'guerrillas', shooting anyone whom they regarded as one or anyone who sympathised with them. It is interesting to note that some informants tended to buy the idea that 'guerrillas' could easily disappear or transform themselves into several forms of life. These ranged from changing into a cow, a donkey, a goat, a dog, a cat, to a hare, a small girl, woman or even a cabbage.[40] However, this was hardly so, and, in any case, the Rhodesian security forces were a professionally trained and highly skilled fighting unit to believe this kind of myth.

It is important to point out some of the implications of this myth, bearing in mind that both the security forces and the guerrillas were involved in myth-making for their own ends. First, for the guerrillas, it gave them some degree of sophistication by being seen as people capable of performing mysterious things. And, secondly, for the security forces, it allowed them to use excessive force and to kill willy-nilly because, for them, they would maintain that it was impossible to make a distinction between who was or was not a guerrilla. According to both Mrs Chikambiro and Morgen Tichafa Tarugarira, the first soldiers who came to Marange, and who often painted their faces in black tar, had this silly belief that a guerrilla or 'terrorist' was something totally different from a normal human being. 'If soldiers were to ask what a guerrilla looked like', reminiscences Mrs Chikambiro, 'we would conveniently say a guerrilla looks like a hare'.[41] This had the effect of reinforcing further the myth of mutation, and possibly gave the security forces an alibi to kill indiscriminately.

The exact number of people shot dead for breaking curfew in Marange, Makoni and Mutasa is difficult to say, and so are the figures for livestock. Causality figures varied from one informant to another, even for the same locality and from as low as twenty to as many as several thousands. For Marange, casualty figures varied from as few as fifty to as many as several thousands.[42] But disparities aside, all the informants pointed out that many of those shot dead were shot on sight and without warning. The security forces' philosophy seemed to be 'shoot first and ask questions later' as the confession by Gordon Wood, an ex-Grenadier Guardsman and deserter from the Rhodesian Army, shows. 'One soldier called me a murderer for shooting two men who turned out not to have weapons. But they were out during curfew, and you can't say: "Excuse me, have you got a grenade or a gun?" You shoot first and ask questions after if you want to continue living. Even so it is all wrong'.[43]

Gwani Kashaya from Marange claims to know several people who were shot dead for breaking the curfew in Marange, including one man who was shot in broad daylight while fetching water from a nearby stream. According to Kashaya, the man intended to administer the water to his patients, as he was a faith healer.[44] There were also those who were shot while on their way home, from a beer drink/party.[45] In Mapararikwa, Kashaya remembers six girls being shot dead, four of them on their way home from a nearby stream where they had gone to do some laundry. The security forces assumed that the young girls were *chimbwindos* (women collaborators) who were on their way to a guerrilla base. The fifth one, about seven years old, was shot for attempting to flee after catching sight of soldiers who were carrying guns. The sixth was shot a few metres from her homestead after she had attempted to sneak out before time to go and see her grandmother who was seriously ill.[46] Other innocent lives were also lost while gathering wild fruits in order to supplement their food.[47]

In terms of livestock, people in the three districts were unanimous that very few cattle were shot for 'breaking' curfew, although they say that several of their cattle were never found after going astray as the curfew militated against any follow-up system once cattle went missing. 'As far as I know I don't remember any cattle which were shot dead by the soldiers for breaking curfew except those which were mistaken for the enemy particularly during the night'[48] said Tarugarira. Several people said that the soldiers did not particularly mind animals except when they suspected that guerrillas were using cattle as a form of cover to enter the locality.

Yet, besides the indiscriminate shooting of curfew breakers, there were other problems and hardships associated with the curfew in these areas. For instance, the curfew obviously disrupted the normal agricultural cycle, and, consequently, people were faced with the threat of starvation. However, none of my informants could remember ever hearing of anyone who starved to death because of the curfew. The curfew also meant that baboons and other wild animals could destroy the green maize fields at will, as people could not 'step out' to chase them away without risking being shot. Equally true, cattle could break out of their pens and devour the green maize without anyone doing anything as long as it was before the gazetted time as anyone who dared to 'step out' was sure to be killed.

For pregnant and expecting mothers and the sick, the curfew was the last thing they ever wanted to hear.[49] For example, while the Marange Clinic remained operational throughout the curfew period, it was also subject to the same times, 6 p.m.-12 midday. This meant that the sick or any other people requiring urgent medical attention could only be attended to after 12 midday for those in Marange, and after 10 a.m. for those in Makoni and Mutasa. This presumably led to deaths, which could have been avoided, although my interviewees do not remember any such deaths. When an African MP stated in Parliament that many pregnant women had died because of the curfew, he drew wrath of the white Minister of Health, who told him, 'Surely the honourable Member is aware that the closure of these services was not the fault of this Minister, or indeed this Government. It was the cause of the vermin who made it impossible to continue running these services and of the local people who supported these vermin'.[50]

Furthermore, the curfew also meant that proper burials of the deceased became a thing of the past. Most of the informants said that the curfew had made the burying of the dead difficult. The deceased were buried in shallow graves hastily dug in order to keep within the framework of the curfew. For the urban dwellers, or at least those who worked in town, it sometimes became impossible to attend the funerals of their close relatives. Clifford Chingwende failed to attend his father's funeral because he could not get transport from Mutare where he was working.[51] Serina Marange said that her aunt's funeral was poorly attended, with no people staying behind to console the bereaved family, as everyone was worried about getting home before 6 p.m.[52] She says that her aunt, a mother of five children, had been shot for breaking the curfew a few minutes before 12 o'clock. MP Nyandoro also told Parliament that Mr Zvinoera, a businessman from Marange, lost his life when he met a security man who looked at his watch and said, 'It is ten minutes to twelve. Why are you out?', before shooting him dead.[53] Moreover, the security forces did not permit anyone shot for breaking curfew to be buried outside the main curfew time table, nor his/her body to be collected for burial outside the stated times unless they sanctioned it. By implication, for anyone shot just after 6 p.m.

his/her body spent the whole night at the mercy of the vultures.[54] At times the security forces prevented the burials of those who would have been killed on the suspicion that they were guerrillas. For instance, security forces are said to have prevented the burial of two bodies they had dumped at Marange Township, claiming that the two were guerrillas. For two weeks the bodies were left in the open to decompose, until Chief Marange had to take the law into his own hands and ordered their burial.[55] Informants say that chief Marange was lucky to get away with a caution for defying security forces' order.

The banning of the herding of cattle by the juveniles implied several things. While some interviewees felt that this move was harsh, others applauded it. Those who felt it was harsh pointed to the shortage of labour, not only to till the fields, but for the various other day to day activities. It meant that adults had to herd the cattle while the kids remained confined to the homestead. Those who applauded it did so for two reasons. Firstly, they felt that children were likely to run away upon coming across people carrying guns, thereby risking being shot unlike adults, and, secondly, that children were not better placed to find enough pastures for cattle within a period as short as six hours. 'Can you imagine something that feeds for twelve hours each day now being restricted to less than six hours. Do you think kids would be able to find better pastures in so short a time?'[56] asked Chandaoneswa Marange. Given the short grazing hours, the quality of cattle naturally deteriorated, while the death rate was frightful due to inadequate grazing time.[57] In the view of one informant, the young boys and girls were banned from herding cattle as they were regarded as 'mobile phones' by the security forces. Furthermore, the curfew prevented any search for any livestock that would have gone astray.

A further consequence of the curfew was to force people to come up with alternative survival strategies. In this regard, the role played by women stands out clearly. With no grinding mills around, the women did everything they could to produce maize-meal. The two options, which were open to them at the time, were equally taxing to say the least. The first option involved making/drilling holes through an iron sheet using nails. Then the rough side of the sheet would be used to make maize-meal, which would collect into a sack or dish or winnowing basket placed underneath the sheet.[58] This maize-meal would then be turned into a finer form through the grinding stone or, alternatively, through the use of a sieve. The other option, which has been in use from time immemorial, was the use of a pestle and mortar, before subjecting the resultant maize-meal to the grinding stone. Of course, this method worked better with bulrush millet (*mhunga*) than with maize.

Again, according to several informants, the other consequence was that many youths were pushed into the war and into 'guerrilla' training because they could not withstand the shocking, callous and heartless murder of innocent people whose bodies would be displayed for everyone to see. In many cases, it turned out that victims were *mujibhas* (male war collaborators). The security forces thought that by publicly displaying bodies of the so-called 'guerrillas', people would be deterred from joining 'guerrilla' training. Instead, several young men left en masse for training. But it must also be pointed out that curfew had a regulating effect on the social behaviour of people, especially on drinking patterns. People were now getting home early to avoid breaking the curfew laws.

The resultant hardships brought upon the people of Marange, Makoni and Mutasa, whether as a direct or indirect result of the security forces or the guerrillas, as far as the inhabitants of these areas were concerned, succeeded in hardening their attitude towards the security forces and the incumbent regime. Consequently, curfew laws and regulations proved counterproductive, as they tended to increase the resistance of the people to the government and therefore hastened the collapse of the Smith regime.

Conclusion

The main arguments of this chapter is that curfew was used by officers of the regime as a licence to kill ordinary civilians with impunity. It has also been shown that there were serious contradictions within the laws and regulations governing the curfew, both in theory and in practice. Through the voices of the people of Marange, Makoni and Mutasa, the chapter has not only captured the peoples' sad memories and experiences, but also demonstrated the very delicate and difficult position of the 'man in the middle.'

Notes

1. The paper's title is borrowed in part from the Catholic Institute for International Relations 1975 publication entitled *The Man in the Middle: Torture, resettlement and eviction.* Here, the 'man in the middle' was seen as that unarmed ordinary civilian who had to contend with demands of the Rhodesian authorities, on the one hand, and the guerrillas, on the other. It must, therefore, be stated that the so-called 'man in the middle' was not as neutral as the term seems to imply as the ordinary person either sided or sympathised with the regime or the guerrillas.
2. The terms 'terrorist' and 'terrorism' are of recent date. According to a French Dictionary published in 1796, the Jacobins had on occasion used the term when speaking and writing about themselves in a positive sense. After the 9th Thermidor, 'terrorist' became a term of abuse with criminal implications and it is in this context that the Rhodesian state used the term. However, in this paper the term 'guerrilla' will be used where previously terrorist had been employed. During the period under study the Rhodesians did not accept the term 'guerrilla'. For instance, MP Dewa, for Matojeni, was asked by the Speaker of Parliament in February

1978 to withdraw the words 'guerrilla forces' in a motion on the subject because in his view it implied 'an aura of respectability to guerrilla activities... ' See Southern Rhodesia, *House of Assembly Debates*, Vol. 97, February, 1978, col. 2327. See also Southern Rhodesia, *House of Assembly Debates*, Vol. 89, January, 1975.
3. The initial fieldwork had its bad memories. On 2 November 1999, I lost about 270 hours of interview tape in a car accident on my way back from the field. I also lost my Mazda 323 in that accident. It was then that I realised I should have taken David Henige's advice seriously as he warns researchers, 'many historians have heard tales about field notes that were lost or destroyed through water damage, fire, mechanical error, errant mails, etc... The most obvious and necessary precaution is making a second tape and keep these in a different place than the originals', writes D. Henige, *Oral Historiography* (Longmans, London, 1982), p. 50.
4. P. L. Moorcraft, *Contact II: The Struggle for Peace*, (Sygma Books, Johannesburg, 1981), p. 66. According to Moorcraft, the Rhodesian army had either closely studied or actually fought in the Malaya counter-insurgency operations and had also learnt their lessons from the British as their army was based not only upon British traditions, but it also employed British tactics as well as Israel Entebbe-style raids.
5. For example, a district assistant shot two Africans in Mzarabani Protected Village for breaking curfew. Moreover, those in the protected villages were not allowed to take food with them to their fields for fear that they might end up giving it to the guerrillas. Thus, people naturally went the whole day without food, causing serious hardships on the people who would have spent the whole day in the fields.
6. Southern Rhodesia, *Rhodesia of House Assembly Debates*, vol. 97, February, 1978, col. 2259-2260.
7. Catholic Commission for Justice and Peace (CCJP), *The Man in the Middle: torture, resettlement and eviction*, (CIIR, London, 1975), p.1-18; See also M. Mushonga, 'The Formation, Organization and Activities of the Catholic Commission for Justice Peace in Zimbabwe: With special reference to the Rhodesian War, 1972-1980', Unpublished B.A. (Honours) Dissertation, University of Zimbabwe, History Department, 1990, p.18.
8. For example, Raymond Kunaka and George Gunda, both Form 2 students at Mazoe Secondary School, were shot by security forces for allegedly being found in the no-go areas in 1975. See Box 322, Jesuit Archives (JA), Prestage House, Harare. See also M. Mushonga, 'The Catholic Commission', pp. 16-17; 58-60.
9. The 6 p.m. to 12 o'clock curfew also applied in the Mushawasha area of the Victoria Province (Masvingo). See Southern Rhodesia, *House of Assembly Debates*, Vol. 97, February, 1978, col. 2274; International Commission of Jurists (ICJ), *Racial Discrimination and Repression in Southern Rhodesia*, (CIIR, London, 1976), p.67.
10. Ibid.
11. Southern Rhodesia, *House of Rhodesia Assembly Debates*, Vol. 97, February, 1978, col. 2243. MP Bwanya also pointed out that there was no curfew along certain sections of the tarred roads, for example between Featherstone and Enkeldoorn because Europeans frequently used them. He thus deplored the variations in curfew regulations.

12. Ibid., col. 2300.
13. National Archives of Zimbabwe, MS 590/10, Rhodesia Security, 1973-1978.
14. Ibid. Maybe the reason for declaring curfew in the African townships of Bulawayo is closely related to the belief that Zipra had an urban warfare approach in its operational areas as opposed to Zanla. James Muzondidya, in his discussion of Coloured feelings of marginality vis-à-vis the 1979 Lancaster House Constitution shows that security in the Coloured areas close to African townships such as Thorngrove had deteriorated as the war intensified and curfew seemed to be the answer. See. J. Muzondidya, 'The most obscene fraud of the 20th century?' The Lancaster House Constitution, African majority rule and Coloured peoples' feelings of marginality', Seminar paper presented to the Human Rights and Democracy Seminar Series, History Department, University of Zimbabwe, 5 October 2000. See also City of Bulawayo, Mayor's Minutes for the year ended 31 July, 1979.
15. Southern Rhodesia, *Statute Law of Rhodesia*, Acts 1-47, 1975, pp. 446-7.
16. Southern Rhodesia, *Statute Law of Rhodesia*, Vol. 2, Chapter 65. col. 251.
17. Ibid.
18. ICJ, *Racial Discrimination and Repression in Southern Rhodesia*, p.59. Two of those twelve shot dead were students from Mazoe Secondary School. A statement by the Rhodesia Ministry of Information alleged that the two were shot in the Nyamaropa border area, 125 km north of Umtali. Investigations later revealed that the two were not shot in the Inyanga area but somewhere in the Mazoe area. See Jesuit Archives, Box 322, Raymund Kunaka File, Prestage House, Mt. Pleasant, Harare. See also M. Mushonga, 'The Formation, Organisation and Activities of the Catholic Commission for Justice and Peace in Rhodesia: With particular reference to the Rhodesian War, 1972-1980', B.A. Honours (History) Dissertation, University of Zimbabwe, 1990. pp. 16-17.
19. Southern Rhodesia, *House of Rhodesia Assembly Debates* Vol. 97, 1978, Col. 2266.
20. Ibid., col. 2234. Bishop Donal Lamont, the Roman Catholic Bishop of Umtali (Mutare) and President of the Catholic Commission for Justice and Peace (CCJP) in Rhodesia and his staff at Avila Mission should have faced the same fate for failing to report the presence of guerrillas. Instead, Lamont was simply deported. The offence committed by Lamont carried a possible death sentence or life imprisonment but the Government neither sentenced him to death nor sent him to prison as they felt that would have given him 'spectacular martyrdom'. According to Lamont, he purposely defied the law in order to focus international attention on the dilemma facing priests and the 'man in the middle' in the Rhodesian war zone.
21. Ibid., col. 2344.
22. Ibid., col. 2245.
23. Ibid., col. 2246-7.
24. Ibid., col. 2270.
25. M. Meredith, *The Past is Another Country; Rhodesia 1890-1979*, (Andre Deutsch, London, 1979), p.136.
26. Southern Rhodesia, *House of Assembly Debates*, Vol. 97, 1978, col. 2235-2236.
27. Ibid., col. 2235-2236.

28. J. Frederikse, *None But Ourselves: Masses Vs Media in the Making of Zimbabwe*, (Otazi, Harare, 1983), pp. 90-91. See also Southern Rhodesia, *House of Assembly Debates*, Vol. 97, col. 2248. MP Nyandoro pointed out that there were many Africans serving long and heavy jail sentences because they failed to report guerrillas, and yet the government did not have the mechanism to say whether or not one failed to report deliberately. Again he made it clear that it was difficult to report the presence of 'our own daughters and sons'.
29. ICJ, *Racial Discrimination and Repression in Southern Rhodesia*, pp. 86-7; See also M. Mushonga, 'The Catholic Commission', p. 18.
30. Southern Rhodesia, *House of Assembly Debates*, Vol. 97, 1978, cols. 2304-2305.
31. Ibid., Col. 2272.
32. Southern Rhodesia, *House of Assembly Debates*, Vol. 90, 1975, col. 1706.
33. Southern Rhodesia, *House of Assembly Debates*, Vol. 97, 1978, col. 2234.
34. Southern Rhodesia, *House of Rhodesia Assembly Debates*, Vol. 97, 1978, col. 2232.
35. Real names of people who gave evidence are used here as none of them requested anonymity. However, my sincerest apologies to them if what I record here was taken out of context.
36. This is because in all the three districts research was confined to within 500 to 1000 metres accessible by road given the small car this researcher was using.
37. Ibid.
38. Interview with Violet Serede, an ordinary villager in Chikumbu village, Mutasa, 27 January 2000; Alexander Nyamatanga, Chemhere village, Makoni, 27 January 2000. One Group interview I had also confirmed this.
39. Interview with Mrs Chikambiro Marange, the wife of the incumbent Chief Marange, Marange homestead, 28 October 1999. See also Southern Rhodesia, *House of Assembly Debates*, Vol. 97, 1978, col. 2274.
40. Interview with Mrs Marange, 28 October 1999; Violet Serede, 27 January 2000; Alexander Nyamatanga, 27 January 2000; Interview with Morgen Muchafa Tarugarira, Marange Township, 29 October 1999. As if to confirm the myth, Never Gandira Marange, in an interview, Marange homestead, 28 October 1999, says that the curfew did not particularly affect them as his late father had the magical powers to suddenly 'disappear' once confronted by the Rhodesian security forces.
41. Interview with Mrs Chikambiro and Mr Tarugarira, 28 October 1999.
42. Never Marange put the figure at 1000, Morgen Tarugarira at 270, Clifford Chingwende at 47. Violet Serede at 4, Alexander Nyamatanga at 23.
43. National Archives of Zimbabwe, MS 590/10, Curfew breakers shot, May 1977.
44. Interview with Gwani Kashaya, 28 October 1999.
45. The following were given to me by Never, Jebwede, Chandaoneswa and Morgen as names of some of those who were shot dead while at /or coming from a beer drink/party. Their names are Gede and his son, Manzwi and his son, Dekete, Kauzini, Benjamin, Kwenga, Gibson Pundo, and Gedion and his son.
46. Interview with Kashaya, 28 October 1999.
47. Interview with Mrs. Chikambiro, 28 October 1999.
48. Ibid.

49. While I have no statistics from my case studies of mothers who died as a result of pregnancy related pains, Hansard of 1978, Vol. 97, records a one such woman in the Hurungwe North area, Mashonaland West.
50. ICJ, *Racial Discrimination*, p.64.
51. Interview with Clifford Chingwende, Marange, 30 October 1999.
52. Interview with Serina Marange, Marange Township, 30 October 1999.
53. Southern Rhodesia, *House of Assembly Debates*, 1978, col. 2248.
54. Interview with Morgen, 29 October 1999.
55. Interviews with Never, Jebwede, Morgen and Chandaoneswa Marange, 29 October 1999.
56. Interview with Chandaoneswa, 29 October 1999.
57. Southern Rhodesia, *House of Assembly Debates*, Vol. 97, 1978, col. 2274-2275.
58. Interviews with Lydia, Mrs Chikambiro, Jebwede and Tarugarira, Marange, 28-30 October 1999.

References

Catholic Commission for Justice and Peace (CCJP), 1975, *The Man in the Middle: Torture, Resettlement and Eviction*, CIIR: London

Frederikse, J., 1983, *None But Ourselves: Masses vs Media in the Making of Zimbabwe*, Harare: Otazi.

Henige, D., 1982, *Oral Historiography*, London: Longman.

International Commission of Jurists (ICJ), 1976, *Racial Discrimination and Repression in Southern Rhodesia*, London: CIIR

Meredith, M., 1979, *The Past is Another Country: Rhodesia 1890-1979*, London: Andre Deutsch

Moorcraft, P.L., 1981, *Contact II: The Struggle for Peace*, Johannesburg: Sygma Books.

Mushonga, M., 1990, 'The Formation, Organisation and Activities of the Catholic Commission for Justice Peace in Zimbabwe-with special reference to the Rhodesian War, 1972-1980', Unpublished B.A. (Hons) Dissertation, University of Zimbabwe, Zimbabwe.

Muzondidya, J., 2000, 'The Most Obscene Fraud of the 20th Century? The Lancaster House Constitution, African Majority rule and Coloured Peoples' Feelings of Marginality', Paper presented to the 'Human Rights and Democracy' Seminar Series, History Department, University of Zimbabwe.

Southern Rhodesia, 1978, *Rhodesia House of Assembly Debates*, Vol. 97, February

Southern Rhodesia, 1975, *House of Assembly Debates*, Vol. 89, January

Southern Rhodesia, 1975, House of Assembly Debates, Vol. 90

Interviews

Alexander Nyamatange, Chimhere Village, 27 January 2000

Chandaoneswa Marange, 29 October 1999

Clifford Chingwende, Marange, 30 October 1999

Mrs Chikambiro Marange, Lydia, Jebwede and Morgen Tarugarira, Marange, 28-30 October 1999

Gwani Kashaya, 28 October 1999
Violet Serede, Chikumbu Village, 27 January 2000
Never Gandira Marange, Marange Homestead, 28 October, 1999

Archival Material(s)
National Archives of Zimbabwe, MS 590/10

10

'Your Obedient Servant or Your Friend': Forms of Address in Letters Among British Administrators and Batswana Chiefs

Mompoloki Bagwasi

Introduction

In the late 1800s, Bechuanaland, now Botswana, and other less powerful nations neighbouring South Africa were in danger of being annexed to South Africa by the powerful Boers who ruled it then. Bechuanaland asked for protection from the British government, and in 1885 it was declared a British protectorate. However, before British protection, the country was ruled by local chiefs who had a great deal of power over the people, the land, and were responsible for issuing mine prospecting permits. The advent of the British in 1885 called for a redefining and regulation of the powers of the chiefs, a step that naturally bred misunderstandings and strains in the relationship between local Batswana chiefs and British administrators.

Using a corpus of 200 letters written during the protectorate period (1885–1966) by and to the British administrators on one hand and letters written by and to Batswana chiefs on the other hand, this chapter aims to explore the type of relationship that existed between the British administrators and Batswana chiefs during the protectorate days. This relationship is assessed by examining the type of address forms used in the salutations and signatures of the letters. The chapter argues that the two groups sought linguistic means of dealing with the strife between them by use of or failure to use certain address forms. For example, the British administrators used the signature 'your obedient servant' when writing to fellow British administrators but rarely when writing to Batswana chiefs, suggesting that a Briton could not be a servant of a Motswana chief. Similarly, the address term 'friend' which connotes equality and solidarity is only found in letters from British administrators to Batswana chiefs but is rare in British administrator to British administrator correspondence. In this chapter, the African liberation struggle and the history of colonisation in Africa is investigated from a language point of view and, thus, contributes towards debates on this issue by adding a language dimension.

Analysis of the letters

The letters used in this analysis are authentic and were obtained from the Botswana National Archives in Gaborone between August 2000 and June 2001. The letters are divided into two broad categories. The first category consists of letters written by the British administrators who mostly worked as officials in the British administration as High Commissioners, Deputy High Commissioners, Resident Commissioners, Governors, Magistrates, etc. This category is further divided into two parts: letters written by the British administrators to other British administrators, and letters written by British administrators to Batswana chiefs. The second category consists mainly of letters written by Batswana chiefs. This category, too, has two parts: letters written by Batswana to the British administrators, and those written by Batswana to other Batswana.

Letters by British administrators to other British administrators

Salutations and openings

In this category 43 out of 45 (or 95 percent) of letters from one British administrator to another employ a formal salutation such as: *Dear Sir, Sir, Your honour*, or the addressee's name or official title. It is only in two cases that elaborate praise or greetings such as 'May it please your excellency' is used in the salutation. This finding suggests that the relationship between the addressee and the reader for one British administrator writing to another is formal and professional, allowing very little intimacy. The following examples illustrate the kind of salutations and opening sentences of letters of this kind.

> Excerpt 1
> My dear Colonel,
> It appears Bathoen became infatuated with a local girl who is no class and she seems to get control of him.
> (Signature of letter not legible, To Colonel Sir Carrington, 6 February 1929 S 5/5).

Excerpt 2
Sir,
I have the honour to inform you in reply to yours of 15 inst. with reference to the inquiry as to whether we intend charging a commission on sums of money transferred to the credit of the deputy commissioner in Bechuanaland at Kimberly, that we have much pleasure in making the said transfers at par.
(Letter from imperial secretary, signature not legible, to High Commissioner 25 April 1884 *HC 65/14*).

The letters written by British administrators to other British administrators do not only have formal salutations but they also include direct opening sentences that immediately present the issue that the author wants to discuss. Merkestein (1998) remarks that British letter writing style is more direct because the norms of British English fellowship dictate that expositions must be rational and since reason and emotion are felt to be diametrically opposed, the overt expression of feelings, attitude and emotions must be avoided as much as possible.

Signatures and endings
The signatures of these letters are also simple, formal and formulaic. In the current data the most popular signature is 'your obedient servant' which is employed in 22 out of 45 letters (or 45 percent). This signature seems to convey reverence and respect for the high status of the addressee and is therefore mostly used by a low status person writing to a high status person. It is also formulaic, used by most of the writers and sometimes not even written in full but abbreviated to 'I am your etc'. The rest of the letters, 23 out of 45 (or 51 percent) use other formal signatures such as 'yours sincerely', 'yours truly', or 'with kind regards I remain'. Once again, the formal and formulaic endings and signatures in these letters suggest a formal, professional and faceless type of relationship in which colloquial and intimate language does not have a place. The letters have one function: to convey official business. The following examples illustrate the type of endings and signatures found in the letters of the British administrators to other British administrators.

Exerpt 3
It occurs to me that perhaps some of the sentences in this communication may appear at a distance to be too strongly expressed. My apology, it could be due to my sense of magnitude of the imminence of the question, which alone could have induced me to write at all.
With every expression of respect, I remain.
Your excellency's humble servant,

John Mackenzie
(Letter from John Mackenzie to Sir Henry Berkly, 2 May 1876 *HC 48/1/2*).

Excerpt 4

I asked him if he is satisfied, he said 'no' and then again he said if you are only riding past it is all right, but you must do nothing.
I have the honour to be etc.
J. Vosthurgen
(Letter from J.Vosthurgen to High Commissioner, 19 February 1889 *HC 25/42*).

Letters by the British administrators to Batswana chiefs

It is through these letters that we obtain an insight into the controversial relationship between the British administrators and Batswana chiefs. It should be noted that during the 1800s and 1900s when these letters were written, white people in South Africa were considered to be superior to black people, so the kind of relationship that existed between British administrators and Batswana chiefs had its roots on the struggles that existed between blacks and whites. Though Bechuanaland did not have a white government in the same way that South Africa and Rhodesia did, it was a British protectorate and the British administered and oversaw the country by means of a small administration based in Mafeking, South Africa. The terms of the protectorate were that the British protect Batswana country from annexation to South Africa but leave the governance of the country to the local chiefs. However, that situation could not be maintained, and the British ended up assuming more power than the chiefs had anticipated (Tlou and Campbell 1984). This obviously caused conflicts and overlaps in the duties and powers of the British administrators and Batswana chiefs, who before the advent of the British administration were the sole rulers of the land and people. The forms of address found in the correspondence between the British administrators and Batswana chiefs serve to shed some light into the kind of relationship that existed between these two groups.

Salutations and openings

The form of address in the letters written by the British administrators to Batswana chiefs is less formal than that found in British administrators writing to other British administrators. The letters mostly employ an informal and intimate address form, 'my friend'. Of the 23 letters written by the British administrators to Batswana chiefs, 18 of them (or 78 percent) employ the salutation 'my friend'. This finding is significant and interesting since it is rare in British administrator to British administrator correspondence. The use of such an informal and intimate address form suggests that although the British administrators were very formal in their correspondence with other British administrators they did not need to be formal in their correspondence and interaction with Batswana chiefs.

The Oxford Reference English Dictionary (1996: 555) defines 'friend' as a person with whom one enjoys mutual affection and regard. Therefore, the address term, 'My friend' in these letters can be interpreted to be a neutral address form that connotes solidarity, equality, intimacy and informality. The use of this salutation establishes a solidarity and closer relationship between the British and the local chiefs and bridges the gap of subordinate and boss between the two groups. It is only in a few instances that formal salutations such as 'Dear sir' or title of addressee or their name is used in these letters. The following exemplify the kind of salutations and openings found in letters from British administrators to Batswana chiefs.

Excerpt 5
My friend Sechele,
When I visited Molepolole last month an address of welcome was presented to me by you and your people and I told you in reply to certain points therein that I was unable to say anything relative thereto without first consulting Mr. Barry.
(Letter from assistant commissioner to Chief Sechele, 24 February 1912, *S 42*).

Excerpt 6
To the kafir chief Khama,
Friend, I have received your letter about complaints against Khamane and will in answer inform you that I have referred the matter to my native of Lurtenburg, Mr Polfiator.
(Letter from S.G.R. Kruger, State President of South Africa, to Chief Khama, 30 March 1885, *HC 5/12*).

Excerpt 7
Chief,
Herewith I give you notice and forbid you absolutely from trespassing on Transvaal ground as is already done by your people and warn you in the name of the South African Republic not to lay your hands upon the crops sown by your people in the boundary of the South African Republic.
(Letter from Native Commissioner, Mafeking to Chief Ikaning, 7 March 1887, *HC 12/18*).

The opening sentences of these letters are also for the most part direct, immediately stating the issue. It is important to note that though the address form 'my friend' connotes solidarity, equality, and intimacy, these sentiments are contradicted in some of the letters where the authors use very bald on record, statements which signify their authority and power over the addressee. For example in Excerpts 7 and 8 above, the writers issue a reprimand or a command that clearly indicates their authority and superiority over the chiefs.

It is also interesting to note the use of the word *kafir* in Excerpt 6 above. *The Oxford Reference English Dictionary* (1996: 770) states that the word 'kafir' originates from Arabic meaning infidel, or not a believer. 'Kafir' was a disparaging and derogatory term used to refer to blacks during white supremacy rule in South Africa. In this excerpt the word 'kafir' is used in juxtaposition with a more intimate address term 'friend' to refer to chief Khama. Such address terms as 'kafir' and the issuing of reprimands and orders suggest that the British administrators did not regard Batswana chiefs as their equals despite the use of this form of address. It would, therefore, seem that the term was deliberately adopted by the British administrators to mask the power struggle and gap between them and the local chiefs as well as a cover up for British dominance over its subjects.

Signatures and endings

In the analysis of letters from British administrators to other British administrators it was noted that 48 percent of the letters employed the formulaic signature 'your obedient servant'. However, it is interesting to note that this signature is found in only 3 out of 23 letters written by British administrators to Batswana chiefs. This finding is significant because it suggests that though the ending 'your obedient servant' might seem formulaic or routine between native speakers or British administrators, it is hardly used in letters to the local chiefs. The near absence of 'your obedient servant' in these letters is a comment on how the British administrators perceived their status in relation to the chiefs. It suggests that though 'your obedient servant' was popular in letters during that era it did not apply in a situation of a Briton writing to a local chief because it could suggest that a Briton could be of a lower status or a servant of a local black chief. That of course was not acceptable.

The endings and signatures of letters written by the British to Batswana chiefs are relatively less formal when compared to those found in letters to other British administrators. The most popular signature found in letters from the British to the local chiefs is 'your friend' and the endings of these letters mostly convey greetings and best wishes. Of the 23 letters written by British administrators to Batswana chiefs 20 of them (86 percent) employ the signature 'your friend' and only 14 percent of the letters employ such signatures as 'with best wishes, rain, I remain'. The following excerpts illustrate the kind of signatures and endings found in letters from British administrators to Batswana chiefs.

Excerpt 8
> I propose to be at Gaberones on Friday next and request you to be present there to meet me and give me an explanation of why you held the meeting and the reason for making use of the words which you are said to have used. Until we meet I shall not discuss the matter with you.
> Let it rain.
> Resident Commissioner, Mafeking.
> Letter from Resident Commissioner to Chief Sebele 9 June 1899, *HC 115*).

Excerpt 9
> With regard to a line between you and Khama, I know no such line yet and I don't see how any line could justly be made without your knowledge and consent.
> With hearty greetings remain always your friend.
> Letter from S.G.A. Shippard to Chief Lobengula, 29 April 1887, *HC122*).

Letters written by the British administrators to Batswana chiefs can generally be characterised as less formal though faceless. The letters have an informal tone which is achieved by a direct presentation of the subject matter without informal openings such as greetings. The informal tone is achieved through use of intimate salutations and signatures such as 'my friend, let it rain, with greetings'.

Letters by Batswana to British administrators

Salutations and openings

The majority of letters, 70 out of 130 (or 54 percent) from Batswana to British administrators employ formal salutations such as 'dear sir', 'your excellency', 'your honour', or the addressee's title or name. This is in contrast to letters from the British to Batswana. The high percentage of formal salutations in these letters is probably indicative of the formality with which Batswana chiefs perceived their relationship with the British administrators: formal, distant and professional. The less formal salutation, 'dear friend', is also used in a significant number of letters, 42 out of 130, (or 32 percent). It has already been argued that this address form is a mark of solidarity and equality though it has also been demonstrated that the use of this address term does not connote equality because the British administrators and Batswana chiefs rarely participated as equals in their interaction. For instance, despite the use of the address form 'my friend', the British displayed their authority by use of reprimands and commands and Batswana authors on the other hand used a lot of self-denigration strategies in their letters to the British administrators. This contrast serves to highlight the power disparity in their relationship.

Since the addressee (British administrator) in all these cases is someone who is believed could bring about an adjustment in that disparity, the use of self-deprecating language is designed to invoke compassion and pity. Batswana writers used the strategy of downgrading in order to attract attention and compassion from their readers. In Setswana speech interaction, such expressions as 'I have nothing to say' or 'I have a little question', make the speaker's opinion or idea seem modest, and, therefore, not pressurising or imposing to the listener. At the same time, such expressions appeal to the addressee's compassion and generosity to listen to those with a small voice. Excerpt 10 below exemplifies common Setswana downgrading strategies of downplaying one's opinion and ideas in front of a superior by using such expressions as 'I have nothing to say', or 'I have a little question'. In addition, the use of the plural marker 'our' in the salutation of the same excerpt is an expression of respect for a person of higher status in the writer's dialect.

Excerpt 10

To *our* senior magistrate,

My best greetings Sir, *I have nothing to say sir*, I *only* ask about the health o f my relative who is there. *I ask only one little question chief.* I hear that my wife says that when I beat her I had her held down, one person holding her by one foot, another by another foot, and another by her hand. I say I hear her words, but if they are hers they are lies.

(Letter from chief Sekgoma Letsholathebe to Magistrate, 13 November 1905, *RC 5/13*).

Sometimes the address form 'chief' was used to refer to British administrators such as resident magistrates, magistrates, etc., as exemplified in Excerpt 11 below. This address form is found in four out of 130 letters and its use suggests a much broader meaning than a leader of an ethnic community. It was also used as a term of respect to refer to an individual in a position of authority.

Excerpt 11

Mr Ellenberger,

Greetings *chief*, to you, your wife and your children. I am writing to inform you that on his return from Gaberones, the boy who had taken our letters to you said that he told him it was well with regard to the letter which I had written to you.

(Letter from Kgabo to Ellenberger, 2 May 1901, *RC 5/12*).

The following excerpts illustrate the kind of salutations and openings found in letters written by Batswana chiefs to the British administrators.

Excerpt 12
> Your honour,
> I greet you and the Bakwena also greet you. I together with the headmen and all of the Bakwena are very much pleased that his honour found an opportunity and the necessity to visit our town and see us.
> (Letter from Sechele paramount chief of the Bakwena to His Honour the Resident Commissioner, 8 September 1911, *S 42/3*).

Excerpt 13
> My dear friend,
> Sir, I write to greet you, and Mrs Wright. Now I send you these few lines to let you know that you will be so kind enough, please sir, to wait until I tell you when I need the corn.
> (Letter from chief Montsioa to W.J. Wright 25 September 1884, *HC 193*).

It is also worth noting that while the letters written by the British mostly opened by going straight into the issue, letters written by Batswana tended to open by a greeting or making a reference to the welfare of the reader before presenting the subject matter. In the best traditions of Setswana hospitality a speaker has to ask about the welfare of the hearer and sometimes that of his family at the beginning of a conversation. An examination of the data shows that of the 130 letters written by Batswana chiefs to the British administrators, 29 of them (or 22 percent) opened with a greeting or inquiry about the health of the recipient or his family thereby employing the Setswana practice of using greetings as conversation openers and as a strategy by which a speaker attempts to please and win the social approval of the listener.

Signatures and endings

Although Batswana chiefs seem to have accepted the superiority of the British as evident in the use of downgraders, and honorific titles such as 'chief', it is interesting to note that only about 15 percent (or 20 letters) of the letters from Batswana chiefs to British administrators were signed 'your obedient servant'. This low percentage among Batswana chiefs is indicative of the fact that although Batswana chiefs acknowledged and accepted the superiority of the British administrators they could not readily accept the position of obedient servant. Batswana writers tended to prefer less formal endings such as 'greetings, your friend, that is all'. Of the 130 letters written to the British, 54 of them (or 41.5 percent) end with a greeting, 34 (26 percent) are signed 'your friend', 13 (10 percent) employ the Setswana conversation ending 'that is all', or the Batswana peace slogan 'pula or rain', thus making the percentage of informal signatures 78 percent. The rest of the letters employ formal signatures such as 'yours sincerely', 'yours faithfully', or 'yours truly'. The following examples illustrate the endings and signatures of letters by Batswana chiefs to British administrators.

> Excerpt 14
>> With regard to this matter we can only inform the government, only the government will know what to do, we have no other will but that of the government. *This is all, Greetings chief,* I shall say no more.
>> *I am your friend,* Baruti.
>> (Letter from Baruti Kgosidintsi to J. Ellenberger 17 July 1901, *RC 5/12*).

> Excerpt 15
>> His people are doing what they wish, they are not waiting for the decision, with regard to my people I have told them not to do nothing as you said. I am waiting for the decision. *With kind greetings* to yourself and to Mrs Surmon and family.
>> I am etc. Sebele.
>> (Letter from Sebele chief of Bakwena to Mr Surmon 25 September 1894, *RC 5/12*).

The letters written by Batswana chiefs to the British administrators suggest a formal and yet friendly and cautious relationship. Batswana writers tend to address the British formally, yet in accordance with their culture they have to greet them and ask about their welfare and that of their families. Letters written by Batswana thus have longer introductions and longer signatures which involve greetings and best wishes. While the British used the signature 'your obedient servant' in letters from subordinate to superior this type of signature was not preferred by the majority of Batswana writers even though they accepted and acknowledged the superiority of the British administrators.

Letters from Batswana to other Batswana

Current holdings contain a few letters between Batswana chiefs because there was not much written communication between them in the early years. The chiefs mostly communicated by word of mouth. The holdings include only 32 letters written by Batswana chiefs to others.

Salutations and beginnings

The majority of letters written by Batswana chiefs to other Batswana have formal types of salutations: 15 letters (or 47 percent) employ such salutations as 'dear sir', 'your honour', 10 of the letters (or 31 percent) employ the title of the addressee or 'chief' is used. These two kinds of formal salutations numbered 25 out of 32 (or 78 percent). However what sets the salutations of the letters from Batswana chiefs to other Batswana apart is the use of kinship terms and totems as salutations as exemplified in the excerpts 16, 17, and 19 below. The use of kinship terms does not necessarily connote a biological relationship between author and reader. The kinship terms are honorific forms meant to show respect and solidarity with the addressee.

> Excerpt 16
> Dear chief Keaboka,
> huti ke a dumedisa. (*Duiker I greet you*). *Chief* I learn that you have paid us a visit a few days ago in connection with some school trouble we are having. *Chief* we are only sorry that when you were here you did not even see one of the teachers. *Chief* we here feel that we are your ears and eyes.
> (Letter from John Malome to chief Keaboka 24 March 1952, BT *Admin 1/22*).

> Excerpt 17
> *Dear father,*
> When a man is rotten all the things which belong to him smell bad too. I speak these words for the sake of the dispute and color bar and persecution of employers of the workers who are recruited in the South African mines in the republic of South Africa.
> (Letter from Khumo Keitumetse to the Office of the President 31 July 1971, *OP 18/2/1*).

Though the majority of the letters have a formal type of salutation a significant number of them open with a greeting. For example, 12 out of 32 (37.5 percent) use greetings as openers in accordance with the Setswana practice. Totems are also used as a way of expressing solidarity. Setswana conversation openers such as 'I have no news', or 'I have nothing to say', which are a modest way of presenting one's opinions or downgrading one's view, are also common in these letters.

Signatures and endings
Most of the letters in this category end with a greeting. Out of 32 letters, 17 (or 53 percent) conclude with a greeting and 4 (or 12.5 percent) employ conversation endings such as 'that is all', or 'pula or rain'. Eleven of the letters (34 percent) employ formal signatures such as 'yours truly' or 'yours sincerely'. The following exemplify the type of signatures found in letters from Batswana to other Batswana chiefs.

> Excerpt 18
> Mr Lampard told me that he will inform the chief that I should getaway from here. He says that even when I meet him I do not take off my hat. This

European comes from Mashonanaland. I am well chief. There is no news. *Greetings to the family.*
Yours B.K. Motheo.
(Letter from B.K. Motheo to Bangwato Deputy Chief 25 January 1940, *DCF 7/2*).

Excerpt 19
We found out that the huts had been entered and searched for fictitious evidence for which the girls were to get dresses. *Father*, there is not much to say. I will stop here. The writer is *your child*.
(Unsigned letter to D. Raditladi 4 January 1937, *S 485/1/1*).

Batswana writers mostly used formal signatures and salutations when writing to other Batswana. Letters to the British administrators on the other hand tended to have more informal signatures. This is interesting since we would expect letters to the British administrators to have more formal signatures and salutations. However, this is not surprising since the British writers also employed more informal salutations and signatures when writing to Batswana than when writing to other British administrators. The informality between these two groups is argued to be an expression of solidarity as well as an avoidance strategy for dealing with the power struggle between the British administrators and Batswana chiefs during the protectorate period. Letters written by Batswana are orientated towards the relationship between the reader and the writer and the format, content and style of the letters help establish or maintain that relationship. The letters by Batswana illustrate a freer register in which there is a place for the explicit maintenance of relationships. As Merkestein (1998: 182) points out, the expression of relationships is central to the social reality of Batswana. On the other hand, letters by British administrators are more formal, they have no place for maintenance of relationships but are focused on expressing the message of the writer.

Conclusion

The available evidence tends to suggest that both the British administrators and Batswana chiefs were aware of the inherent power struggle between them. The two groups seemed cautious of this inherent problem, and they both sought linguistic means of dealing with it such as use or failure to use certain address forms when writing to each other. For example, the address form 'my friend' which connotes equality and solidarity is only found in letters written to Batswana chiefs by British administrator and in letters written to British administrators by Batswana chiefs but rarely used by Batswana chiefs or British administrators when writing to fellow British administrators or fellow Batswana. The use of this address term masks the unequal power relationship and tension that existed between the two camps. The failure to use the signature 'your obedient servant' by British administrators when writing to Batswana chiefs also suggests that the British did not perceive themselves as being subordinate to Batswana chiefs. The superiority of the British administrators is demonstrated in these letters by the issuing of commands and reprimands and the inferiority of Batswana chiefs is demonstrated by use of down graders and repeated use of honorific titles when writing to British administrators.

This chapter argues that language has played a very crucial role in the African liberation struggle and it is worth looking into in order to further support and broaden already existing evidence. While most studies on the history of the African liberation struggle have concentrated on the political issues they have largely ignored the battle of words that has always gone alongside with these. This chapter is thus an attempt to generate interest in scholars in this field to look more closely at how language use can lend more evidence to their historical and political findings.

References

Campbell, A., 1979, *The Guide to Botswana*, Johannesburg: Winchester Press.
Merkestein, A., 1998, 'Deculturizing Englishes: the Botswana Context', *World Englishes*, 17 (2).
Oxford Reference English Dictionary, 1996, Oxford: Oxford University Press.
Tlou, T. and Campbell, A., 1984, *History of Botswana*, Gaborone: Macmillan Botswana.

Archival Materials - Letters

John Mackenzie to Sir Henry Berkly, 2 May 1876 *HC 48/1/2*
Imperial secretary to High Commissioner 25 April 1884 *HC 65/14*
Chief Montsioa to W.J. Wright 25 September 1884, *HC 193*
S.G.R. Kruger, State President of South Africa, to Chief Khama, 30 March 1885, *HC 5/12*
Native Commissioner, Mafeking to Chief Ikaning, 7 March 1887, *HC 12/18*
S.G.A. Shippard to Chief Lobengula, 29 April 1887, *HC 122*
J. Vosthurgen to High Commissioner, 19 February 1889 *HC 25/42*
Sebele chief of Bakwena to Mr Surmon, 25 September 1894, *RC 5/12*
Resident Commissioner to Chief Sebele, 9 June 1899, *HC 115*
Kgabo to Ellenberger, 2 May 1901, *RC 5/12*).
Baruti Kgosidintsi to J. Ellenberger, 17 July 1901, *RC 5/12*
Chief Sekgoma Letsholathebe to Magistrate, 13 November 1905, *RC 5/13*
Sechele paramount chief of the Bakwena to His Honour the Resident Commissioner, 8 September 1911, *S 42/3*
Assistant commissioner to Chief Sechele, 24 February 1912, *S 43/2*
British administrator to Colonel Sir Carrington, 6 February 1929 S 5/5).
Unsigned letter to D. Raditladi, 4 January 1937, *S 485/1/1*
B.K. Motheo to Bangwato Deputy Chief, 25 January 1940, *DCF 7/2*

John Malome to chief Keaboka, 24 March 1952, *BT Admin 1/22*
Khumo Keitumetse to the Office of the President, 31 July 1971, *OP 18/2/1*

Printed in the United States
54815LVS00004B/325-348